Moments of Crisis

Moments of Crisis

Religion and National Identity in Québec

IAN A. MORRISON

UBCPress · Vancouver · Toronto

28 27 26 25 24 23 22 21 20 19   5 4 3 2 1

Printed in Canada on FSC-certified ancient-forest-free paper (100% post-consumer recycled) that is processed chlorine- and acid-free.

Library and Archives Canada Cataloguing in Publication

Title: Moments of crisis : religion and national identity in Québec / Ian A. Morrison.
Names: Morrison, Ian A., 1977– author.
Description: Includes bibliographical references and index.
Identifiers: Canadiana (print) 20190119411 | Canadiana (ebook) 2019011942X |
ISBN 9780774861762 (hardcover) | ISBN 9780774861779 (paperback) |
ISBN 9780774861786 (PDF) | ISBN 9780774861793 (EPUB) |
ISBN 9780774861809 (Kindle)
Subjects: LCSH: Nationalism—Québec (Province)—Religious aspects. |
LCSH: Nationalism—Québec (Province) | LCSH: Québec (Province)—Religion.
Classification: LCC FC2920.N38 M67 2019 | DDC 320.5409714—dc23

Canadä

UBC Press gratefully acknowledges the financial support for our publishing program of the Government of Canada (through the Canada Book Fund), the Canada Council for the Arts, and the British Columbia Arts Council.

This book has been published with the help of a grant from the Canadian Federation for the Humanities and Social Sciences, through the Awards to Scholarly Publications Program, using funds provided by the Social Sciences and Humanities Research Council of Canada.

Printed and bound in Canada by Friesens
Set in Sabon Next LT Pro and Myriad Pro by Apex CoVantage, LLC
Copy editor: Robert Lewis
Proofreader: Lana Okerlund
Indexer: Judy Dunlop
Cover designer: Lara Minja

UBC Press
The University of British Columbia
2029 West Mall
Vancouver, BC V6T 1Z2
www.ubcpress.ca

Contents

Acknowledgments

Over the long course of writing this book, I was provided with a great deal of assistance and support. Some people helped me to sharpen the content and arguments of the book, others were helpful readers and editors, and still others were of great personal support. Many of these important people remain in my life, but I have lost contact with others. Nonetheless, I will always appreciate their help. I thank my colleagues and students at the American University in Cairo, Dr. Joseph Fernando, Dr. Stephen Fowler, Professor Engin Isin and the members of my dissertation committee, and the staff at Table 55. I also thank Yoke, my family, and my friends for their patience, understanding, and love throughout the writing and research process. Without them, it would not have been possible to complete this book.

This project was made possible by grants from the Social Sciences and Humanities Research Council of Canada, the Government of Ontario, the American University in Cairo, York University, and Trent University.

Moments of Crisis

Introduction

From shortly after the arrival of French traders, missionaries, and colonists on the banks of the Saint Lawrence River in the early seventeenth century, the French-speaking people residing in what is now the Canadian province of Québec have engaged in an ongoing process of defining, asserting, and protecting their cultural and linguistic particularity in the face of a variety of social, political, and cultural challenges. In forging and protecting their identity as a people, they have engaged in shifting relations of differentiation from, and elective affinity and identification with, a series of others who they have encountered: people of the First Nations, French elite, English, Americans, and people of other groups who have migrated to the territory.

Although references to the Canadiens, as they were then known, as a nation date to the period following the 1760 English Conquest of New France, it was at the beginning of the nineteenth century that their identity and demands began to be articulated in terms of nationalism. Although the reasons given by scholars for the rise of nationalism in this period vary, they agree that it was during this time that "the bonds of birth, class, and station and the values of aristocracy, hierarchy, and deference" began to lose their dominance and "the ties of ethnicity began to exercise their pull" (Mann Trofimenkoff 1982, 50).

Since the first invocations of French Canadian nationalism by groups of Patriotes in the early nineteenth century, politics in Québec have been dominated by questions of national identity, sovereignty, and the place of Québec and French Canadians within Canadian federalism, North America, and the international state system. The nature of this nation and concern with its survival in the face of various threats have been ongoing subjects of discussion within the social sciences and political discourse.

Key to the definition of the French Canadian and later québécois nation has been a shifting conceptualization of the relationship of religion and the secular to national identity. Until the latter half of the twentieth century, religion was a crucial marker of identity, differentiating French Canadians from various groups with which they came into contact and in relation to which they derived their distinctive identity. Once a nation defined predominantly by and through its Catholicism, Québec has, in recent times, come to be seen, and to see, its national identity as secular. Catholicism has been transformed from a lived experience of the people into a historical relic representing the cultural heritage of the nation. In this sense, québécois society and the French Canadian people are often seen as a latecomer to, and an archetype of, secularization. The narrative of secularization provides a means to convey the historical continuity of the nation despite a radical transformation or even reversal of that which is said to be definitive of its way of life. This process has involved both transformations in the dominant self-understandings of national identity and shifts in the meaning of religion and the secular.

On November 7, 2013, the Québec government tabled Bill 60, *Charter Affirming the Values of State Secularism and Religious Neutrality and the Equality between Women and Men, and Providing a Framework for Accommodation Requests*. This bill, popularly known as the Charte de la laïcité (Charter of Secularism) or the Charte des valeurs québécoises (Charter of Québécois Values), was meant to provide a resolution to longstanding concerns about the accommodation of religious symbols and practices in the public sphere. The nature of such accommodations has been the focus of an ongoing, prominent, and heated debate in Québec since the early 1990s.

The debate to which the Charter of Values sought to respond was never simply one related to concerns about the interpretation of the legal principle of reasonable accommodation. Both the content and the highly affective nature of this debate revealed that at its core were questions of the nature of québécois national identity. Indeed, since the early 1990s, questions concerning reasonable accommodation and the nature of québécois identity have had a near permanent presence as the focus of editorials, political debates, and talk-show conversations, becoming what Marie McAndrew has labelled a discursive "social happening" (Clément 1994) and a topic that has been debated "ad nauseum" (McAndrew 2006, 1). At stake in these debates has been the determination of the values upon which the boundaries of pluralism and, therefore, belonging in Québec are to be based. In other words, the debate surrounding the accommodation of religious practices in the public sphere is part of a larger consideration of the nature and limits of national identity and, therefore, of the nation itself.

The resolution to these debates offered by the Parti Québécois (PQ), which framed itself "as the guardian of cultural survival" (Cooper 2013, 26), was the Charter of Values. The PQ asserted that once enshrined in law, québécois values could officially serve as the foundation for future discussions and decisions related to pluralism. For proponents of the Charter of Values, an unbridled pluralism threatens to undermine the secular state, the progressive social values achieved through a history of struggle against the dominance of the Catholic Church, and the particularity of québécois identity itself. Consequently, what they consider the national values definitive of this identity – particularly secularism and women's rights – need to be immunized against this threat through their codification and enshrinement in law as fundamental values of Québec society. Those values deemed properly québécois are to serve as the basis upon which permissible difference, and consequently membership in the nation, will be judged.

Conversely, opponents of the Charter of Values argue that codifying national identity through the enshrinement of essential québécois values is tantamount to a closure of authentic contemporary québécois identity, a rejection of a modern, civic conception of the nation – a *citoyenneté québécoise* open to difference – and the institution of an inauthentic identity at odds with the lived experience of contemporary Québec. Moreover, they argue that it marks a return to an ethnic nationalism that Québec society has been gradually attempting to move away from. For all sides, then, the debate surrounding the Charter of Values is one of upmost importance. The debate concerning reasonable accommodation is meant to address and resolve what has come to be seen as a crisis not only of governance but also of national identity, one that has come to be viewed by both sides as an existential crisis.

Commentators, including the leaders of the 2007 provincial commission formed to investigate and offer solutions to the question of reasonable accommodation, have dismissed the idea that Québec is facing a crisis of national identity (Bouchard and Roy 2007), with some deeming the controversy simply a "circus" (Heinrich and Dufour 2008) "manufactured" (Cooper 2013) by journalists and political leaders seeking to benefit from it. Indeed, many of the most inflammatory and cataclysmic statements regarding the threat that pluralism poses to the Québec nation have been voiced by individuals living in locales with largely homogeneous ethnically French Canadian populations, individuals who would have had little interaction with migrants or ethnic or religious minorities and who were therefore distanced from actual processes of integration. However, it cannot be denied that, whether manufactured or not, the debates surrounding reasonable accommodation have produced a reaction at the level of affect. Although it can be argued that certain members of the media and the political class have cynically deployed the threat of migration, pluralism, and "foreign" religiosity, this sentiment has resounded at an affective level with a portion of the population of Québec who feel that their identity is under threat and thus that the nation is in a state of crisis that needs to be imminently resolved.

The notion of a national crisis in Québec is not, however, unique to this recent period; rather, it echoes earlier, periodic pronouncements of threat and crisis and feeds into a notion that the québécois nation is particularly unstable – a "worrier nation" (Stasiulis 2013) prone to a melancholic form of nationalism (Maclure 2003) and bouts of self-doubt (Bouchard 2012; Mac Kay 1996). Even within dominant strains of Québécois nationalism, the Québec nation is considered to be in perennial, if not perpetual, crisis owing to historical events and geopolitical phenomena. This sense of crisis has been voiced with urgency at particular points in the history of Québec in response to perceived existential threats, both endogenous and exogenous. As in the case of the debate over the Charter of Values, earlier moments of crisis involved the emergence of a perceived threat to the dominant, often taken-for-granted conception of national identity. In response to this threat, various solutions were voiced in the form of alternative conceptions of the nation, visions of national identity that claimed to be able to immunize the nation from the threat and thereby resolve the crisis.

In each moment of historical crisis, a threefold operation can be observed. First, there is a concurrent pronouncement of a threat and that which is threatened: the hegemonic conception of national identity and, consequently, the nation. In day-to-day experience, one is not faced with a crisis of national identity or required to provide a pure, unproblematic definition of the nation or its foundational values and characteristics. However, stating that there is a threat to the nation requires the simultaneous articulation of an understanding of that which constitutes the essential features of the nation. For the nation to be threatened by modernization, it must be defined as traditional. For the nation to be threatened by secularization, its essential religiosity must be articulated. In the same way, for the nation to be threatened by pluralism and the perceived regressive religious practices of minorities, a self-understanding based on notions of progress, secularity, and women's rights must be articulated.

Second, this articulation of a national essence opens a space for a questioning of this understanding of the nation and its capacity to contend with the threat, as well as for a coming to the fore of alternative conceptions of national identity that purport to be better able to respond to the crisis at hand. Thus the pronouncement of a crisis offers the terrain for a struggle over the definition of the nation. These new, or at least newly prominent, conceptions of the nation and its essential characteristics are often incompatible with the hegemonic conception of the nation, at times presenting the dominant conception as a threat in and of itself. Third, through this struggle, the hegemonic definition of the nation may be displaced by an alternative conception.

Thus, through a moment of crisis, the nation is both reconstituted and reproduced. However, it is not reproduced in an identical form. In a sense, then, this reproduction of the nation through crisis involves the constitution of a new nation. As I argue throughout this book, it is in moments of crisis that the nation is articulated and rearticulated, reinforced and definitionally transformed, undone and consolidated, and thereby reproduced in novel form. It is this operation of crisis followed by reproduction, transformation, and reconsolidation that this book explores in relation to moments of crisis in the history of national identity in Québec.

That which defines the essence of the nation can, and does, change. Yet within both sociological and nationalist narratives, the nation is required to have a continuous history, one in which, despite these definitional differences, it appears as a continuous transhistorical entity. The nation must be seen as a like object despite the sometimes radical disparities in that which is historically said to define it. A nation must be seen, and crucially felt, as an enduring entity. Therefore, for a narrative to be successful in maintaining a sense of identity, it must be able to account for changes in the nature of the nation over time. It must be able to point to what is common despite temporal (or sometimes spatial) transformations. Crucial to this process is the development of narratives of continuity such as modernization, secularization, maturation, and the gradual realization of authenticity. In these narratives, the national subject is transformed, sometimes radically, both through the abandonment of characteristics once thought and felt to be essential and through the institution of new fundamental characteristics, without these transformations being felt as an abandonment or loss of identity.

The dominant narrative device deployed in accounts of transformations of Québec society is secularization. For the most part, accounts of secularization in Quebec involve one of two narratives. The first narrative explains secularization as an accomplishment realized through the efforts of a small group of enlightened intellectuals to combat backwardness, superstition, and the clerical control of society and, thereby, to bring about the modernization and secularization of society (Behiels 1985; Dion 1993). The second narrative portrays secularization as the product of a socio-historic process linked to industrialization, modernization, and capitalization (Guindon 1988; Linteau, Durocher, and Robert 1979; Young 1994). It is through the narrative device of secularization that a continuous transhistorical identity can be forged between a historical nation once defined by its essential religiosity and a contemporary society for which secularity is deemed a fundamental value and social form.

In each of the moments of crisis that this book investigates, religion and the secular prove crucial to conceptions of québécois identity. The centrality of the religious and the secular to historical understandings of québécois identity and the prominence of secularization in narratives of transformations of the Québec nation provide a valuable entry to analyzing moments of crisis, struggle, and transformation in québécois identity and are revelatory of both the fragility and endurance of national identity.

Crisis

In recent years, we have been inundated with what commentators have come to refer to as "crisis talk" (Tazziolo and De Genova 2016, 8). Not only are we said to be in the midst of crises of national and "civilizational" identities (Morrison 2013a, 2014), but we are also faced with a multitude of social, political, cultural, economic, humanitarian, environmental, medical, spiritual, and moral crises. Among the many contemporary declarations of crisis, democracy is said to be in crisis due to a rise in populism and authoritarianism and a shrinking of the public sphere/subject. The academy is said to be in crisis due to neoliberal reforms and anti-intellectualism. Humanity is said to be facing a crisis of antibiotic resistant bacteria and rapidly declining male fertility. The world, or at least human civilization, is said to be facing a crisis of environmental degradation owing to global warming. As "an omnipresent sign in almost all forms of narrative today," crisis appears as both "the defining category of our contemporary situation" (Roitman 2012) and, due to its seemingly counterintuitive normality, "utterly banal" (Tazziolo and De Genova 2016, 2). We are, although not for the first time, said to be witnessing an age of crisis.

Yet, despite its apparent omnipresence, in the sense that the term "crisis" is deployed in much academic and popular discourse, it is understood as an exceptional state. The term is used to designate an aberration – an abnormal state of affairs marked by an instability that threatens the existence of that which is thought to be experiencing crisis. This exceptional condition is said to be the result of error, corruption, or contamination, in the absence of which the imperilled entity, institution, or phenomenon would have continued to operate unproblematically. For instance, the global economic crisis of 2008 is often deemed to be the consequence of some combination of poor policy decisions, deregulation, financialization, securitization, irresponsible consumer behaviour, and the unethical or criminal actions of bankers. Thus the roots of the crisis are not located in capitalism itself but in individuals and institutions whose actions and decisions put capitalism at risk of collapse. Similarly, the migrant or refugee crisis that Europe is said to be facing is professed to be the consequence not of the nation-state system but of phenomena in the countries that the migrants are fleeing (e.g., war, revolution, oppressive governments, the persecution of minorities, natural disasters, and poverty), in the countries to which they wish to migrate (e.g., lax or overly robust border controls and inefficient methods of integration), or in the moral or cultural failings of individuals (e.g., profiteering human smugglers, inassimilable or dishonest migrants, and xenophobic, overly permissive, or naive host populations).

If a crisis is understood to be an exceptional event brought about by externalities or inessential corrupted elements of that which is said to be in crisis, it follows that there exists a normal, noncrisis state of affairs from which the state of crisis can be differentiated and that the crisis threatens not only to disrupt but also to annihilate. In line with such a perception of an imminent, existential threat, invocations of crisis are often accompanied by assertions that "we are reaching the point of no return," or they make use of imagery of "contamination," "the barbarians at the door," "tidal waves," or "being swamped." Moreover, although intervention leading to the restoration of pre-crisis normality may be possible, the threat is understood to be so dire that steps need to be taken imminently or restoration will not be possible. To make use of the biomedical analogies often at play in depictions of crises, it may be possible to save the host through radical interventions – excisions, expulsions, and prophylaxis – but such measures must be undertaken before the illness has become terminal. Moreover, if the crisis is successfully averted, steps can be taken to immunize the host against future crises.

Therefore, at risk in crisis as it is understood above is not mere transformation but transformation understood as loss. For example, in the case of the financial crisis, the risk was not that capitalism would be transformed by the crisis but that capitalism would cease to be. Similarly, in the case of crises of national identity, the fear is not that the demographic makeup, institutions, or values of the nation are changing but that such changes represent the collapse of national identity and, consequently, of the nation itself.

It is the dread of impending loss that allows for declarations of crisis to operate strongly at the level of affect. Although declarations of crisis may or may not be a response to fear, they reflect or are invoked in order to provoke a deep sense of urgency and anxiety. Consequently, declarations of crisis can be deployed as a powerful tool to achieve political or ideological purposes and, therefore, are often greeted with skepticism (Klein 2007). Engin Isin (2004) has highlighted the use of crisis talk in the formation and governance of what he refers to as "neurotic citizens," subjects who are governed not through calculating rationalities but through fears, anxieties, and insecurities. As has often been noted, neoliberalism operates through a perpetual invocation of crisis – whether of individual firms, sectors, or the economy as a whole – and attendant demands for downsizing, rationalization, marketization, and/or austerity to resolve each crisis, which in a short time is met with further declarations of crisis requiring further downsizing, rationalization, and so on. Similarly, critics of the "war on terror" assert that fear of perpetually impending attacks is stoked in order to justify the expansion of the state's security apparatus and the limitation of the rights of citizens and migrants.

The invocation of crises of national identity, such as those in Québec, can be seen in such a light. Whether truly believed or merely deployed cynically, arguments are often made that group identity and, consequently, the group itself are threatened by the presence of outsiders and/or the introduction of cultural elements that are at odds with or undermine what individuals and groups hold to be core national values. In response, measures are offered to remedy the situation by restoring the identity to its proper, authentic form and thereby defending the group. As mentioned earlier, the PQ and its supporters claimed that the introduction of the Charter of Values was necessary in order to contend with a crisis of national identity owing to increased pluralism and demands for the accommodation of religious practices in the public sphere. Champions of the Charter of Values felt – or deemed it politically useful to argue – that changes in the composition of Québec society and the move toward a civic conception of nationhood, unless grounded in properly québécois values, threatened the existence of the Québec nation. They contended not only that the nation was changing but also that this change would eventually amount to a loss of the nation. With the exception of a few marginal voices on the far right, the Québécois did not articulate fear of the physical or demographic elimination of a people but fear of the extermination of the nation through the loss of culture and identity. In other words, migration and the move toward a pluralistic, civic conception of nationhood were seen to fuel the disappearance of fundamental aspects of group membership. A similar feeling of impending loss was articulated by opponents of the Charter of Values who felt that the codification of official québécois values would amount to the loss of a civic, modern form of identity and belonging and a move toward an artificial identity not representative of lived experience in Québec.

Although crisis is most often articulated as a disruption of the normal and desirable, it can also, as Janet Roitman (2012) asserts, be "mobilized in narrative constructions to mark out a 'moment of truth' ... instances where 'the real' is made bare." Understood in this way, moments of crisis allow for a glimpse of the true, fundamental nature of the phenomenon or entity. For instance, as Hannah Arendt's (1951) and Giorgio Agamben's (2000) seminal analyses of the figure of the refugee make clear, the plight of refugees, particularly the stateless, is not fundamentally the consequence of the failure of international actors and international law to adequately enforce human rights; rather, the refugee is a product of, and lays bare the nature and limitations of, the international system of nation-states. Given that, within the nation-state system, rights are granted on the basis of citizenship within a nation-state, this system does not permit access to rights on the basis of the status of being merely human. Consequently, a refugee crisis is not one that can be resolved by reforming international law or by choosing to enforce existing law. Approached in this manner, the crisis of the refugee is one that exposes the fundamental truths of the nation-state system, truths that are obscured by international human rights discourse.

Similarly, within Marxist analysis, capitalist economic crises are not understood as the consequence of accidents or errors but are seen as the product of contradictions inherent to capitalism itself. Karl Marx (1894) and subsequent Marxian economists argue that, as a consequence of the tendency of rates of profit to fall, the capitalist system must periodically engage in the destruction of the value of capital in order to restore profitability. In contrast to Keynesian economics, Marxian analysis asserts that the boom and bust cycle of capitalism, as inherent to capitalism itself, cannot be alleviated through government intervention. As a result, crisis is a fundamental characteristic of capitalism, and moments of crisis provide an opportunity for us to observe its inescapable instability.

The Crisis of Identity

Reflecting on the increased centrality of identity as an object of analysis in socio-cultural studies and political scholarship in the early 1990s, Stuart Hall (1996, 1) noted "a veritable discursive explosion in recent years around the concept of 'identity.'" In contrast to the promised final victory of a stable, liberal international order at the end of the Cold War, in the period referred to alternatively as postmodernity, late modernity, or advanced or late capitalism, the intensification of globalization in its various forms – economic, political, institutional, technological, and cultural – was accompanied by the seemingly paradoxical consolidation and fragmentation of identity. Ethno-national and religious identities and the accompanying phenomena of ethnic conflict and fundamentalism appeared to be on the rise. At the same time, what had been the dominant forms of group representation and identification, particularly those associated with the modern nation-state, were becoming fragmented, giving rise to the increased prominence of what would come to be known as identity politics. Consequently, identity became a topic of greater political importance, recognized as being both in crisis and the cause of crisis.

In the writing of Charles Taylor (1994), Zygmunt Bauman (1996), and other prominent scholars of identity of the period, identity is portrayed as a modern invention. Not only is identity deemed to be a product of modernity, but so too are its crises. As a modern phenomenon, identity – like modernity – is always in flux, with markers of identity, such as gender, class, or nation, increasingly unable to serve as a singular frame of reference within late modernity (Maclure 2003, 9). Yet "at no time did identity 'become' a problem; it was a 'problem' from its birth – was *born as a problem* (that is, as something one needs do something about – as a task), could exist only as a problem" (Bauman 1996, 18–19). Stripped of the certainties of the fixed identities determined by one's proper social position in traditional or premodern societies, the task of what Bauman refers to as the "disembedded" subject of modernity was "to find escape from uncertainty" (19). However, this task of identity formation is made difficult by the nature of modernity itself.

The first of the difficulties noted in this literature involves the social aspect of the process of identity formation. Identity, as an individual's or group's sense of self, is not forged in isolation; rather, it is influenced by relations of recognition through the images of oneself that are presented to one by others. As Taylor (1994, 35) asserts, what is distinctive of modern identity "is not the need for recognition but the conditions in which the attempt to be recognized can fail." Questions of identity did not arise in premodern times because the fixed social categories that situated all members of society were both accepted and taken for granted. Therefore, recognition operated unproblematically. With the advent of modernity, as Marx and Friedrich Engels (1848, 111) famously note, "all that is solid melts into air." Modernity continuously undermined all traditional categories, beliefs, and institutions that failed to accord with its own logics. With the dissolution of traditional hierarchies and the givenness of social categories in modernity, recognition came to be a problem. Freed from traditional social categories, recognition was no longer certain. The problem then became how to maintain an identity in the face of the unsettling force of modernity. In the words of Bauman (1996, 23), "whatever you may build in the sand is unlikely to be a castle."

Moreover, in the eighteenth century, identity came to be intimately associated with notions of authenticity (Taylor 1994, 28). Identity was no longer limited to how one was identified within traditional social categories; rather, one was called upon to express one's true self, an identity that may not have accorded with the manner in which one was identified. As Taylor writes, not only is it individuals who are called on to be true to themselves and who suffer the damage of mis- or nonrecognition, but it is also a people who must do so: "Just like individuals, a Volk should be true to itself, that is, its own culture" (31). In modernity, then, recognition and identity became the site of individual and group struggles for self-fulfilment and self-determination.

Bauman (1996, 18) argues that although postmodernity does not give rise to the "problem of identity," it transforms the nature of the problem: "If the modern 'problem of identity' was how to construct an identity and keep it solid and stable, the postmodern 'problem of identity' is primarily how to avoid fixation and keep the options open." Within modernity, individuals and groups struggled to discover and maintain their authentic particularities in the face of universalizing forces of capitalization, rationalization, and colonialism in its various guises. However, despite the intensification of these processes in postmodernity, Bauman asserts that "well constructed and durable identity turns from an asset into a liability" (24). He attributes this transformation to the late-capitalist requirements of flexibility. The neoliberal economy has largely done away with stable jobs-for-life. As a result, the postmodern subject will not develop strong attachments to, and identifications with, particular workplaces, colleagues, or professions. Combined with increasing geographical mobility, this circumstance also means that throughout life one will not have stable social, cultural, or professional circles but will constantly be forming, discarding, and re-forming relationships and attachments to people and places. Because one cannot know how long a personal or professional relationship will last, deep attachments or identifications are disadvantageous. The modern anxiety over health – "of keeping the standard stable and unscathed" – is displaced by the postmodern preoccupation with fitness – "the capacity to move swiftly where the action is and be ready to take in experiences as they come" (24). To this account of the changes wrought by postmodernity, we can add the increased number of possible forms of self-identification and venues for recognition offered by travel, migration, and communication technologies. The result of this proliferation is said to be a hybridization of identity and a decentring of those identities that had gained the most prominence and seeming stability in modernity, central among them national identity.

In his valuable contribution to the study of identity in Québec, Jocelyn Maclure observes that since the early 1990s, Québec has been "in the throes of an exceptionally intense interrogation of its own identity."

This "fascination in Quebec with identity issues" is attributed to what he labels "identity indeterminacy," a phenomenon experienced by "every citizen ... on a daily basis" (Maclure 2003, 4). Unlike the commentators mentioned earlier, for whom this questioning of identity is considered a reflection of the perpetual québécois fixation on, and anxiety about, issues of identity, Maclure argues that intense questioning of identity emerges when dominant conceptions of identity become inoperative (8). Identity, then, "is not an objective, natural condition" but "a narrative project or a 'persuasive fiction'" – the product of particular narratives (9).

Approaching the question of identity through the method of Foucauldian archaeology, Maclure attempts to understand the limits imposed on conceptions of national identity by the two dominant discourses of identity in Québec, what he labels melancholy nationalism and anti-nationalist liberalism. Through this analysis, he hopes to make it possible to "go beyond" such narratives in the construction of a new form of national identity (Maclure 2003, 12). He attributes the cause of the crisis of identity in the early 1990s to the inability of these dominant conceptions of national identity to contend with globalization and Québec's "problematic status within the Canadian federation" (5).

In attributing the crisis of identity in Québec in the early 1990s to a narrative failure owing to disruptive exogenous and endogenous factors, Maclure's analysis is consistent with the approach of Bauman, Taylor, and the broader constructivist school of national identity, discussed in detail in the following chapter. These disruptive factors contribute to what Maclure (2003) labels "the challenge of pluralism," a challenge that provoked a re-evaluation and reinterpretation of dominant conceptions of *québécité* and that is made more difficult to contend with as a consequence of the limitations imposed on national identity by the prevailing narratives of the time. Cultural and economic globalization, including the phenomenon of mass migration, has resulted in a hybridization of identity for those living in Québec, one of multiple identifications and feelings of belonging, which has displaced the centrality of, and attachment to, a single national identity based on a shared territory and historical memory. At the same time, within Canadian federalism, Québec has continued to be subject to mis- or nonrecognition, which has limited the scope of national sovereignty and, until recently, prevented official recognition of Québec as a nation. In other words, Canadian federalism did not provide the Québécois with a vision of Québec that corresponded to an authentic self-image, prompting the need for the articulation of an identity other than that imposed by Canadian federalism (4–8).

Identity, Crisis, and Reproduction

The "identity indeterminacy" that Maclure refers to is portrayed as a product of increasing transnational or subnational identifications that create problems for both the stability and centrality of national identity resulting from the dynamics of postmodernity. Maclure's analysis, despite repeatedly referring to the persistence of the importance of the nation as a fundamental source of identity, does not account for the enduring and highly affective nature of national identity in the face of the fluidity of modernity and the fragmentation of postmodernity. As a result, although he provides a compelling account of the nature and limitations of dominant discourses of national identity in Québec at a particular moment, his account does not demonstrate why, despite being "detranscendentalized" (Maclure 2003, 10), national identity continues to produce strongly affective attachments and responses.

In other words, although Maclure's analysis offers an important account of the reproduction of an ongoing questioning of the nature of national identity in Québec since the mid-twentieth century, it does not provide an account of the reproduction of national identity itself in the face of such questioning and crisis. Thus, although Maclure (2003, 12) suggests that the goal of his analysis is, following Michel Foucault, "to 'free ourselves from ourselves,' to *become other,*" this cannot be accomplished unless we also examine why we tend to reproduce ourselves in particular forms. We cannot adequately think beyond our attachment to a certain narrative of the nation if we do not first examine why and in which ways we reproduce ourselves as national subjects.

Adopting an approach similar to the critical analyses of crises of capitalism and the nation-state system described above permits such an examination. By giving primacy to the nature of national identity rather than to particular expressions of national identity and moments of crisis, we can engage with questions of national identity in a manner that allows us to appreciate both its inherent fragility and the way that it endures despite this fragility. In doing so, we can avoid reducing crises of national identity to the consequence of either the features of a given nation that make it prone to crisis or the exogenous factors that act on and disrupt the nation. Instead, these features, events, or forces can be treated as phenomena that may, at particular moments, allow symptoms of crisis to become conscious.

Recent claims of national or civilizational crises in Québec and elsewhere, which portray a need to protect already secularized societies from the threat of "foreign" religiosity, engage in what Jacques Derrida (1992, 1995, 1996, 2003) refers to as a logic of immunity. According to Derrida (1995, 73n), "the immunitary reaction protects the 'indemnity' of the body proper in producing antibodies against foreign antigens." Such immunity processes are present in all attempts to produce or maintain what he refers to as "ipseic" definitions of discrete, binary identities. As Derrida and others have demonstrated in their investigations of various oppositional structures, such as between nature and culture, faith and knowledge, man and animal, the religious and the political, the national and the foreigner, and the European and the non-European, such definitions function through the construction of borders demarcating the unified self from its external other. Within this logic of immunity, religiosity is depicted both as an impediment to the integration of foreigners into secular Western societies and as an element that, if not contained, poses a threat to these societies. As a result, religion appears not as an endogenously generated entity that must be cleansed from the social body but as a contaminant that is external to an already purified, secularized West (Morrison 2013a, 153).

The logic of immunity presupposes the pre-givenness of both an identity and its other. The only difference acknowledged within the logic of immunity is that of the exterior. However, as the discussion of identity and alterity in the following chapter explains, difference is not that through which we can identify the particularities of already existing identities or communities; rather, it is the condition of possibility of all identity. A nation, like all identities, is not a thing-in-itself that encounters other predetermined identities. It is always involved in a relation of supplementation with what Derrida (1992) refers to as "the other shore," that which is constituted as non-national. As a result, "there is no culture or cultural identity without this difference *with itself*" (9–10). Otherness is always present within the self. Thus, as Julia Kristeva (1991) famously asserts, we are all "strangers to ourselves." The self is composed of various antagonistic elements that can never be integrated into a unified, ipseic identity.

The contentious debates about the Charter of Québécois Values, similar to those concerning attempts to formulate a definition of Europe to be included in the various proposals for a European Constitution (Morrison 2013a, 2014), are demonstrative of the conflict inherent to all identity. Not only have these debates involved competing thick (ethnic) and thin (civic) definitions of the collective, but the thin definitions themselves are also composed of internally antagonistic elements. A civic nationalism is defined on the basis of citizenship and in opposition to a nationalism that is grounded in ethnic belonging. However, a nation, like all forms of identity, is constituted on the basis of differentiation from others. As a result, a civic nationalism cannot be grounded in universalism. Although the basis of membership may be legal and territorial, the values underpinning the vision of citizenship must refer to particular national values, themselves the product of particular acknowledged or unacknowledged ethnic histories. As a result, civic nationalism contains elements of that against which it attempts to differentiate itself.

The only difference that ipseic definitions of the nation permit or acknowledge are those of the exterior. Immunitary processes attempt to protect the self from internal contradictions through denial, by exteriorizing one of the contradictory elements of the self, or by attempting to create an identity or continuity between these contradictory elements. However, a unified, ipseic national identity cannot be realized. The question of national identity cannot be resolved by buttressing its immunity against external antigens or by resolving internal contradictions.

Unlike immune processes, which seek to protect the host body by defending it against that which is foreign to it, "the process of autoimmunization ... consists for a living organism ... of protecting itself against its self-protection by destroying its own immune system" (Derrida 1995, 73n). The concept of autoimmunity reveals that each identity contains a force that promotes its self-destruction. It is this "internal-external, non-dialectizable antimony" (Derrida 2003, 35) that works against, and makes impossible, any ipseity. Thus the logic of autoimmunity upsets the oppositional structure of interiority and exteriority. Rather than exteriorizing or resolving the difference at play in national identity, it acknowledges the undecidability at the heart of seemingly contradictory identities.

The question of national identity is at once perpetual and always the product of a particular immanence. The integrity of any unified conception of national identity is always under threat from the autoimmune processes that work to undermine the dualistic structures upon which the conception rests. As a result, a closure or final resolution of national identity is never possible. As a unified, ipseic national identity can never be realized, the nation will always be subject to periodic crises (Morrison 2013a).

In this sense, unlike in the work of developmental psychologists such as Erik Erikson (1968, 1980) and the historical analyses of Québec's abnormality or immaturity discussed in Chapter 3, identity crisis is not understood as a pathological deviation from normal patterns of maturation or as a predictable period of ontological uncertainty, such as adolescence or midlife. If identity is a site of incessant struggle, contending with the crisis of identity is not a matter of "working through" moments of crisis once and for all and thereby developing a healthy personal or national narrative that accords with a given reality; rather, in accepting crisis as a basic feature of identity, we are called to find ways to reorient our relation of attachment to the threatened object so that change need not feel like a devastating loss.

In contrast to an understanding of crisis as abnormal and resolvable or as an epiphenomenon of other social processes, this alternative approach to studying crisis allows us to question the relationship between crisis and that which it is said to threaten. In this way, it asks us to question whether crisis is an external or inherent feature of a given system, entity, or phenomenon and, therefore, whether crisis is something that can or should be eradicated. In other words, we must question the necessity and desirability of that which is given or to which we have developed a form of affective attachment that Lauren Berlant (2011) labels "cruel optimism."

National identity, like all identity, is fundamentally riven by latent internal conflicts that may become manifest in periodic moments of crisis. The ever-present conflictual nature of identity, which may be repressed through the successful deployment of narrative devices, becomes manifest when a given narrative is made inoperative as the consequence of certain events, encounters, or forces. However, crisis is not the product of the failures of a particular narrative but a fundamental feature of identity that moments of narrative failure allow us to glimpse.

The recent declaration of national crisis in Québec provides an opening through which it is possible to engage with the nation as an aspect of our historical way of being. It offers an opportunity to explore the limits of this way of being and to understand and re-evaluate our attachments. With the declaration of a crisis of national identity, the inherently conflictual nature of the nation and identity, which may have previously functioned at a low level of visibility, is exposed. As in the case of Québec since the early 1990s, the failure of a narrative of the nation, announced as a crisis, provokes a questioning of the grounds for identity. When we articulate the threat faced by a nation, the nature of what is threatened, which is often taken as self-evident, must also be voiced. The hibernating assumptions of national identity must be articulated and illuminated. As a result, they are moved out of the shadows of the background and into the light of the foreground, permitting an interrogative spotlight to be shone on them. This exposure enables us to probe the parameters not only of particular conceptions of national identity but also of the fragile yet enduring nature of national identity.

Through an examination of moments of crisis in national identity in the history of Québec, this book provides an alternative historical narrative of the nation, one in which crisis serves as the locus of dissolution, transformation, and consolidation. In doing so, it does not attempt to determine an institutional or legal solution to questions of pluralism. Unlike the authors of much of the already existing analysis of current debates in Québec, I do not propose a framework for a reasonable, adequate, just, or efficient response to the presence of religion or the religious in the public sphere. In other words, I do not attempt to determine the proper limits of freedom of religion or propose an ideal model of the public sphere or subject in order to make possible or maximize cohesion, equality, toleration, or justice; rather, through an analysis of the nature of national identity, the book explores and problematizes the assumptions on which such debates rest. In doing so, it opens up a space for, and reveals the challenges of, developing alternative forms of community, belonging, and identity that, rather than trying to solve the problems of the fragility of national identity, are open to the possibilities that this fragility offers.

1 National Identity, Contingency, and Durability: Historicizing the Nation

Identity, whether individual or collective, is constituted by two criteria: temporal continuity and differentiation from others (Baumeister 1986). The stability and self-evidence of identity are made possible by the fact that – unlike differences between self and other, which are felt to be significant – temporal differences, if acknowledged, are not considered meaningful enough to disturb a sense of historical continuity. A disruption of either of these criteria of identity can result in ontological uncertainty – a questioning of our sense of self or the solidity of the "we." In other words, a disruption of temporal continuity or differentiation from others produces a crisis of identity.

In this chapter, I examine the understandings of temporal continuity and differentiation from others present within the two prominent contemporary approaches to critical analysis of the nation, nationalism, and national identity, namely constructivism and Lacanian psychoanalysis. The constructivist approach, exemplified by the work of Benedict Anderson (1983), offers an important critique of essentialist nationalist narratives by demonstrating the manner in which nations and national identities are historically constructed. Psychoanalytic approaches influenced by the work of Jacques Lacan via Slavoj Žižek (1993) have argued that constructivists fail to account for the deeply affective and, consequently, enduring nature of national identity. However, this focus on the reproduction of the same has come at the expense of providing a historical account of transformations in images, forms, and institutions of identity and belonging. Although it importantly accounts for the reproduction of national identity based on particular symbols and experiences of national belonging, it tends to decentre analysis of transformations in the self-understanding of national identity. Thus, because the approach offered by Žižek and his school of thought focuses on the affective strength of national bonds and on the often violent reactions that occur when these bonds are felt to be threatened, it fails to contend with the manner in which national identity reproduces itself not by a reproduction of the same but through a transformation of that which is said, and felt, to be definitive of the group.

Through an examination of both the promise and limitations of these approaches, I argue that in order to understand the manner in which the nation is both transformed in, and persists through, moments of crisis, there is a need to reframe conceptions of contingency and alterity. In undertaking this task, I focus on the notion of an inherent difference from oneself, evident in the processes of immunity and autoimmunity at play in the formation, maintenance, and transformation of identity and community. Moreover, I describe how a focus on contingency and transformation allows for the writing of a counternarrative of national identity, one that permits an understanding of change and endurance without relying on notions of transhistorical identity provided by narrative devices such as secularization.

The Nation as Construct

Writing in 1972 in reference to what he argued was a profound alienation at the heart of then contemporary French Canadian identity, Jean Bouthillette (1972, 25), stated, "We have not disappeared, but we are no longer identical with ourselves." Bouthillette's statement reveals the paradox of speaking of transhistorical identity. What does it mean to speak of a we, a common identity across time, while at the same time acknowledging that the group that we speak of today is not identical with, and may display characteristics at odds with, the historical group with which it is identified? In other words, how can we understand historical difference within that which must, according to the logic of the nation, be understood as transhistorically identical?

For some nationalists and scholars of the nation, the answer to such questions is apparent. For them, the nation and national identity are an outgrowth of evolving yet enduring primordial ethnic identities and affiliations (Geertz 1963; Smith 1986). If the nation is rooted in a common ethnicity, ancestry, and/or historical experience, it is unproblematic to speak of it as a continuous transhistorical identity. The loss or transformation of cultural features once held to be definitive of the nation appears as an episode within a broader narrative of ethnic continuity. Crisis, trauma, or what certain nationalist historians refer to as moments of "collective drama" (Cantin 1997; Dumont 1995) can result in the developmental path of the nation going astray if once core features of national identity are displaced by a damaged, inauthentic, or alienated form of self-conception. It is in this sense that Bouthillette can write of an alienated "we" that, in some regard, is no longer identical to itself.

In contrast to such primordialist or substantialist understandings of the nation, constructivists offer an account of the nation as a recent creation. They argue that rather than an essence constituted by determinable transhistorical ethnic characteristics, the nation is an entity whose emergence was made possible by particular historical forces and circumstances and that it must be continuously enacted through practices and rituals. The nation is perceived as a form of community brought about by the homogenization and subsequent internalization of cultural artefacts, symbols, values, beliefs, and customs by members of any society that permits nationals to perceive themselves as separate and different from "others," facilitating, in turn, the spread of nationalism.

In the more instrumental understanding of the construction of the nation, nationalism is portrayed as a tool deployed by the elite in the advancement of their interests. National identities are described as ideological inventions designed to legitimize the centralization and unification of the state associated with capitalist development (Calhoun 1997, 21; Hobsbawm 1990; Tilly 1990).

Others within the constructivist tradition understand nations as historically constructed "discursive formations" whose emergence and hegemony were made possible by certain technological, political, economic, and social developments (Calhoun 1997, 3–6). Anderson, perhaps the most influential contemporary scholar of the nation and nationalism, is exemplary of this perspective. Differentiating his approach from that of others, such as Ernest Gellner (1964, 169), who, he argues, portray the nation as an invented community marked by "falsity" and "fabrication," Anderson (1983, 15) argues that "any communities larger than primordial villages of face-to-face contact (and perhaps even these) are imagined." To say that nations and other communities are imagined is not to say that they are imaginary; rather, the term "imagined" refers to the types of images and image formation that are key to the constitution of particular communities (McCrone 1998, 6). Thus nations should not be distinguished from other forms of community on the basis of falsity or authenticity "but by the style in which they are imagined" (Anderson 1983, 15).

Nations are "imagined" in terms of both their internal composition and their external boundaries. Members of even the smallest nation do not know most of their fellow nationals, yet each possesses an image of a connection and communion with the other (Anderson 1983, 15). First, the nation is imagined as limited. Each nation has external boundaries determined by that which is imagined to define the line between the last national and the first alien. Second, nations are imagined as sovereign, with the nation-state serving as "the gage and emblem of this freedom." Finally, nations are imagined as a deep horizontal community (16). Camaraderie between nationals is imaginatively maintained, notwithstanding the presence of inequality and exploitation.

According to Anderson (1983, 30), imagining the nation was made possible by the rise of what he, following Walter Benjamin (1973, 265), refers to as homogeneous empty time. This understanding of the relationship between time and space, marked by temporal coincidence, is crucial to a form of identification that allows for the nation to be imagined. The nation requires a particular understanding of history, identity, and community within which "the idea of a sociological organism moving calendrically through homogeneous empty time is a precise analogue of the idea of the nation, which is also conceived as a solid community moving steadily down (or up) history" (Anderson 1983, 31). For Anderson and others within the constructivist tradition, the task for scholars of the nation is to understand the processes through which this contemporaneous and transhistorical identification was forged.

For Anderson, the development of print capitalism, particularly newspapers, was central to creating the unity of the time-space of the nation (Anderson 1983, 37–40). Standardized, vernacular print languages created unified fields of communication between geographically dispersed people, who, through this communication, became aware of their ostensible fellowship with other readers within a linguistic community. The bourgeoisie and other groups sought to align themselves with this new understanding of community first by publishing dictionaries of the nation's language, its history, and its literatures and later through the development and transmission of official nationalisms.

Among the most influential of early attempts to attend to questions of the origins and nature of the nation is Ernest Renan's address at the Sorbonne in 1882. Within this address, many of the key elements of constructivist thinking, particularly the historical contingency and fragility of the nation, are laid bare. In addressing the question "what is the nation?" Renan sought to counter essentialist conceptions of the nation found in the writings of militant nationalists of his time, such as Heinrich Treitschke (Smith 1998, 9). He argued that the nation was a recently emergent historical entity "brought about by a series of convergent facts" (Renan 1882, 45). The essential elements of a nation cannot be equated with dynasty, race, language, religion, common interest, or geography. The nation, he argued, is none of these material things; rather, it is "a spiritual principle, the outcome of the profound complications of history" (52).

This spiritual principle is constituted by two closely related factors, one of which Renan related to the past and the other to the present. Related to the past is the "possession in common of a rich legacy of memories" (Renan 1882, 52). In relation to the present, the nation involves a daily plebiscite concerning the veracity of these memories and "the will to perpetuate the value of the heritage that one has received in an undivided form" (52). The unitary power of memories is based on what Renan deems the most legitimate of all cults, the cult of the ancestor. Thus the common memories that form the nation concern the heroic deeds, glories, sacrifices, and suffering of ancestors. Of these memories, the most important and most powerful are those associated with suffering, as "they impose duties, and require a common effort" (53).

Renan is careful to acknowledge that the unity of the nation, like the common memories that serve as its basis, relies fundamentally on a process of forgetting. The forging of a common memory involves forgetting the "deeds of violence which took place at the origin of all political formations" (Renan 1882, 45). He asserts, for example, that the cohesion of the French nation requires the French to forget the brutality of the massacres that accompanied the unification of northern France with the Midi in the thirteenth century (45).

As Derrida's (1988, 184) reading of Renan suggests, forgetting acts as a form of repression; "it is active, selective, meaningful, in one word interpretive." Consequently, the national forgetting that Renan describes is an active process. Rather than being "simply a psychological effacement, a wearing out or a meaningless obstacle making access to the past more difficult, as when an archive has been accidentally destroyed," national forgetting occurs "because there is no bearing something which was at the origin of the nation, surely an act of violence, a traumatic event, some sort of curse that one does not admit" (184). In other words, collective forgetting is not only the result of the irrelevancy of the past to the present, as Jocelyne Dakhlia (2001, 72) claims, but also involves what Adrian Forty (1999, 18) has called "artfully selective oblivion." Only through forgetting can a nation be assured of its existence, and only through forgetting is it possible to make promises for the future (Derrida 1988, 185).

Although an ongoing process of forgetting is necessary for the constitution and maintenance of the nation, it is also the centrality of forgetting that renders the nation inherently fragile. Renan (1882, 45) asserts that as a consequence of the long process of the formation of the French nation, "no French citizen knows whether he is Burgundian, an Alan, a Taifale, or a Visigoth." However, forgetting does not mean the effacement of memory. As Derrida (1988, 185) emphasizes, "as long as some remember originary deeds of violence" or "recall the purity of their origin ... the nation remains unassured of its essence or of its existence." Repression is not annihilation. That which is repressed is always present and always threatening to surface and undo the historical work of national formation. Thus, for the nation to persist, the originary violence – the denial of internal difference constitutive of the nation – must remain active through the ongoing work of forgetting.

It is in relation to the threat that remembering poses to the nation that Renan (1882, 45) notes the danger of historical study. Here, Renan seems to be referring to what Friedrich Nietzsche (1874, 74) labels critical history – a selective, temporary suspension of forgetfulness that permits a critique of the past and the present. As every past contains violence, weakness, and injustice, it is always worthy of condemnation. The temporary suspension of forgetfulness allows us to forget the generality of historical injustice in order to denounce a particular aspect of the past.

History, however, can also often work in the service of the nation. First, in its antiquarian form, rather than undermining that which is, history preserves and reveres (Nietzsche 1874, 67). Through its use of the "we," it allows members of the nation to see beyond the transience of their existence in order to "find the contentment of the tree in its roots" (73–74). Here, we have a form of history – present in certain forms of primordialist or substantialist theories of the nation – where "the formation of the nation ... appears as the fulfillment of a 'project' stretching over the centuries, in which there are different stages and moments of coming to self-awareness" (Balibar 1991, 86). Within such a "retrospective illusion" of project and destiny, as Etienne Balibar labels it, "generations which succeed one another ... have handed down to each other an invariant substance" (86). In this form of historical analysis, the fabrication of tradition and culture provides an invaluable means of constructing or enhancing national bonds (Guibernau 1996, 76; Hobsbawm and Ranger 1983).

Although such analysis can undermine a given nation, the temporariness and selectiveness of critique often mean that analysis stops short of critiquing the concept of nationality itself. Consequently, this form of history can give birth to a new or renewed national consciousness among members of the group who have become aware of attempts to efface their difference within the project of nation building. For example, historical research pointing to the violent annexation of a region or incorporation of a people into the French nation or the discovery of Burgundian or Tafalian roots in certain segments of the population need not necessarily lead to the undoing of the French nation as a whole. It may, however, provide impetus for the formation of a Burgundian or Tafalian national consciousness. Thus, as Anderson (1983, 66) argues, despite attempts by particular elites to forge the nation in their own image, "the nation proved an invention on which it was impossible to secure a patent" – an image "available for pirating by widely different, and sometimes unexpected hands."

Within the constructivist tradition, therefore, the construction of a nation is said to depend on an internalized perception of national identity. For some, this means that nations are, in fact, "made by nationalism," in that they "exist only when their members understand themselves through the discursive framework of national identity" (Calhoun 1997, 99). Others are not convinced that an unequivocal causal arrow can be drawn from nationalism to nation or vice versa. Such scholars nevertheless concur that the articulation of nation and nationalism is at the epicentre of nationalist practices, which precariously construct boundaries separating "sacred kin and alien kind" (Manzo 1996, 3). These boundaries, according to Kathryn Manzo, are "made to appear timeless and beyond question. But precisely because national boundaries are constructed and always contestable, the reproduction of the national and alien requires constant practice. It occurs continuously in a range of social institutions such as schools and media, and in daily routines associated with 'policing, suspicion, and crossing (or refusal of entry)'" (38). As the nation is subjectively constituted on the basis of its spiritual principle and maintained through a daily plebiscite, the constructed nature of the nation requires that the nation and nationalism be perpetually practised. Crisis occurs when the results of this daily plebiscite are uncertain because the historical narrative has failed to provide the means sufficient for forgetting the violence and difference at the roots of what must appear as identical and temporally continuous. Within the constructivist tradition, therefore, the nation appears as (1) historically constructed, (2) subjective, (3) requiring ongoing reproduction, and thus (4) crucially fragile.

Affect and the Endurance of the Nation

This constructivist understanding of national identity, despite remaining the dominant perspective within studies of nations and nationalisms, has been challenged by scholars who have argued that it is unable to account for the persistence of the nation "as a relatively unshakeable unifying principle for human communities" (Stavrakis and Chrysoloras 2006, 146). Although they accept the nation as a relatively recent product of history, they ask why, if identity is a fluid construction and the product of particular social and political events and processes, national identity has continued to endure and even thrive.

One answer to this question is posited by Anthony Smith, who argues that the endurance of national identity is the result of the nation's grounding in deeply rooted ethnic identifications and practices. Consequently, understanding the paradox of national identity requires an "intermediate position between ... 'perennialism' and 'modernism'" (Smith 1986, 17), one that can "bring out the differences and similarities between modern national units and sentiments and the collective cultural units and sentiments of previous eras" (13). National identity is not constructed on the basis of a tabula rasa but from pre-existing ethnic material. The strength of attachment to the nation is a result of the relationship of members to deeply rooted ethnic cultural symbols and practices that have been incorporated into the national imaginary. The enduring quality of the nation is provided by the historic solidity of the ethnic bonds operationalized within nationalism rather than by the emptiness of the imaginary bonds of the recently emergent national community.

However, as Lacanian scholars Yannis Stavrakis and Nicos Chrysoloras (2006, 147) argue, Smith's insight "merely displaces the terms of the paradox." In deferring the source of deeply held attachment to early forms of community, it fails to acknowledge that these forms of attachment are themselves also socially and historically produced. The question that must be asked is what, then, is the nature of the attachments that allow certain forms of collective identity to endure? As a result, any account of the nation must address the role of affect in the construction and reproduction of national identity.

Anderson (1983, 129) himself admits that the constructivist approach is unable to adequately explain the deep attachment of members to the nation: "It is doubtful whether either social change or transformed consciousnesses, in themselves, do much to explain the *attachment* that peoples feel for the inventions of their imaginations [or] ... why people are ready to die for these inventions." What is missing in the constructivist account is an explanation of how the nation – an imaginary social formation constructed on the basis of the emptiness of time and the arbitrariness of language – is able to inspire self-sacrificing love. It is one thing to imagine a form of identification that prevails despite the geographical dispersion of, and the relations of inequality and exploitation among, its members, and it is another thing to account for the feelings of fraternity that this imaginary identification is said to produce (Ziarek 1995, 14). Although a common public language can help in the process of identification, it is affect that is able to convert this commonality into a meaningful attachment and to transform language and other "empty signs into emblems of 'communion' ... reif[ying] the arbitrary signifiers into the expression of empathy" (14).

In order to understand the particular form of psychic investment that grants the nation its force as an enduring and profound object of identification and attachment, a number of scholars have argued that it is necessary to approach the study of the nation with the aid of psychoanalytic insights and tools. Central to many recent psychoanalytic studies of national identity is the Lacanian concept of enjoyment (*jouissance*).

In his investigations of group psychology, Sigmund Freud (1921) argues for the need to understand the libidinal organization of groups. The "power" that holds a group together, he asserts, is the same as that which "holds together everything in the world," namely the life instinct, or Eros (92). The attachment to particular forms of collective identity is, therefore, not merely the product of discourse but also rooted in the body's libidinal drives (Stavrakis and Chrysoloras 2006, 150).

Lacan reconceptualizes Freud's idea of libido in terms of enjoyment, viewing libido as that which animates desire. Within Lacanian psychoanalysis, entering into the social/symbolic world of linguistic representation requires the sacrifice of enjoyment as fullness. As a consequence of this necessary sacrifice, the subject is always marked by a lack. However, it is this very lack that produces desire. The imaginary promise of recapturing this lost pre-symbolic enjoyment sustains desire. Although impossible to attain, the fantasy of overcoming the limits socially imposed on our enjoyment motivates both individual action and collective political projects, such as the nation. As Stavrakis and Chrysolaras (2006, 151) argue, political projects that promise the "good life" or "just society" are exemplary of this type of motivation. It is the desire to attain full enjoyment that propels individuals and groups to invest themselves in utopian political projects as attempts to imagine or institute social forms that will overcome the limitations on enjoyment inherent in current politico-social arrangements. Fantasy, then, promises the possibility of resolving social antagonism by establishing a harmonious social form in which the lack is covered over (Stavrakis and Chrysoloras 2006, 151; Žižek 2017, 210).

The fantasy of fulfilment is not, however, sufficient to account for the force of identification. If faith in the promise of fullness is not to be gradually extinguished, it must be periodically renewed through limit-experiences that provide a sense of temporary or partial enjoyment. In these experiences, such as a victory in war or sport or the acting-out of a sexual fantasy, the subject momentarily experiences "something akin to an attainment of her identification" (Stavrakis and Chrysoloras 2006, 151). However, as fullness is unattainable, the enjoyment experienced in these moments can be only partial. As Lacan (1998, 111) writes, "'That's not it' is the very cry by which the jouissance obtained is distinguished from the jouissance expected." The partiality of limit-experiences is what reproduces the fantasy of fulfilment. If fulfilment could be attained, desire would be extinguished. Therefore, it is a constant deferral of fullness and the promise of its future attainment that fuel desire. We continually pursue identification because we only ever partially experience it.

Within this framework, the nation can be defined by the way a group organizes its collective enjoyment, what Žižek (1993) labels the "Nation-Thing." Although this thing can be recognized only by the visible "way of life" definitive of a given community – its rituals and symbols – there is always "'something more' in it, something that *is present* in these features, that *appears* through them" (201). The force of the Nation-Thing is the result of the reflexive structure of belief that renders it meaningful for the members of the nation: "'I believe in the (national) Thing' equals 'I believe that others (members of my community) believe in the Thing.'" Consequently, "the national Thing exists as long as members of the community believe in it; it is literally an effect of this belief itself" (202).

It is this reflexive structure that Žižek (1993) argues differentiates Lacanian analysis from constructivism. Symbolic identification does not have enough force to compel attraction and attachment to the nation. What gives "substance" to the attraction is enjoyment. As a result, Žižek asserts, "a nation *exists* only as long as its specific *enjoyment* continues to be materialized in a set of social practices and transmitted through national myths that structure these practices" (202).

The Nation-Thing, however, is not merely positively constituted. As with all identity, national identity is made possible through ongoing relations of alterity. Difference not only accentuates a sense of identity but is also the condition of possibility of all identity (Stavrakis and Chrysoloras 2006, 149–50). What determines the Nation-Thing is that it appears to us as "'our Thing' ... as something accessible only to us, as something 'they,' the others, cannot grasp" (Žižek 1993, 201). If we are asked to explain what it is that defines our national identity, we can list only those things that we see as unique to our way of life – "the unique things that we enjoy, that others do not have" (Keohane 1992, 20).

But this understanding is still only one dimension of the character of identification – the purely formal/semiotic relation of alterity. What is missing is the more substantive/affective dimension. To understand "the passage from *form* to *force*" (Stavrakis and Chrysoloras 2006, 149), psychoanalytic accounts of national identity point to Freud's insistence on the duality of drives. Every unifying affective investment also involves the mobilization of a differentiating hatred and aggressiveness directed toward others. The life-giving Eros is always accompanied by the destructive Thanatos. This duality is what Žižek (1993, 203) refers to when he states that "the basic paradox is that our Thing is conceived as something inaccessible to the other and at the same time threatened by him." Although the outsider's difference is necessary for the constitution of national identity, it appears as threatening to the nation.

What is threatening to the nation is the excessive way that the other organizes their enjoyment, an excess that is felt to limit our capacity to fully enjoy our way of life. What bothers us about the other's cultural practices is not that they are simply strange, being incomprehensible to us or symbolically at odds with our own practices, but that they restrict our own pursuit of enjoyment. In Kieran Keohane's (1992, 25) application of the notion of excessive enjoyment to québécois nationalism, the Québécois are jealous of the political power of the rest of Canada, "the special relationship with the land that we suspect Natives of enjoying ... and the 'prosperity of Americans.'" However, it is not a matter of desiring the form of enjoyment that others have but a matter of resenting the way that these practices are seen to interfere with, or steal the enjoyment of, the Québécois. Canadian federalism and Indigenous claims to land and sovereignty can be seen as interfering with, or at least making more complex, Québec's sovereignty; American prosperity can be equated with the extraction of Québec's resources and the loss of jobs in the province. It is in this sense that the Lacanian perspective employs the notion of the "theft of enjoyment" (Žižek 1993, 201).

As the attainment of fulfilment is never possible, it cannot be stolen by the other. Imputing to the other the theft of enjoyment, therefore, conceals "the traumatic fact that *we never possessed what was allegedly stolen from us*" (Žižek 1993, 203). In this sense, the hatred of the other's enjoyment is really a hatred of the limitations of our own forms of enjoyment (206). When we complain about the excessive enjoyment of the other, what we are really pointing at is not the incompatibility of their cultural practices with ours but the inherent antagonisms within our own community (205). As a result, the other – that which steals our enjoyment – plays the role of the scapegoat.

In moments of crisis, when the givenness of the Nation-Thing is found wanting and, consequently, national identity appears to lack fullness or stability, the nation attempts to retain its hegemonic status by blaming others for this lack (Stavrakis and Chrysoloras 2006, 150). This displacement of inner-group social antagonisms onto the other is not merely ideological but also constitutive of the fantasy organization of desire that sustains the nation (Žižek 1993, 206). On the one hand, the "beatific" dimension of the fantasy of the promise of fulfilment through the nation is maintained by the partial or momentary enjoyment that the nation provides. On the other hand, the "disturbing paranoic fantasy ... tells us why things went wrong" (Žižek 2017, 210). In other words, blaming the other allows us to continue to invest in the nation while providing us with a reason why it has *not yet* delivered on its promise. Thus, blaming the other "preserves our faith in the existence and the possibility of recapturing our lost enjoyment ... but projects its full realization onto the future, when we will manage to get it back from the Other who has stolen it from us" (Stavrakis and Chrysoloras 2006, 152). In effect, keeping enjoyment at "a healthy distance," as something that can be achieved in the future, delays enjoyment and thus maintains the nation as an object of an as yet unfulfilled desire (152).

The role of fantasy in the maintenance of national identity is evident in the nationalist narratives of the fall of a golden era, in which, prior to its disruption by some evil other, the nation was harmonious. Although such an era is a "chimera," this fantasy serves to foster national solidarity and desire for the nation (Stavrakis and Chrysoloras 2006, 153). Such nationalist narratives both promote historical identification and compel successive generations to identify with the nation and to resist the external forces seeking to prevent the nation from attaining its lost full enjoyment. At the same time, "national solidarity is maintained through the ritualization of practices which offer some limited enjoyment as well as through the reproduction of the above-mentioned myth of national destiny in official and unofficial public discourse" (153).

Lacanian theorists of the nation argue that this understanding of the nation enriches the constructivist conception of the nation as a discursive formation with psychoanalytic concepts of enjoyment and desire that account for its endurance as an object of deep, ongoing affective attachment (Stavrakis and Chrysoloras 2006, 154). Moreover, they assert that the notion of the shared enjoyment of the Nation-Thing, as that which fills the emptiness of the national imaginary, offers a means of understanding the solidity of national identity without resorting to essentialism. As mentioned earlier, the Nation-Thing, visible to us as our unique way of life, is delineated only in relation to the manner in which our organization of enjoyment differs from that of others. As a result, it is empty of an essential content, with difference serving as the condition of its possibility.

Problematizing Alterity: Contingency and Fragility

It is in the description of the role of alterity in identity formation that some of the limitations of Lacanian accounts of national identity become apparent. Like Žižek's (1993, 202) assertion that "the national Cause is ultimately nothing but the way subjects of a given ethnic community organize their enjoyment through national myths," the Lacanian perspective often slips into conflating, or at least failing to adequately differentiate, ethnic and national identity. This periodic resort to the use of ethnicity is illustrative of a more general propensity for markers of difference to appear as given rather than as historically produced and thus changing and changeable.

The Lacanian description of the Nation-Thing portrays the content of the way of life that the nation must protect against the perpetual threat of the external other as defined only by what members believe is unique to their group. However, the logic of protection that they describe is one of reproduction as reproduction of the same. In moments of crisis, the nation is renewed by reinvesting in and protecting a predefined distinctive way of life. In this sense, the history of the nation appears as a heroic and/or tragic history of the sometimes bloody struggles undertaken in the name of protecting a nation's static way of life. This historical conception of the nation is consistent with Balibar's (1991) aforementioned description of nationalist history as one in which successive generations pass an invariant substance to the next.

Within such an account, the nation may have a history, but that which is said to define it as invariant is positioned outside of history. However, as the radical transformations in that which has been said to define québécois identity make clear, although nations periodically enter into moments of identity crisis resulting from particular historical events and encounters, they persist not only by a renewal of the same but often also despite the loss or transformation of that which is felt to be definitive of their way of life or national character. Therefore, providing a non-nationalist account of a nation requires writing a history of that which appears to be timeless.

By allowing us to be untimely, history enables us to escape what is most taken for granted and to engage in a questioning of unquestioned values (Nietzsche 1887, 8). However, doing so requires that we think genealogically, treating history not as a teleological unfolding or the work of conscious subjects but as a narrative of the struggles that have led to the emergence of particular ways of being and the sacrifice of other possible ways of being. Therefore, thinking genealogically implies that what is taken for granted today cannot be considered the necessary product of historical development, as no emergence or development is natural. On the contrary, all that is given must be seen as the result of struggles, sacrifices, and domination. Accordingly, genealogy attempts to view historical events in their dispersion or singularity, examining moments of reinterpretation when forces encounter one another and transform what is given as natural (Geuss 1994, 329). Since what is given is always the result of struggle and domination, there is nothing that possesses an essential meaning or purpose. The meanings and purposes assigned to things are the product of struggles involving interpretation and reinterpretation.

Identity and alterity are never pre-given or stable across time. They relate only "to concrete historical situations and to the preoccupations relevant to each of those historical situations" (Van Alphen 2011, 1). As a result, both that which members of a nation hold to be definitive of national identity and that against which the uniqueness of their identity is measured "are changeable products of the ongoing process of constituting a self-image" (15). The problem of what Isin (2002a) labels "the logics of exclusion and enclosure" is that the identity of the other is taken to pre-exist rather than being constituted in the formation of the self. For example, migrants in Québec came to be defined by their religiosity only in the process of the constitution of Québec as a civic nation defined by its secularity. Thinking critically about the nation requires questioning the givenness of categories of otherness and approaching them as internally, rather than externally, related to the constitution and reconstitution of a group's identity (4).

Lacanian accounts of national identity are also limited by the deployment of a restrictive conceptualization of difference itself. Within the framework outlined above, the complexities of alterity are reduced to a simplistic model of "us" versus "them." Differences in the organization of enjoyment play the role of defining the boundaries of the group on the basis of those who share in a common way of life. However, as Isin (2002a, 4) argues in his history of citizenship as alterity, the depiction of a dialectical distinction between inside and outside is strategic and political. The notion of a zero-sum game involving discrete and binary groups has always been used by dominant groups to naturalize relations of difference and domination, with "dominated others appear[ing] as the distant and transitive (barbarians), rather than the near and immanent (strangers, outsiders, aliens)" (5).

Within a logic of alterity, identity is formed not only on the basis of differentiation from an already constituted external other but also through the elective affiliation, recognition, and incorporation of certain groups and through dissociation and estrangement from others, including those once situated as part of the interior. As a result, individuals and groups are differently located within often multiple, fluid, and overlapping relations of distance, immanence, difference, and similarity. Thus social categories as well as spaces of interiority and exteriority are not pre-given but "are systems of orientation and stakes in the struggles that create and situate individuals in certain positions *within* the social space" (Isin 2002a, 25).

Although group identities are always formed under particular historical regimes of classification and categorization, these categories are not unified or stable. Groups should be viewed as solidaristic, agonistic, and alienating assemblages, the product of various historic strategies and technologies of affiliation, dissociation, recognition, and misrecognition. As a result, the conditions that make possible the formation and transformation of group identities cannot be determined theoretically but must be disclosed through genealogical investigation (Isin 2002a, 25).

Strangely, despite being rooted in psychoanalysis, Lacanian accounts of national identity tend to downplay Freud's most fundamental insight, namely that we are different from ourselves. As a result, the vital role of internal difference and conflict in the formation and transformation of identity and community as well as the role that externalization of difference plays both in the construction of the self and in formenting xenophobia are largely overlooked. Freud's writings continually assert that who we are, including our actions, outlooks, and tendencies, is the product not only of the conscious subject but also of an interplay of forces and components of the psyche and of conflicts and compromises between the external and the internal as well as between often antagonistic internal elements.

The role of this difference from oneself in the formation of individual and collective identity is perhaps most strongly articulated in the work of Julia Kristeva (1982, 1990, 1991). Unlike with the scapegoat mechanism articulated by Žižek and others, in which the perceived threat posed by an external other serves to paper over endogenous antagonism and thus allows the nation to appear as unified, in Kristeva's (1991, 98) thought, the figure of the foreigner serves as a "scar," fracturing the imagined unity of the national body (Ziarek 1995, 2). Although the scapegoat mechanism works through a logic of immunity, seemingly protecting the nation from perceived external contaminants, what is overlooked in this perspective is the centrality of autoimmunity to both the constitution and reproduction of identity and community.

Kristeva (1991, 96) describes the foreigner – "the one who does not belong to the state in which we are, the one who does not have the same nationality" – as a liminal figure within the modern nation-state system. Kristeva's foreigner, in a manner similar to Arendt's (1951) figure of the refugee, appears as an immanent other. The foreigner dwells among us but, as a non-national, is not one of us. Even, or perhaps especially, when legally incorporated as a citizen of the nation-state, the modern figure of the foreigner occupies a space of liminality between inside and outside. As a result, the foreigner is abject, "what disturbs identity, system, order. What does not respect borders, positions, rules. The in-between, the ambiguous, the composite. The traitor, the liar, the criminal with a good conscience, the shameless rapist, the killer who claims he is a savior" (Kristeva 1982, 4). The foreigner, as abject, aids in the construction of the boundaries of the nation but also serves as "a 'symptom' ... Psychologically he signifies the difficulty we have of living as an *other* and with others; politically, he underscores the limits of nation-states and of the national political conscience" (Kristeva 1991, 103).

Abjection, for Kristeva, is the always temporal and unstable process through which a subject defines itself by establishing borders. As Kristeva reminds us, it is always an unfinished process because the abject is produced by the body and continues to haunt it. "The twisted braid of affects and thoughts" that Kristeva (1982, 1) labels abjection does not have a definable object. Although the abject shares with objects (as other) the quality of being opposed to the I, the abject is not an object that the I faces, in relation to which the I feels autonomous, and against which the I can define itself; rather, the abject "draws me toward the place where meaning collapses" – toward the ambiguity of the border between subject and object, or I and other. The abject is excluded but intriguing; it repulses yet excites. Even "from its place of banishment, the abject does not cease challenging its master" (2).

To clarify the concept of the abject, Kristeva provides two main examples. The first is the loathing of food, visible in the repulsiveness of the skin on the surface of milk (Kristeva 1982, 2). She describes this repulsion in visceral language that itself produces nausea. It is through this repudiation of food that the I begins to appear. "'I' want none of that element ... 'I' do not want to listen, 'I' do not assimilate it, 'I' expel it" (3).

Through the abjection of that which is not desired, the I is born, or in Kristeva's (1982, 3) words, "I give birth to myself amid the violence of sobs, of vomit." This process of developing the self can appear in early infancy and continue throughout one's life. It is the beginning of the boundary that develops between the mother and the child – a boundary that is tenuous, desirable, and undesirable all at the same time. In this sense, the abject is also what stops the subject's desire from being fulfilled, for it relies on separation while simultaneously desiring unity.

The second example of the abject is the corpse, which Kristeva (1982, 4) labels the "utmost of abjection." The corpse is abject as it wavers between the worlds of the living and the dead. The corpse is the total abjection of the I, for it is the I that is expelled, breaking down the borders that separate the dead from the living.

In order to understand the feelings of horror in the face of the foreigner – "the prickly passions aroused by the intrusion of the *other* into the homogeneity" of the nation – Eva Ziarek (1995, 20) argues that it is necessary to clarify the experience of the uncanny manifest in certain relations of otherness. As Ziarek asserts, the experience of the uncanny is not, as in the work of Emmanuel Levinas (1986), an encounter with the irreducible alterity of the other; rather, as described in Freud's writings, the uncanny is "an immanence of the strange within the familiar" (Kristeva 1991, 183). Encountering the foreigner does not reinforce the nation's sense of identity in relation to an external other but instead produces "an unsettling recognition of the subject's own strangeness" (Ziarek 1995, 20).

Like Žižek, Kristeva argues that, as symbolic identification is insufficient to produce and sustain attachment to the nation, the symbolic must be supplemented by affect. However, unlike in Žižek's account of the productive role of affect in the constitution and maintenance of national identity, for Kristeva the role of affect is ambiguous. As the national community is always threatened by the eruption of repressed internal differences, the affective attachment that fills the void of symbolic identification can itself become a threat (Ziarek 1995, 16). Rather than producing a sense of national unity, the communal desire to "invalidate the arbitrariness of signs" (Kristeva 1991, 186) generates a threatening experience of strangeness to oneself – an awareness of difference and antagonism within the nation.

In this way, as Ziarek (1995, 16) suggests, the encounter with otherness, which produces a sense of difference from the external other, cannot be separated from the disruptive force of the uncanny: "As the primary reminder of the ghostly character of the imaginary identification, the figure of the foreigner disorients the judgment about belonging to the common world and thereby reveals the glaring gaps and discontinuities beneath national affiliation." It is in reaction to such disturbing feelings of strangeness to oneself that Kristeva locates the roots of xenophobia. Unable to acknowledge or accept such difference, we turn on the foreigner as "the figure of otherness as such" (4).

Consequently, Kristeva (1991, 192) argues that attaining a sense of national solidity and resolving the crisis of national identity cannot be accomplished through the expulsion or absorption of others, as "the difference within us ... [is] the ultimate condition of our being with others." The only way to develop a nonviolent way of being with others, she asserts, is to renounce the imaginary unity of the nation and accept the ever-present alterity within the self (Ziarek 1995, 6).

The depiction of alterity in the formation of identity and subjectivity presented by Kristeva and Isin is thus more complicated than a simple model of self and other. Rather than a relation of us and other that provides stability for national identity, they provide an account of constantly shifting relations with variously located others and elements of the self, engagement with whom can both reaffirm and disturb feelings and discourses of national identity. A history of the nation must, therefore, recount (1) the historical contexts and regimes of classification that make possible historically contingent encounters with otherness, (2) the manner in which the national group encounters a variety of internal and external others, (3) the reaction to such encounters through particular strategies of recognition and misrecognition, incorporation, and expulsion, and (4) the ways that the content of that which defines national identity is transformed through these encounters.

Historical Narrative, Continuity, and Transformation

Although nationalism requires an image of the nation as temporally continuous, the content of that which is said to be distinctive of the nation's way of life changes. Narrative devices that can account for these transformations within a broader framework of continuity, such as common ancestry, maturation, modernization, or secularization, are therefore required to provide the solidity necessary for members of the national community to continue, at least for a time, to affectively invest in the nation as a locus of future fulfilment. Thus, in order to account for the manner in which national identity persists despite historical transformations in that which the members of a nation define as essential to national identity, it is necessary to bolster the Lacanian perspective with an account of the role of transhistorical narratives in the reproduction of national identity either despite or through such transformations. It is with the aid of such an approach that the promise of the development of an understanding of the nation that "incorporates into the same theoretical/analytical logic discursive construction and jouissance, desire and aggressivity" can be realized (Stavrakis and Chrysoloras 2006, 154).

All identities exist within and are made possible by historical regimes of classification and categorization. However, events and encounters periodically undermine or introduce new systems of classification, disturbing the relative stability that they provide for identity. Within such moments, the forces of repression at play in the erasure of historical and contemporary difference and antagonism are weakened. It is in such moments, when the ever-present difference from oneself becomes consciously manifest, that we can observe crises of identity.

The sense of self that may have been taken for granted no longer appears as self-evident. In the face of such disturbance, the national community, in order to attempt to immunize itself against dissolution, must clearly and definitively articulate both the features of the nation and that which threatens it in a manner that allows for the maintenance of an affective attachment to the nation. This articulation takes one of two forms: in the attempt to re-establish the solidity of the nation, either the national character or way of life can be rearticulated in a manner that re-enforces that which is already defined as properly national, or it can be redefined in a manner understood to better contend with or domesticate that which appears as threatening. Whether rearticulated or transformed, "the harmony, unity, and homogeneity that are attributed to groups are always a result of its dominant members being able to inculcate such a vision and represent the group as harmonious" (Isin 2002a, 29). However, when the vision of the historical continuity of the nation is disturbed – either because a prevailing nationalist narrative fails to account for change or to continue to adequately resound at the level of affect with members of the national community or because alternative narratives fail to achieve hegemonic status – national identity and the nation are faced with a crisis.

To understand how a nation endures despite and through such crises, it is necessary to examine the manner in which narratives of historical continuity are developed and deployed in the aid of the nation. Citing Synne Corell (2010, 30–31), Auestad (2014, xx–xxi) writes, "there is no obvious connection between the 'we' of today and the 'them' of the past; thus, it is of interest to ask to what extent historians present an earlier population as part of today's 'we.'" An analysis of the manner in which continuity appears in narratives of the nation is of particular importance in developing an understanding of how national identity persists despite the often radical transformations in that which is said to be definitive of the nation. For this reason, Homi Bhabha (1990a, 3) can assert that "to study the nation through its narrative address does not merely draw attention to its language and rhetoric; it also attempts to alter the conceptual object itself." Examining the manner in which historical narrative accounts for transformations in, and even reversals of, that which is said to manifest the Nation-Thing – its particular way of life, character, or values – allows for a historicization of that which nationalism portrays as outside of history.

Secularization

Among the most powerful narrative devices deployed in the service of national continuity is that of secularization. Although it has come under sustained attack academically, secularization remains one of the most prominent lenses through which historical change is understood. By the early 1970s, various theories purporting the progressive marginalization, privatization, and decline of religion owing to the modernization of society had achieved the status of "reigning dogma" in the fields of sociology and the social history of religion (Swatos and Christiano 1999, 209). Central to these theories is the sociological idea of secularization, a notion conceptually and etymologically related to the Latin term *saeculum*. Originally referring to an age or an era, *saeculum* had developed three closely related usages by the fifth century: the first temporally differentiated the transitory secular world from the heavenly world-without-end; the second spatially differentiated a secular from a monastic world; and the third normatively differentiated a lifestyle at odds with the wishes of God from one in line with religious teachings (Casanova 1994, 12; Swatos and Christiano 1999, 210). The notion of the secular, therefore, is grounded in a twofold division: a division of worlds (heaven and earth) and a division of the earthly world into the religious world (the church) and the secular world (*saeculum*) (Casanova 1994, 13).

That the conception of the secular is founded on a division of the world into secular and sacred spheres is evident in the original usage of the term "secularization" to demarcate a particular historico-legal process. Until its emergence as a sociological concept in the late nineteenth century, "secularization" referred to two processes: the canonical process whereby clergy residing in cloisters returned to the "world," thereby becoming "secular"; and the historical process of the appropriation and expropriation of church property that followed the Protestant Reformation and the ensuing wars of religion (Berger 1967, 106; Casanova 1994, 12–13; McLeod 2000, 1; Swatos and Christiano 1999, 210; Turner 2003, 350).

It was in a form consistent with this original sense of the term that Max Weber (1920) introduced the concept of secularization into the sociological lexicon. Weber designated secularization as the process through which Protestant theology's relocation of the calling from the religious to the secular sphere broke down monastic walls, which dissolved the dualistic system of sacred and secular worlds, resulting in the formulation of a single world. Thus, as José Casanova (1994, 13) argues, in its legal and sociological origins, secularization refers to the relocation of persons, things, functions, and meanings from the religious sphere to various secular spheres.

From this initial limited use of the notion, secularization, with the development of sociology as a discipline, came to designate a range of ideas present in the classical sociological analyses of religion and social change by major figures of classical sociology, including Émile Durkheim, Sigmund Freud, Karl Marx, Georg Simmel, and Max Weber. It was not until the 1960s and 1970s, however, with the work of sociologists such as Robert Bellah (1964), Peter Berger (1967), Thomas Luckmann (1963), David Martin (1978), Talcott Parsons (1963), and Bryan Wilson (1966), that a systematized account and empirical studies of secularization were developed.

By the early 1970s, these accounts had become dominant within the field of the sociology of religion. Although the diverse theories that had come to be grouped under the generalized heading of "the secularization thesis" offer multiple and sometimes contradictory meanings for the concept of secularization, they share a set of core principles. As Casanova (1994, 7, 211) argues, the generalized secularization thesis is based on three propositions that suggest the transition from premodernity to modernity has led, or will lead, to (1) a decline in religious beliefs and practices, (2) the structural differentiation of society into religious and secular spheres, and (3) the marginalization of religion in the private sector.

According to Steve Bruce (2002, 2), the foremost contemporary champion of the secularization thesis, the basic proposition of all conceptions of secularization is that, at both the individual and the societal level, modernization "creates problems for religion." Bruce maintains that it is not a mere coincidence that modern societies are generally secular. He argues that secularization, at the individual level, should be conceived of as a process resulting from industrialization that has rendered religion less plausible for, and compelling to, individuals in modern society (36). At the societal level, religion is said to have lost all of its functions, appearing as a relic of some prior level of social evolution – a "now useless appendage to the modern cultural repertoire" (Swatos and Christiano 1999, 212).

Within such accounts, "failures to secularize" are treated as anomalies to be accounted for rather than as refutations of the secularization thesis. According to Bruce (2002, 41), "unevenness" in the process of secularization does not disprove the paradigm; rather, "what matters is the overall direction of trends and their long-term stability." In their attempts to account for the apparent stability or resurgence of religion in modern society, Bruce (2002) and Martin (1978) have resorted to a form of idealist and progressive developmental history in which cases of religious resurgence or nonsecularization are viewed as anomalies from the otherwise rational developmental process of secularization. For Bruce (2002, 30), religious belief and power have diminished, and will continue to do so, "except where [religion] finds work to do other than relating the individual to the supernatural" – work that he encompasses under cultural transition and cultural defence.

Martin's (1978, 3–4) much more systematic "general theory of secularization" deems secularization a "universal" process that "tends to occur, other things being equal." Variance in this universal process is said to depend on crucial events within particular states – such as the success or failure of the Reformation, the outcome of the English Civil War as well as the American, Russian, French, and Dutch Revolutions, and the nonrevolution in Lutheran countries – events that correspond to various patterns of secularization, including the American, the British, the French (Latin), the South American (extended Latin), the Russian, the Calvinist, and the Lutheran patterns. For both Bruce and Martin, therefore, the persistence of religion is viewed as an anomaly within the development of a normalized secular society. Despite the allowance for variations in the course of secularization, such a theory remains within the realm of teleological thought, attempting not to account for a diversity of historical experience but to explain impediments to the universal mechanism of historical development.

Since the earliest attempts to treat the nation and nationalism as objects of academic inquiry, a central and recurrent question has been the relationship of these phenomena to religion (Morrison 2016). Within much of the literature on the emergence of the nation, religion serves as a historical form of group identification and ideology against which the modern phenomena of the nation and nationalism are defined. Renan (1882, 51), for instance, suggests that in modernity, religion cannot serve as the basis for nationhood because it "has ceased almost entirely to be one of the elements which serve to define the frontiers of peoples."

From Renan to Kristeva (1990, 1991), the emergence of the nation and nationalism are seen in much of the literature as a consequence of historical processes of modernization and secularization in the material and/or ideational realm that lead to a conflict with or an evolutionary turn away from religion. As a result, by promoting a decline in supernatural belief and/or the institutional power of religious authorities, as well as a material and cultural reorganization of society, modernization furnished the grounds for the emergence of the nation and nationalism. Whether understood as the product of the secularization of religious groupings and dogmas or as a new, secular form of identification and social action, the relationship between the nation, nationalism, and religion is depicted as one of opposition and exteriority.

The dominance of the paradigm of modernization and secularization is also evident in aspects of the literature that, in opposition to constructivism, view the nation as a primordial or perennial form of group identification. In opposing the notion of the nation as a form of false consciousness that pervades some modernists' accounts, scholars associated with the primordialist or perennialist tradition, such as Smith (1986), John Armstrong (1982), and Clifford Geertz (1963), assert the ethnic core and/or primordiality of national groupings and sentiments. Although these scholars assert that nationalism and modern social arrangements did not create the nation, they acknowledge the manner in which modernity transformed early forms of group identification. Within a significant proportion of this literature, the nation is described as a modern form of earlier associations, one in which religion may play a reduced role in the constitution or self-understanding and maintenance of group boundaries.

When applied to nations, secularization permits a narrative of historical continuity that accounts for, and permits changes in, the culture, beliefs, and social, political, and religious institutions of the nation. Within this narrative, the nation, society, culture, and ethnicity appear as transhistorical objects that are acted on by external social forces. The characteristics of these objects are transformed by engagement with these forces, but the objects themselves persist, although in modified forms. Thus the characteristics of a nation can change while the nation endures. It is in this sense that a historical identity can be constructed between French Canadians prior to the mid-twentieth century – defined primarily on the basis of adherence to a rural, traditional, Catholic life (see Chapter 2) – and the modern, secular Québécois of contemporary Québec.

As discussed in Chapter 5, secularization as a narrative of continuity relies heavily on the transformation of religion, or at least certain markers of religion, from lived experience and belief into a symbol of national heritage. This reliance has been particularly evident in the debates surrounding the Charter of Québécois Values. Among the precise rules outlined in the Charter of Values are restrictions on the presence of religious symbols within state institutions. Controversially, however, certain Christian symbols, including a crucifix mounted on the wall of the National Assembly in Québec, have been exempted from this ban owing to their ostensible importance as symbols of Québec's Christian heritage. The place and protection of Catholicism as part of Québec's heritage are also reinforced through ongoing government programs that fund the restoration of churches in the name of "protecting our sacred heritage." By defining Catholicism in terms of heritage within a narrative of secularization, a common identity can be drawn between a religious past and a secular present. In this way, the nation as an object maintains its transhistorical continuity despite a reversal of that which is said to be among its definitive characteristics.

In opposition to narratives of secularization, an alternative form of analysis of religious change interrogates and seeks to denaturalize the very categories, narratives, and morality on which the secularization paradigm depends. Rather than accepting the basic categories presented as given within discourses of secularization, these historical investigations seek to denaturalize the categories of religion and the secular and to interrogate the forces involved in, and the effects of, their constitution and naturalization. Talal Asad, for example, argues that the definition of religion that today appears to be self-evident, one that posits religion as an autonomous, transhistorical, and transcultural phenomenon, has "a specific Christian history." In tracing the definition of religion as an autonomous sphere to particular historical strategies of delineation and confinement, he demonstrates that the contemporary definition of religion is the product of specific processes of power and knowledge that have made possible the emergence of various subjects, practices, and knowledges. The definition of religion as an abstract, universal phenomenon is not simply the result of benign scientific discovery or an increase in religious toleration but must also be seen in relation to, for instance, European colonial encounters with the noncolonial world and the attempt to differentiate Europe from this other (Asad 1993, 28, 42; 2003, 33–36).

Bryan Turner's (2003) historical analysis demonstrates that, like religion, the secular is also not transhistorically identical but has been constituted, redefined, and employed as a technique of struggle and domination throughout history. In addition, Foucault's work suggests, following Weber, that what is important in critical social analysis is not a determination of levels of belief in society but an analysis of the manner and efficacy of the deployment of that which is defined as religion in the governance of individual behaviour (Foucault 1978).

Thus a critical history of "secularization" involves the delineation of the forces involved in the constitution of a field of knowledge in which particular definitions of religion and the secular emerged and were deployed. Such an analysis makes possible an understanding of the place of religion in modern society without relying on naturalized essential definitions of religion or the secular. By historicizing these categories and the narratives and practices in which they are implicated, historical analysis provides an opportunity to rethink the relationship between religion and modern society and between religion and national identity.

Identity is always dependent on a particular historical regime of categorization and definition that makes possible certain encounters with otherness. As a result, the relation between nation and religion, like the possible narratives of continuity or discontinuity that can account for this relation, depends on historically specific, shifting conceptions of the religious and the secular toward which the nation orients itself through technologies of affiliation, dissociation, incorporation and estrangement. Each of the following chapters of this book addresses a particular moment of crisis in national identity in the history of Québec when religion appeared as a cause of and/or a solution to the crisis at hand. However, within the moments described throughout this book, both that which is defined as properly religious or secular and the relationship of these beliefs, realms, institutions, and behaviours to national identity undergo radical transformations and reversals.

2 The Rise of Clerico-Nationalism: Modernity, Assimilation, and *Survivance*

In the mid-nineteenth century, in a context of upheaval and existential anxiety over the English government's clearly articulated policy of assimilation of the French Canadian population, a particular discourse of historicity became dominant in Lower Canada. For nearly a century, the various manifestations of this discourse, traversing disparate fields, ideological camps, theoretical models, and normative positions, remained largely unquestioned (Jean 2006, 58), guiding academic, artistic, and government practice. Within this discourse, the term "modern" designated not only a historical epoch but also the nature and form of society – the way of being proper to that historical period, as distinct from the premodern. Although various nations and societies existed within the temporal parameters of modernity, not all were considered modern. The premodern, therefore, could be present within modernity. Within this discourse of the modern, French Canadian society, due to the perception of its social structures and collective mentality as "oriented toward another and preceding economic condition" (Hughes 1943), came to be seen as exemplary of an ancient, premodern, traditional, or folk society existing within the modern world.

The continued presence of the premodern within the modern, however, was considered extremely precarious. The very survival of premodern difference was perceived as threatened by contact with the transformatory, assimilationist force of modern cultural, political, and economic arrangements. Due to this perceived tendency toward the modern norm, the presence of the premodern in modernity was understood to be an exceptional, if not temporary, phenomenon. Given the proximity of modern English and American societies, the survival of French Canada, deemed a "primitive" peasant society (Miner 1939; Redfield 1939) belonging to the "middle ages" (Vattier 1928, 171), appeared as something requiring explanation. Thus the very existence of French Canadian society as a vestige of the premodern within the modern world became an object of concern; it was either a society whose very survival appeared as a "heroic cultural miracle" (Fournier 2001, 337) requiring investigation and explanation or one whose continued survival required strategic intervention.

In the latter half of the nineteenth century and the first half of the twentieth century, sentiments that conflated the dominance of religion with the premodern appeared within statements of the British government, officials of the Catholic Church, and prominent social scientists in French Canada. Both champions and adversaries of modernization viewed the dominance of religion as the defining feature of French Canadian society. At the same time, within this dominant discourse, the secular appeared as the modern norm – an essential quality of modern society. Premodern or traditional society was seen as one in which there was little social differentiation, and religion dominated all areas of society.

This distinction fits within a particular conception of religion and history in which forms of religion are equated with particular forms of society, which can be mapped along a plane of historical development conceived of in terms of modernization. Thus, within this discourse, the secular and the religious are qualities ascribed to specific stages of social evolution as characteristic of the way of being and form of society proper to modernity and premodernity respectively.

This chapter attends to the emergence and becoming dominant of this historical sense of the secular as that which is characteristic of the modern in Québec, as well as how this conception of the relationship between history, religion, and the secular provided the grounds for a particular conception of national identity to become dominant in Québec. An interrogation of that which is given necessitates a delineation of that which appears at a particular period as dominant and unquestionable. The chapter, therefore, outlines the manner in which this discourse appeared in various fields and was shared by seemingly antithetical positions and by rival political and ideological outlooks. In other words, the chapter undertakes the primary work of archaeology – an examination of the archive of the epoch under consideration. The archive is not the sum of all things said in an epoch or of all things said about a particular object. The chapter by no means attempts to present everything that was said about religion or the secular in Québec between the mid-nineteenth and mid-twentieth century; rather, the archive is approached here as the manifestation of the historical a priori – the law of what can be said within a particular historical regime of categorization.

Thus the presentation of this discourse in statements from various fields is undertaken to demonstrate the limit of what could be said at a particular moment. By limit, I refer not only to a negative limitation of the sayable but also to the positivity of discourse – the "general system of the formation and transformation of statements" (Foucault 1969, 146). Consequently, what will be addressed in this chapter are the rules governing the discourse in which the secular appears as that which is characteristic of the modern and how the dominance of this discourse permitted the victory of a particular conception of the nation, one that allowed it to persist through a period of crisis.

The definitions of religion, the secular, and the French Canadian nation that emerge are treated as the outcome of the victory of certain forces and the defeat of others. The crystallization of the meaning and sense of anything is the result of the victory of particular forces in an ongoing interpretive struggle over the manner in which the object of contestation is to be understood. As forces take possession of a thing, affinities are forged between the victorious forces and that to which they give meaning. As a result, the nature of the entity comes to be defined through, and by, the victorious forces alone (Deleuze 1962, 3–5).

That these forces are successful in fashioning a definitive meaning for a thing does not, however, mean that this outcome of interpretive struggle reflects a greater degree of insight into the essence or truth of the thing. As the essence of an entity is merely the sense that is attributed to it at a particular moment, the forces that battle over its interpretation cannot be defined by their proximity to, or sustenance of, truth or falsity. That in Québec in the mid-nineteenth century the secular emerges as that which is proper to the modern is not the result of social science, theology, or any other form of inquiry being able to acquire a more precise knowledge or to gain clearer access to the essence of the secular; rather, it is simply the result of the momentary victory of certain forces over others, made possible in a particular historical context.

That the meanings attributed to religion, the secular, and the French Canadian nation appeared as taken for granted and essential is not the consequence of human progress in the attainment of knowledge but the consequence of victorious forces becoming reactive (Deleuze 1962, 53). A force can be characterized as reactive if it attempts, by fixing meaning to an entity, to deny the constitutive role of conflicts of interpretation in the provision of sense. In equating the ahistorical essence of an object with a historically emergent meaning, reactive forces mask the historical contingency of the entity itself.

Consequently, when those forces that provided meaning to the secular in mid-nineteenth-century Québec became reactive, the historicity of a particular conception of the nation was obscured. The secular and the religious did not appear as the product of incessant struggles of interpretation in which the victory of certain forces made possible the crystallization of sense at a particular moment; rather, they appeared as ahistorical markers of difference distinguishing the premodern from the modern.

Not only do reactive forces deny that the meaning attributed to a thing is the result of historical struggles of interpretation, but in fixing meaning and sense, they also obscure the fact that what appears as given, stable, and singular is never in a state of final equilibrium but is itself the site of perpetual struggle. Thus, when forces become reactive, the ongoing becoming of being is masked (Deleuze 1962, 71–72). As every force is related to another in a battle for dominance, the victory of a given force does not mean the elimination or rendering dormant of all others. As Deleuze argues, the history of a thing is not only "the succession of forces which take possession of it" but also "the co-existence of the forces which struggle for possession" (3). Behind the visage of unity, stability, and homogeneity presented by victorious forces is an incessant struggle that conditions the possibility of reinterpretation. Such thought undermines the traditional opposition of the multiple to the one, suggesting instead that the one is always multiple and that difference is always present.

Consequently, to assert that the emergence of the secular as that which is proper to the modern is the outcome of the victory of certain forces is not to imply that previous understandings of the secular disappear. These seculars are in fact appropriated, reorganized, and remobilized by the victorious forces. Dominant forces do not discard the techniques and strategies utilized by other forces but instead appropriate others to make possible or consolidate their dominance. For instance, the understanding of the secular that emerged in Québec in the mid-nineteenth century did not discard the Augustinian *saeculum* as the temporal interval between the fall and the eschaton; rather, in the context of the upheavals of the early nineteenth century and the appropriation of techniques and strategies of theology, historical romanticism, and the nascent disciplines of sociology, anthropology, philology, and comparative religion, a crystallized meaning of the secular was able to emerge as that which was proper to the modern.

It is the emergence of particular, related understandings of the secular, the religious, and the French Canadian nation that this chapter addresses. First, the context of this emergence in mid-nineteenth-century Québec is described. I argue that the secular as a characteristic of the modern emerged in the mid-nineteenth century in the wake of upheaval and concern over the future of the French Canadian nation. Second, the chapter outlines how religion is associated with the premodern and how the secular is associated with the modern in various fields and across apparently oppositional discourses. Thus this chapter investigates a discourse of religion and the secular shared by Lord Durham's *Report on the Affairs of British North America* (1839), early French Canadian historians and social scientists, ultramontane clerical authorities, and American anthropologists associated with the Chicago School. All viewed the French Canadian nation and its society, particularly the pervasiveness of religion, as a relic of the premodern.

Rebellion, Upheaval, and Crisis

In the 1830s, Lower Canada along with Upper Canada and much of Europe found itself in the throes of rebellion and social and political upheaval. By the 1830s, after fermenting since 1805, frustration and discontent concerning the impotence of the elected Assembly had developed into "an explosive situation" (McInnis 1982, 253). By 1834 a dispute between the French Canadian seigneurial class and the English commercial class over conflicting interests in taxation policy had grown into a demand by the French Canadian Parti Patriote for electoral reform, backed by a veiled threat of revolt (248–51).

Beginning with the 1805 taxation dispute, the desires of the elected Assembly, dominated by the French Canadian bourgeois and professional classes, were repeatedly frustrated by the unelected colonial Legislative Council, which was largely supported by the English elite. In 1834 the Parti Patriote, under the leadership of Louis-Joseph Papineau, put forward a document that became known as the Ninety-Two Resolutions. The document, adopted by the Assembly, listed a variety of grievances voiced by the French Canadian population, called for full control of revenues by the Assembly, an elected Legislative Council, and maintenance of the traditional system of land tenure, and expressed criticism of the leading figures of the colonial elite and their supporters (McInnis 1982, 250).

Perhaps most significant, however, were repeated statements conveying admiration for American political institutions and the implied threat of rebellion and independence (McInnis 1982, 250–51). The increasingly liberal, republican, and at times anti-clerical tone of Papineau and his supporters caused a split in the reform movement. Moderates such as John Neilson, who sought to attain constitutional reforms based on the British model, those who only sought protection for language, religion, and traditional institutions, as well as officials within the Catholic Church who feared both the consequences of revolution and the anti-clericalism of Papineau's more radical followers all opposed the more radical tone of the Patriotes.

In 1837, three years after their issuance, the Ninety-Two Resolutions were rejected by the British government. The rejection of these demands, combined with an agrarian crisis in Lower Canada, gave rise to increased hostility and resentment toward the British authorities and the colonial elite (McInnis 1982, 256–57). A series of demonstrations and public meetings led by a group called the Fils de la liberté expressed this discontent. Fearing revolt, the colonial authorities issued warrants for the arrest of Papineau, Dr. Edmund Bailey O'Callaghan, and other radical leaders.

On November 23, armed Patriotes repelled British troops attempting to execute the warrants, and in the following month, after Papineau and O'Callaghan had fled to the United States, the military twice forcefully dispersed gatherings of Patriotes and brought the 1837 Rebellion to an end. In 1838 a second attempted rebellion was quickly quelled by the execution of seventeen men for the crime of sedition (McInnis 1982, 257).

In November 1840, on the basis of recommendations meant to suppress the possibility of future conflict through the promotion of assimilation outlined in Lord Durham's *Report on the Affairs of British North America* (1839), a Crown-appointed council imposed union on Upper and Lower Canada. These territories subsequently became known as the provinces of Canada West and Canada East. The Act of Union reinstated representative political institutions in the form of a common legislative assembly, which provided equal representation to each of the two provinces despite the far greater population in Canada East (Mann Trofimenkoff 1982, 81; McInnis 1982, 273). To further promote the process of assimilation, French was proscribed as an official language, and to increase dependence, and thus additionally discourage isolationism, Canada East was saddled with a disproportionate share of the combined public debt (Mann Trofimenkoff 1982, 81).

The Durham Report

As Robert Leroux (2001, 351) asserts, it was in the aftermath of the failure of the 1837–1838 Rebellions that "the first systematic reflections on the future of French Canadian culture appear[ed]." In various fields, attempts were made to define French Canada and to determine and affirm its specificities. The first of these attempts appears in Lord Durham's *Report on the Affairs of British North America* (1839). In the aftermath of the defeated Rebellions, the British government appointed Lord Durham (John George Lambton) as high commissioner and governor general of British North America and tasked him with preparing a report detailing the causes of rebellion and proposing measures to avert future conflict. Initially welcomed by the reformers within Lower Canada due to his reputation as a supporter of responsible government, the emancipation of Catholics in Britain, and other Whig causes, Lord Durham soon became a figure of scorn and derision.

Although Durham (1839, 7) clearly articulated his condemnation of oligarchic rule in Lower Canada, he believed that the rebellions were the consequence of an issue much more fundamental than that of the structures of governance and representation – "a far deeper and far more efficient cause – a cause which penetrated beneath its political institutions into its social state – a cause which no reform of constitution or laws ... could remove, but which must be removed." According to Durham, the cause of conflict was a fundamental, irreconcilable racial conflict between the English and French. Rather than observing "a contest between a government and a people," he witnessed "two nations warring in the bosom of a single state." This feud, extending into every field of activity, was deemed "the origin or the essence of every dispute" in Lower Canada (7).

Rooting this intractable conflict in racial or national difference, Durham concluded that it could be resolved only through a policy of assimilation of the French Canadian population. This solution was arrived at based on two related premises. First, the mentality and institutions of French Canada were deemed inferior to those of Britain. In a sentiment that appears repeatedly in various statements discussed throughout the course of this chapter, institutions deemed fundamental to the French Canadian nation were deemed to be artefacts of a different age, namely those of France during the period of the colonization of North America. According to Durham (1839), these institutions "were, perhaps, more than those of any other European nation, calculated to repress the intelligence and freedom of the great mass of the people." The "same central, ill-organized, unimproving, and repressive despotism" that was present in France during the *ancien régime* continued and extended itself over the French Canadians of Durham's age (11). The system of governance permitted no public participation, the seigneurial system promoted feudal dependence and desire for only immediate satisfaction, the necessity of education was "not appreciated," and most importantly, Church authorities "established their institutions around" the French Canadian and "continued to exercise over him [their] ancient influence" (12). "Above all," he suggested, the problem was the attachment of the people to the Catholic Church, which had "produced the effect of confining [French Canadian society] within its ancient limits" (30). French Canadians were deemed to be a people who remained "entirely separate" from "recent history, manners, and modes of thought" as well as "a people with no history, and no literature" (132). Given that their institutions remained those of a prior age, Durham concluded that it was not surprising that the French Canadians "remained the same uninstructed, inactive, unprogressive people" that they had been at the time of French colonization (12).

The second of Durham's premises was that given the backward nature and inferiority of French Canadian institutions and mentality, prior colonial policies of institutionalizing the retention of these institutions had doomed the French Canadian population to a state of misery and destitution as an underclass. Rather than permitting the natural course of assimilation toward a modern English norm, these policies had forced the French Canadians into becoming "labourers in the employ of English capitalists" (Durham 1839, 131).

Faced with the superiority of modern English institutions, the only way that the French Canadian nation had survived thus far and could continue to survive was in isolation from any foreign, modern influence: "The province should have been set apart to be wholly French, if it was not to be rendered completely English" (Durham 1839, 30). Thus not only was assimilation seen as a compassionate policy that would permit French Canadians to transcend the misery inflicted upon them by their retention of institutions, practices, and a mentality that were said to be "ancient," but it was also the natural result of contact with the institutions of a superior, modern way of life.

The Construction of a Heroic Past

This unfavourable portrayal provoked among French Canadians "a sense of urgency ... to define themselves, to affirm their specificity and to elaborate a historical memory" (Leroux 2001, 351). Durham's contention that French Canadians were a defeated people whose way of being was at odds with the modern world instigated a turn toward the past. In the immediate aftermath of the Durham Report, in a move generally viewed as an effort to counter the report's portrayal of French Canadians as "a people with no history," the first attempts to produce a history of French Canada were undertaken.

Published in three volumes between 1845 and 1848, François-Xavier Garneau's *Histoire du Canada depuis sa découverte jusqu'à nos jours* was among the first of these undertakings. It sought to refute the image of French Canadians as an immobile, defeated people by portraying a glorious past of heroic struggle and great feats (Falardeau 1964a, 15). In a manner similar to that of French romantic historians of the era – such as Augustin Thierry, Adolphe Thiers, and Jules Michelet – Garneau portrayed national antagonism as the driving force of history. French Canadian history was not that of a defeated people but one of heroic struggle against various external forces, including nature, Aboriginals, and French and English imperialists. Surviving against all odds, the French Canadian people had, with a remarkable spirit of liberty and enterprise proper to the new world, embarked on adventures of settlement, exploration, Christianization, and warfare (Mann Trofimenkoff 1982, 91).

In the third volume of *Histoire du Canada*, Garneau suggests that the specificity of French Canada is characterized by the three pillars of religion, law, and language. In a manner that would later be expounded on by Émile Miller, Léon Gérin, and Lionel Groulx, Garneau asserted that these elements of French Canadian society were imported to Canada in the age of discovery and were infused with a particular spirit born of the difficult conditions faced by the early settlers. It was French Canada's particularity in these three areas that differentiated it from the other nations against whom it was engaged in struggle. Moreover, it was these elements that had aided and, if afforded sufficient support and protection, would continue to aid the French Canadians in their historic struggle for survival (Mann Trofimenkoff 1982, 92; Rioux 1976, 77).

By 1848 Garneau, who less than ten years earlier had championed Papineau and his fellow rebels, was advocating that French Canada should above all seek to avoid risk. Areas of confrontation and competition with the English, including both the economic and political fields, should be avoided, as they were fraught with danger for a small nation such as French Canada; instead, French Canada should turn toward the maintenance of its three traditional pillars, seeking only the adequate protection to do so.

In Garneau's study, the French Canadian nation appears as one whose essence is to be found in the religion, laws, and language of seventeenth-century France, adapted to the conditions faced in the new world by the early settlers of New France (Rioux 1976, 77). As the essence of the French Canadian nation is to be found in the past, the very survival of this nation depends on maintaining its religion, law, and language in the face of assimilationist pressure. In Garneau's historical study, therefore, we can perceive an identification of French Canada with a particular historical form of society.

Clerico-Nationalism

Like Garneau, the Catholic Church in French Canada responded to the Durham Report and the enforced union of Upper and Lower Canada with antipathy and incredulity. The Catholic Church had, after all, been a key ally of the British in their struggle against the forces of both reform and rebellion, threatening any Catholic who participated in rebellion and dissent with the denial of sacraments or excommunication. Since the Conquest, the continued existence of the Catholic Church in Canada had rested on the will of the colonial authorities. At the same time, the British depended on the church to promote loyalty to colonial authorities and stamp out French Canadian dissent. As Lucia Ferretti (1999, 39) states, in exchange for permitting the existence of the church and allowing it autonomy in internal affairs, the bishops demonstrated a boundless loyalty to the Crown. In exchange for the church's application of sanctions against disobedient Canadiens and its public support each time England risked losing the colony, London would recognize the church in its societal roles.

After the Act of Union, the church adopted a more critical attitude toward the colonial authorities. It could no longer rely on its proximity to the British authorities as a source of security and began to preach distrust of the state (Bélanger 2000). At the same time, however, in their critique of the colonial authorities, the clerical elite were not willing to align themselves with the liberal nationalists of the Parti Rouge and the

Institut canadien, who they viewed as an even greater threat. In the 1840s, faced with this dual threat of liberalism and assimilation, the Catholic Church in Québec turned to a program of religious renewal, guided by the theological doctrine of ultramontanism and by the bourgeoning force of nationalism.

Since 1789 the Catholic Church in Europe had seen its position undermined by the forces of republicanism. Not only did the French National Convention of 1795 proclaim a separation of church and state, but congregations were also prohibited, clergy were persecuted, seminaries were closed, and church property was confiscated. Even with its official recognition under the Concordat of 1801, the Catholic Church remained, in line with laws introduced in 1790, merely one of five authorized religious groups whose finances and appointments were strictly controlled by the state (Ferretti 1999, 34).

In this environment, a new Catholic ethos emerged in France known as ultramontanism. In the aftermath of the French Revolution, the earliest indications of ultramontanism appeared in the works of Louis de Bonald, Joseph de Maistre, and cleric Hugues-Félicité de Lamennais. Faced with the turmoil of post-revolutionary France, these thinkers argued that "the normal functioning and even the survival of society depended on the supremacy of religious over civil authority and the maintenance of the monarchical system" (Eid 1978, 22). In contrast to those advocating Enlightenment rationalism as the basis for the rational ordering of the arbitrary, de Maistre argued that what holds societies together is "not a formal ordering of the arbitrary, but rather the *content* of the arbitrary, or devotion to a particular *mythos*" (Milbank 2006, 55).

According to early ultramontane thinkers, a mythos capable of sustaining a healthy society must be in accordance with social facts. As de Bonald argues, following the stoïc conception of conservation, everything in the universe seeks to conserve itself. In order to do so, the individual, in the struggle against other forces, is in need of supplementary mediating powers in the form of hierarchic, triadic relationships such as between father, mother, and child, sovereign, executive, and subject, and God, priest, and the faithful (Milbank 2006, 56). For any society to conserve itself, it must conform to this hierarchic, triadic relationship. Only the reinstatement of this hierarchical social arrangement, which ultramontane thinkers contended was consistent with the French *ancien régime,* could halt the dissolution of society brought about by the revolution. Moreover, in conformity with this hierarchical system, it was argued that the primary loyalty of Catholics should be to the papacy rather than the state.

It was consistent with this thought that Pope Gregory XVI opposed the Catholic struggles of national liberation against foreign, Protestant monarchs in the Netherlands in 1830 and Poland in 1831. In his encyclical *Cum primum,* he argued that these uprisings against monarchical regimes were revolts against a "sacred social order" and "legitimate power" conferred by God (Ferretti 1999, 37). This ultramontane orientation positioned the pope as the leader of the movement to restore the pre-revolutionary order and to reinforce the power of the Vatican in the face of nationalist threats. Protestant and orthodox monarchies turned to the Vatican to placate movements for Catholic emancipation, and bishops turned to the Vatican for help in their conflicts with civil authorities and for guidance in internal matters.

In the wake of the French Revolution, an influx of clergy from the most conservative orders in France arrived in Lower Canada, fleeing the persecution and desacralization of their country. They brought with them not only tales of the horror of the French Revolution but also the incipit ideas of ultramontane thought. To them, Lower Canada appeared as a "lost paradise" that had escaped the "filth" of the French Revolution (Sarra-Bournet 2001, 27). In a manner that would soon find expression in the words of French Canadian clergy, the newly arrived clergy saw French Canada as the natural extension of the "lost paradise" of the pure, pre-revolutionary France of the *ancien régime* (Rioux 1976, 77).

In French Canada, the chief proponents of ultramontanism in the nineteenth century were Jean-Jacques Lartigue, the first Catholic bishop of Montréal; Ignace Bourget, who succeeded him; Louis François Laflèche, the first bishop of Trois Rivières; and Jules-Paul Tardive, the publisher of the newspaper *La Verité.* Unlike the vision of French Canada as a lost paradise of Catholicism advocated by the French clergy, these figures saw the religiosity of French Canada as already under threat by "the intense Protestant propaganda that was flooding the countryside" (Mann Trofimenkoff 1982, 88). Aided by the collection of statistical data,

Catholic authorities determined that Catholicism in 1840 was "insipid" (88). There was too much religious indifference, there were too many nonpractising Catholics and apostates, and a variety of social vices were taking hold of the people.

Beginning in the 1830s and intensifying in the 1840s, the Catholic Church in French Canada embarked on a crusade to renew and reinforce the piety of the French Canadian people in order to promote a healthy social order and resist assimilation. The primary figure in this movement was Bourget. With the help of former French bishop Charles de Forbin-Janson, Bourget promoted religious fervour through the organization of religious retreats, brought new religious orders to Québec to augment the small numbers of French Canadian clergy, and presided over the establishment of lay religious organizations such as the Société Saint Vincent de Paul, over the founding of the female religious orders the Soeurs de Charité de la Providence, Soeurs des Saints Noms de Jésus et Marie, Soeurs de la Miséricorde, and Soeurs de Sainte Anne, and over the expansion of the Soeurs Grises (Mann Trofimenkoff 1982, 88–89).

The role of the Catholic Church in the provision of education and social services was also expanded. Religious orders were responsible for education at all levels and were expected to care for "the poor, the deprived, the disgraced, the old and the sick" (Mann Trofimenkoff 1982, 89). As Claude Bélanger (2000) describes, the expansion of the role of the church was such that "no major initiative, whether educational, social, cultural, and even economic or political, was possible, and potentially successful, without the clergy being involved or providing its blessing."

Central to their adaptation of the ultramontane doctrine to the context of Québec in the form of what would come to be known as clerico-nationalism were two related notions. First, ultramontanism "superimpose[d] the historical disjunction between modern and pre-modern Western society on the cultural differences between the French of Quebec and the English of the rest of North American society" (Beyer 1985, 38). Thus not only was the French Canadian nation seen as different from post-revolutionary France and from the English of North America, but its differences were also presented in temporal terms. French Canada, particularly its religiosity, was equated with the premodern, as opposed to the modern nature of post-revolutionary France and English North

America, both of which were marked by, among other things, irreligion and secularity.

Second, the survival of the nation was tied to the ability to maintain and promote the healthy social order of *ancien régime* France on North American soil. According to clerico-nationalist thought, every nation was divinely ascribed a mission (Laflèche 1866, 42). Nations that did not remain true to their anointed mission would face destruction through the wrath of God. In the words of Laflèche, the French Canadian nation was founded for the purpose of "the conversion of the poor unbelievers who inhabit [North America], and the extension of the Kingdom of God by the formation of an above all Catholic nation" (47).

Consistent with the statements of Garneau, ultramontanist thought conceived of the French Canadian nation in terms of a unity of the Holy Trinity of "*nos lois, notre langue, notre religion,*" which represented the "unity of language and of faith, and the uniformity of customs, habits, and institutions" (Sarra-Bournet 2001, 27, 42). In the writings of Laflèche and Groulx, these characteristics are linked both to the families that originally settled New France and to the geographical isolation of New France itself. In this setting, free of the influences of the European Reformation, Enlightenment, and modernization, the Catholic Church was able to fashion this *petit peuple* according to "divine laws," resulting in the formation of "social, juridical and cultural structures of a superior essence and quality" (Groulx 1949, 5).

Groulx (1949, 6) suggested that, unlike the French, who had fallen prey to "the problems of the modern spirit," the French Canadian people were protected by the church from "the immoderate temptations of foreign cultures." Thus, in contrast to the citizens of revolutionary, fallen France, the French Canadians were portrayed as an incarnation of "the French of the great century ... from 1660–1680, an era when France was the premier nation of the world" (4, 7).

Within clerico-nationalist discourse, then, the French Canadian nation was constituted as possessing "by its spiritual birth, a blood richer, more august, than any of the great bloods of the earth ... [the blood of] a divine race, the sons of God" (Groulx 1949, 4). It was the characteristics born of these circumstances that the clerico-nationalists believed would aid French Canada in its mission in North America and permit its survival.

Particularly after 1840, the theme of national survival in the face of continuous threats became the major focus of French Canadian nationalism. That the French Canadians had survived was seen as nothing short of a miracle. Their survival was perceived as further evidence that God was on their side and had a mission for them "as a Catholic people in a universe of Protestant and materialist forces": they were to bear witness to "true spiritual principles" (Bélanger 2000).

It was believed that fidelity to this mission would protect the French Canadian people from external threats. According to this discourse, the French Canadian people were threatened by external forces promoting political and economic alternatives that would undermine the religious and structural foundations of the nation. These forces, all of which were conceived of as consequences of modernization, manifested themselves not only through the assimilationist policies of the Durham Report and the Act of Union, and the liberalism promoted by the Parti Rouge, but also through the social forces of rationalization, industrialization, urbanization, and social differentiation. All of these forces were said to promote a process of secularization that undermined the proper religious structure of French Canadian society through the advancement of false religion (Protestantism) and irreligion (liberalism).

According to clerico-nationalist thought, to fulfil its mission and promote its survival, French Canada had to observe a functional hierarchy in which the church was followed by the family and then by all other functions that served to fulfil the goals determined by the first two (Beyer 1985, 42; Laflèche 1866). Consequently, each family and each individual within the nation were said to have been divinely assigned a special mission as part of the overall mission of society. By following their individual missions, the members of the French Canadian nation aided the functioning of their family, the church, and the nation as a whole.

Hierarchy was conceived not only in terms of function but also in terms of what Peter Beyer (1985, 43) calls implicit stratification. Central to the hierarchical organization of society was the dominance of the clerical elite. Although the *habitants* (French Canadian farmers) were seen as leading the life most conducive to the fulfilment of the nation's mission, the survival of the nation required that they be controlled by a clerical elite. Beyer suggests that this control "was not [meant] to maintain the privileges of elite strata since such did not exist in anything but an attenuated and fluid way" (44); rather, it was meant to serve two purposes. First, as in the hierarchy of the Catholic Church, clerical authorities were seen as divinely appointed guardians of the people's morals and minds. As Laflèche instructed, "Let us each say in his own heart, 'I hear my *curé*, my *curé* hears the Bishop, the Bishop hears the Pope and the Pope hears Our Lord Jesus Christ'" (Francis, Jones, and Smith 1992, 48). By following the instructions of clerical authorities, the *habitants* were following the wishes of God. Second, this control permitted the clerical elite to maintain a communication barrier between the bulk of the French Canadian population and the outside world. By acting as a communicative buffer between the nation and the outside world, the clerical elite hoped to promote and maintain the French Canadian peasantry as "a communicatively closed social group within which communication could at least ideally be seen as communication among equals" (Beyer 1985, 43).

Given the importance of stratification and the ultramontane conceptions of monarchical rule, the clerical elite in French Canada generally favoured hereditary and monarchical political structures. According to Laflèche, limited monarchy was the ideal form of government because it was most consistent with the hierarchical, paternal structure of the authority of the church and all other legitimate authority. Unlike democracy and aristocratic rule, limited monarchy was seen as founded on the family and religion. Democracy, in contrast, reversed this paternal hierarchy by placing, in effect, the children (the people) in charge of the family (the nation). By designating the people and their interests as the source of sovereignty, it rejected God as the source of all power. Aristocracy, although superior to democracy, destabilized social unity since it promoted differentiation between social groups (Beyer 1985, 45; Laflèche 1866). As a result, ultramontane leaders preferred British rule to that of the United States.

In general, after 1840 the Catholic Church in French Canada remained largely ambivalent to the political institutions of Canada, promoting an ideology of anti-statism. The policies of government and of political institutions were evaluated based on whether they "denied or confirmed the subordination of the political sphere to the functional hierarchy dictated by the organizational goals of French Canadian society as defined by the religious elite" (Beyer 1985, 45). As a result, the French Canadian Catholic authorities engaged with the political system only when they believed that the state was attempting to usurp their role or to influence the direction of French Canadian society. Despite reserving the right to manipulate the electoral decisions of their flock, as evident in the Catholic Programme of 1871, as well as the use of subtle hints such as "Heaven is blue, Hell is red" (referring to the blue Conservatives and the red Liberals and Parti Rouge), the clerical elite also "shunned politicians, and heaped scorn on political parties" (Bélanger 2000). Political parties were seen as a divisive force, in opposition to the uniting force of the clerical elite. As Bélanger (2000) argues, Groulx was typical of this antipathy to electoral politics, proudly stating in his memoirs that he frequently did not vote, as one could not expect anything good from politicians.

Besides the role of the clerical elite, two other characteristics of French Canadian society – language and its rural existence – were viewed by clerico-nationalists as buffers against external threats. The French language was seen as a vital aspect of the culture inherited from their ancestors and thus as a symbol of their connection to one of the great civilizations of Europe (Bélanger 2000). Perhaps more crucially, however, it prevented the contamination of French Canadian society by Protestant and modern values. As the famous phrase coined by Henri Bourassa at the turn of the twentieth century asserted, not only was language "*la gardienne de la foi*" (the guardian of the faith), but it was also the protector of the nation. As French Canadians were a minority in Canada and North America, linguistic difference was seen as central to the preservation of their Catholic values.

In the face of rapid industrialization at the end of the nineteenth century, rural agriculturalism was considered a further bulwark against the external threat posed by this process. Rural life isolated the *habitant* from the temptations and the influence of the English, who were associated with the city. Cities were seen as "a vast impersonal and godless universe, a place full of dangers for one's soul and nationality, an occasion for sin"

(Bélanger 2000). Moreover, given that the majority of the population of Montréal was anglophone by the middle of the nineteenth century, as was nearly half the population of Québec City, "in the theatres, cinemas, dancing halls, clubs, and taverns found in the cities, the nation was subjected to foreign influences and shed its traditional beliefs and values" (Bélanger 2000). In contrast, in a rural, agricultural setting, a life centred on the family, steeped in tradition, and concentrated on religion was possible (Eid 1978, 241).

Farming, rural life, and agricultural colonization, as promoted by the Back to the Land Movement, were considered the way of life proper to the mission of the nation. As stated in the ultramontane periodical *Nouveau Monde,* agricultural economic activity was "the real source, the base and the foundation of the nation's wealth" (Eid 1978, 243). In contrast to commerce and industry, which were said to be based on "fictive values," rural agricultural society was conducive to the pure, simple life proper to Christianity, a life of few material needs and temptations (243). Projects of economic development that focused on industry and commerce rather than agriculture were consistently opposed as anti-patriotic.

Both the need to create geographic, cultural, and communicative barriers to the external world as well as the notion of functional hierarchy are the basic tenets of clerico-nationalist thought. These two elements are the basis of a perspective that equates the survival of the French Canadian nation in the North American context with the continuation and internal reinforcement of a social structure and way of being associated with the premodern and with the externalization of those things associated with modernity, particularly the autonomy of politics, education, and the economy from religious values and control (Beyer 1985, 43). The French Canadian nation was seen as incompatible with the modern, its existence possible only through isolation from the forces of modernity.

Religion, Modernity, and the Nation in French Canadian Literature

The opposition of the French Canadian nation to modernity is present not only in the statements and practices of the clerical elite of the era but also in much of the literature and social and political thought of the period. In the wake of the Durham Report and the Act of Union, spurred by Garneau's *Histoire du Canada depuis sa découverte jusqu'à nos jours,* historically oriented nationalist literature made an appearance in the form of the historical dramas of Édouard Hamon, the "novels of the soil" of Philippe Aubert de Gaspé, Antoine Gérin-Lajoie, and others, and the poetry of writers such as Gérin-Lajoie and Octave Crémazie. This historical literature sought to glorify the French Canadian past and its associated way of life. These literary works addressed three major themes consistent with the tenets of clerico-nationalism: the need for clerical guidance, agriculturalism, and the concern for the future of the French Canadian nation.

As regards the first theme, the heroic figures of French Canadian history depicted in the literature of the later nineteenth and early twentieth centuries were all members of the educated, urban, upper classes, spoke standard French, and were familiar with classical French literature (Moss 1989, 339). In contrast, the *habitant,* representing the vast majority of the French Canadian population, was presented as simple, rural, uncorrupted, and speaking a Canadian dialect of French. In the words of Louis-Honoré Fréchette (1880, 108), in contrast to the sophistication and grandeur of the elite, they were "a brave little people."

This depiction of the French Canadian people was not meant as denigration. In fact, as is evident in novels such as de Gaspé's *Les anciens Canadiens* (1864), Gérin-Lajoie's *Jean Rivard* (1862), and Ernest Choquette's *La terre* (1916), the rural, agricultural life and religious outlook of the *habitant* were praised as exemplary of the way of being proper to French Canadians. In keeping with the aspect of clerico-nationalism that Michel Brunet (1957) labels agriculturalism, farming was considered the economic activity assigned to the French Canadian people by God. It was an activity associated with purity and simplicity, during which one was in communion with the forces of nature and with God (Bélanger 2000). As the character Jean Rivard exclaims in Gérin-Lajoie's 1867 novel, "If only I were a farmer ... Farmers form the most virtuous class of the population ... The enlightened and virtuous farmer is to my mind the best type of man" (Rioux 1976, 76–77).

This second major theme in the literature of the period suggested that as simple, pure, and pious people, the French Canadians should not worry themselves with, or contaminate themselves through, exposure to modern and/or alien influences. Moreover, given their nature, the French Canadian *habitants* were suited to a simple way of life, not to that of modern English Canada or the United States. In a manner consistent with the ultramontane nationalism of the French Canadian Catholic Church, the literature of this epoch generally suggested that the *habitants*, under the guidance of the elite, should simply maintain their traditional way of being, focusing on agricultural labour and religious practices. Due to their nature and training, it was the elite, for the most part church officials, who could concern themselves and interact with the world external to French Canadian society. In doing so, they would act as both a buffer against external influences and a champion of rights, which would enable the protection of the nation. Afforded these protections, the mass of the population could simply continue to lead lives proper to the French Canadian national mission.

The third major theme in the literature of the period was a concern with threats to national survival. One such threat, elaborated by Édouard Hamon in his play *Éxil et patrie* (Exile and Homeland) (1882) and by Gérin-Lajoie in his song "Un Canadien errant" (A Wandering Canadien), was faced by those French Canadians who had been displaced from traditional French Canadian society through exile or economic emigration. This concern, shared by early French Canadian social scientists (Leroux 2001, 361), related not only to the misery resulting from such dislocation but also to the threat of emigrants falling prey to assimilationist forces. Removed from the form of society and mode of living proper to their national essence, these individuals were seen as especially vulnerable to assimilation. Consequently, those French Canadians who chose to emigrate to the city, nonfrancophone communities, or the United States were accused of moral failing and religious and patriotic disloyalty (Eid 1978; Laflèche 1866).

The demographic impact of the emigration of significant numbers of French Canadians to the United States proved to be a source of concern for the survival of the French Canadian nation. Particularly after Confederation, emigration appeared as a factor that could further threaten the ability of the French Canadian nation to fend off assimilation. Already faced with their own status not only as a defeated people but also as a minority within Canada, emigration increased their numerical disadvantage and scattered them throughout the continent.

In response, French Canadians engaged in a systematic, ongoing process of counting themselves. Given the importance of demographics, "every loss was a catastrophic loss" (Bélanger 2000). Each census became a document requiring detailed examination, and articles and reports tracking the struggles of French Canadian communities outside of Québec proliferated. The church and the provincial government attempted to combat this numerical decline through an ongoing campaign known as *la revanche des berceaux* (the revenge of the cradles), which took place between 1840 and 1960. During this time, French Canadian families maintained a birth rate of nearly ten children per family. However, concern over numerical inferiority and the status of emigrants and communities outside of Québec remained a persistent theme.

Within the literature of the period, therefore, one can locate the identification of the French Canadian nation with the rural, agrarian, and religious way of life proper to that of the settlers of New France. Not only was this way of life proper to the nature of the French Canadian people, but it was the social structure of this form of society that would afford them the guidance and protection necessary to avoid assimilation. Thus the construction of a heroic past and the associated glorification of the way of being related to this past created a relationship between the past and the way of being proper to French Canadians that rendered this way of life incompatible with the modern world.

Religion, Modernity, and the Nation in the Social Sciences

In social and political thought, the question of the nature and survival of the French Canadian people became an object of concern following the Durham Report and the Act of Union. As "patriotism requires a perfect knowledge of one's country," nationalists threw themselves into the study of French Canadian society (Fournier 2002, 43). In fact, the motto of Groulx's nationalist journal *L'Action française* was "Étudions les sciences sociales" (Study the social sciences). As in the literature and religious thought of this era, the French Canadian nation was portrayed as incompatible with modernity in the domains of social and political thought.

The attempt to aid in the mission and survival of the nation through social science research is particularly evident in the treatment of three recurring foci of inquiry: history, demography, and language. French Canadian intellectuals of the period, in a manner similar to Garneau's historiographic study of the glorious past of the French Canadian people, not only aimed to refute Durham's denigration of the French Canadian people but also sought to provide insight into the historical conditions that had permitted, and would permit, the nation to flourish.

These goals were particularly evident in the writings of one of the first French Canadian social scientists, Edmund de Nevers. De Nevers's studies of the past were conducted not to provide a historical narrative or description but to determine what the past might reveal about the destiny of the French Canadian nation (Leroux 2001, 352). It was in the past that de Nevers located the model for a utopia of the future. As he outlined in *L'avenir du peuple Canadien-français* (1896), this utopia would be based on two aspects of the specificity of the French Canadian people, namely their links to the great culture of *ancien régime* France and the agricultural way of life of the *habitant*. Montréal could become the metropole of this society through the development of culture, letters, and arts, whereas the countryside could remain an agricultural society. In this way, the specificity of the way of life proper to French Canada could be maintained and its autonomy protected, as it would not fall behind in cultural achievements.

For this to be possible, de Nevers suggested, political reform would be required. Employing Renan's definition of the nation, de Nevers suggested that Canada did not constitute a nation but was made up of two nations. The English and the French, despite possessing an agreement to live together, "share neither a common past nor common objectives" (de Nevers 1896, 252). In order for both people to live together, de Nevers suggested a form of federalism along the lines of the Swiss model. Failing such an agreement, he saw annexation by the United States as inevitable.

For Émile Miller, one of the first intellectuals in Québec to engage in the study of geography, the physical and cultural traits of the French Canadian people were born out of a historical relationship between man and nature. According to Miller, the French Canadian people, whom he referred to as "the 'Neo-French' and the 'Laurentians,'" were marked by two characteristics: "the Franco-Canadian soul, blessed with the three qualities essential to the existence of homogeneous people (unity of faith, language, and convergence of aspirations); the Quebec dialect, with its outdated words, expressions of archaic flavour, numerous 'Canadianisms,' and physical appearance (high forehead, aquiline nose, wide square shoulders, medium stature, remarkable superiority of structure and musculature)" (Fournier 2002, 44). These characteristics were seen to be the product of particular historical and geographical circumstances. A homogeneous people with a unifying language was possible due to Québec's isolation from France and other foreign influence and due to the protections offered by a rural religious society controlled by the clergy. Physically, the French Canadian people were formed by, and predisposed to, agricultural labour. Thus Miller's work asserted that the relationship between early French Canadians and nature had resulted in the formation of a particular people marked by specific cultural and physical characteristics.

Esdras Minville also undertook a series of detailed historical studies of the French Canadian nation. He argued that it was necessary to clearly distinguish between the political and the sociological in order to formulate a vision of the future for the French Canadian people. According to Minville (1992, 146), "the nation is a sociological entity that must be distinguished from a political state if one wants to find a new way of living that will be good for all the groups that are at this moment included within the boundaries of the same state." Minville determined that the historical forces responsible for the formation of the French Canadian nation were "French genius" and "Christian inspiration." As a result, French Canada is primarily a "Christian nation" defined by the "pervasive presence and strength of religion" (Fournier 2002, 44; Leroux 2001, 364). Consequently, its main characteristics are spiritual, communitarian (particularly seen in the strength of the family and the parish), and qualitative (the search for a greater degree of humanity in the world) (Fournier 2002, 45). Although Minville (1992, 143–44) asserted that French Canadians constitute "a cultural community distinct within the large political formation called Canada," he viewed the utilitarianism and materialism of America as the main threat to the nation (Fournier

2002, 45). In order to survive, the French Canadian nation would have to be protected from these influences.

For each of these intellectuals, the essence of the French Canadian nation can be found in a way of life associated with the settlers of New France. Central to this essence are the religious orientation of the people and the structure of the society. Not only did these features shape the French Canadian nation, but they were also the source of its greatest strength and chance of survival in the modern world. As de Nevers (1896, 255) stated, the French Canadian people must not forget that they "have been handed a privileged task." The collective will that this task promotes is what enables them, despite being "lost in the middle of a population of innumerable foreigners," to maintain their status as a "great people" (255).

In addition to history, language also received significant attention from these intellectuals. It was as "a vehicle of tradition and history" that language was seen by de Nevers (1896, 24) as vital to the maintenance of the French Canadian nation. Language allows for a better understanding of a people's history, creating a connection with the past that allows for the promotion of collective memory and a sense of community. As well as recounting historical facts, language conveys "the emotions that have been felt by generations of humans which are no longer here, the variety of their impressions, the complexities of their sensations, their beliefs, their misery, their happiness" (124). As a result, the French language had to be "conserved with a jealous zeal," for it was through the French language that a connection to the historic mission of the French Canadian people could be maintained (131). Thus any threat of linguistic assimilation was a threat to the nation itself.

In a manner similar to that of the clerical elite, social scientists of the period were also deeply concerned with issues of demographics. The position of the French Canadian nation as a numerical minority within Canada was of central concern given the threat that this position posed to their survival. The importance placed on demographic considerations for the survival of the nation is perhaps most evident in Édouard Montpetit's (1938, 272) assertion that "we have survived by our numbers."

The demographic concern of social scientists focused on two issues: infant mortality and emigration. A common refrain in historical and sociological studies of French Canada was that despite having a population of only 65,000 at the time of the Conquest, it had been able to survive due to a substantial fertility rate (Leroux 2001, 360). However, as Montpetit noted, the birth rate of the French Canadian people, which in the late nineteenth century was among the highest in the Western world (362), came with an infant mortality rate that was much higher than in any other Canadian province (Montpetit 1938, 271–72). As a consequence, the English population, bolstered particularly in the rest of Canada by immigration, threatened to gain further numerical advantage. Thus Montpetit argued that measures to improve hygiene and education were needed in order to counter this tendency (Leroux 2001, 362). Emphasizing the gravity of the situation, Montpetit (1938, 362) asserted, "Less coffins, more cradles, this is the challenge of the future."

The second demographic concern, that of emigration, was present as early as the work of de Nevers. As in the case of infant mortality, this concern was one of numbers. As an increasing number of French Canadians emigrated to the United States seeking industrial employment, the policy of *la revanche des berceaux* increased in importance. De Nevers (1896, 115) noted that "the majority of those who have left over the past thirty years have not returned to the Province of Québec." This emigration posed a threat to the future of the French Canadian nation since political borders now divided them "as two fractions of a people" (115). Given the threat that emigration posed to the nation, de Nevers was dumbfounded that "such large numbers of our compatriots shy from the noble work of the pioneer and instead compromise their health and dull their intelligence in the oppressive atmosphere of the factories of New England" (221).

In the work of these social scientists, the essential elements of the French Canadian nation were equated with those of an earlier time and thus threatened by modern conditions and forces of assimilation. In their statements, the traditional structures and way of being of French Canada were portrayed as the basis for the survival of the nation in the context of modern threats. It was the maintenance of traditional society and its barriers to modern forces of assimilation that could provide hope for the survival of the nation.

In the late eighteenth and early nineteenth centuries, a second group of social scientists offered very different conclusions. The structures of

French Canadian society were perceived by this group as a hindrance to, rather than essential for, the survival of the nation. Despite differing in their valuation of the structures of French Canadian society, however, these social scientists also associated these structures, particularly religion, with the premodern.

Following Confederation in 1867, two minority groups within Canada – the Aboriginal peoples and the French Canadians – came under sociological and ethnological scrutiny. Within a large number of studies, the particularism of these groups came to be seen as either a handicap or a museum artefact (Fournier 2002, 42). This outlook is especially apparent in the work of Léon Gérin, often considered the first French Canadian sociologist (Leroux 2001, 354). Toward the end of the nineteenth century, Gérin undertook three different monographic studies of rural Québec, the most famous of which is *L'habitant de Saint-Justin* (1898). He argued that French Canada was composed of a series of local communities whose structures and way of life were organized solely around tradition. Much of his study involved observation of the Casaubon family in the rural village of St. Dominique. He asserted that the traits he observed in this family, specifically their lack of initiative, creativity, and curiosity, were representative of the close-mindedness of French Canadians.

Gérin argued that these traits were a result of the Catholic communitarianism that characterized French Canadian social organization. As he was a proponent of the theory of particularism, the statement was a harsh judgment of French Canadian society. Particularism asserts that the bases of economic, social, and political progress are the education of the individual and training in personal initiative, both of which are related to the transition from the community-based family to the particularist family (Fournier 2001, 335; 2002, 43). According to Gérin, family-based Catholic communitarianism "contributed to the maintenance of Québec as a 'backward' society somewhat disjointed from the course of history" (Jean 2006, 58).

Through historical analysis, Gérin further associated the structure and mentality of French Canadian society with the premodern. He formulated a detailed social history of New France that involved an analysis of the provinces and regions of France from which the bulk of settlers had emigrated. He concluded that it was peasants from north-west France who were best able to adapt to the conditions of North America (Falardeau 1968, 18). The peasants and the clergy who accompanied them brought along the feudal outlooks and social structures of *ancien régime* France, which were dominated by traditions largely interpreted and governed by religious authorities. As a result, he asserted, the clergy played the central role in the socialization process (Leroux 2001, 364). According to his progressive view of historical development, these structures were able to remain intact only due to the unique context of isolation in North America.

However, in the face of contact with modern economic forces, which Gérin saw as "pressing determinants," these structures had become an obstacle to survival (Caldwell 1995; Fournier 2001, 336). In order to survive in the midst of modern economic arrangements, Gérin asserted, it would be necessary for Anglo-Saxon particularism – characterized by frugality, initiative, creativity, autonomy, and the formation of a business elite – to replace Catholic communitarianism (Caldwell 1995; Fournier 2001, 336; 2002, 43). These characteristics could be developed only through educational reform. He suggested the need for a move away from a form of education dominated by the clergy and the family, which focused on community, and toward a form of education concerned with the individual and modern economic values, one that would permit "an entry into modernity" (Fournier 2001, 335; 2002, 43).

Another social scientist of the period who equated French Canadian society with the premodern was Marius Barbeau. A student of Robert Ranulph Marret and Marcel Mauss (Fournier 2002, 43), Barbeau conducted several ethnological studies of Aboriginals and French Canadians as an ethnologist employed by the Geological Commission of the Federal Department of Mines and the National Library of Canada. In the early twentieth century, these organizations formed anthropological divisions in order to gather "authentic data" about these populations "before it was too late" (n6).

As part of his studies of French Canadian society, Barbeau collected songs, legends, tales, and objects, all of which were said to be traditional. Within Barbeau's reports, French Canadian society and culture appeared as "objects of amazement and marvel" whose traditional practices and institutions were "artefacts destined for the museum or the learned journal, to be appreciated by specialists and other 'cultured' onlookers" (Fournier 2002, 43). Thus, by the late nineteenth century, as manifest in the writings of Gérin and Barbeau, tradition had become an object of discourse and a focus of social scientists.

In the twentieth century, the perceived cultural uniqueness of French Canada also attracted American sociologists associated with the Chicago School, who were eager to observe and analyze traditional societies. The most prominent among these scholars were Horace Miner and Everett C. Hughes. Miner and Hughes were primarily concerned with French Canada as a society that was in the preliminary stages of a transformation from a traditional to a modern form. In their analysis, they applied the concept of folk society to French Canada. This term, which had previously been applied to other "peasant" societies, such as that of the Yucatán Peninsula in Mexico, differentiated French Canada from the modern world of industry and city life as well as from "primitive" tribal societies, whom they were said to closely resemble (Jean 2006, 58; Redfield 1939, xiv). The first of these studies was undertaken by Horace Miner, a student of anthropologist Robert Redfield. Conducting fieldwork over a few years in the community of St. Denis, a small village approximately 150 kilometres from Québec City, Miner sought to provide a detailed description of the structure and culture of French Canada, which he saw as exemplary of a folk society. Being labelled as a folk society meant that French Canada was considered to be at an intermediary stage "in the equation of culture and civilization" (Redfield 1939, xiii). On the one hand, it was said to closely resemble the societies of "primitive peoples" (xiii). Like other societies that are "more primitive and outside the European world" (xiv), French Canada was seen as exhibiting a simplicity of social structures, a lack of structural differentiation, strong familial organization, and perhaps above all, the pervasiveness of religion (Miner 1930).

Miner observed the Catholic Church and the Catholic religion to be dominant in all aspects of French Canadian life:

> The church provides sacred justifications and explanations for the necessary toil of the native, offers rituals to carry the individual from

> birth to death, and supports and sanctifies the large-family system. In its local institutions and in the local priest it provides the framework for community government and the moral leader of the community. And when the local ways are threatened ... the church is there, in the sermons of the priest, to minimize the danger of contagion. (Redfield 1939, xvii)

Thus, throughout their entire lives, French Canadians were immersed in religion, took part in religious rituals, and conducted themselves according to religious doctrine not out of coercion but out of belief (Miner 1939, ch. 5). Religious practices were seen by Miner and other anthropologists of the Chicago School as promoting the homogeneity and sense of social inclusion characteristic of traditional societies.

Despite being an "isolated peasant group" that shared many of the traits of primitive societies, French Canada, as a folk society, was not considered "another Melanasian or American Indian society," as it was said to be of the modern, urbanized world (Redfield 1939, xiv). French Canadians engaged in a money economy, sold their goods in urban markets, paid taxes, and through the clergy had contact with the wider modern society (Miner 1939, ch. 11; Redfield 1939, xiv). However, the influence of the modern world was regulated by the Catholic Church: "She has stood between the changing world and the *habitant,* preventing the admission of elements in accordance with the faith and with local culture" (xvii).

Despite the strength of the barrier formed by the church, Miner saw the dissolution of French Canadian society as inevitable. Due to professionalization, emigration, and contact with the modern economy, elements of modern culture were said to be increasingly infiltrating French Canadian life (Miner 1939, ch. 11). Miner argued that these cultural elements would slowly wear down the hold of traditional values, which seem to have been understood as stable only in isolation. Moreover, the pervasiveness of religion and the power of the Catholic Church were seen as making this inevitable transformation one fraught with hardship.

Redfield (1939, xviii) asserted that French Canadian society, "as a body of beliefs and practices, is static; but as an adjustment between sources of wealth and means of exploitation, it is expansive." Although the church promoted a high birth rate and the settlement of more land, the only land available was of increasingly poor quality and, therefore, unable to support the population (Miner 1939, ch. 11). Due to the pervasiveness and the static nature of religion, French Canadian society had not made the necessary adjustment toward smaller families. Miner argued that as a consequence of the inability to find adequate land, the excess population was increasingly forced to engage in industrial labour, thus undermining the traditional society. However, the retention of folk culture, particularly its aversion to education, meant that although French Canadians were inevitably entering the modern world, they were doing so at an extreme disadvantage.

A few years after the publication of Miner's study, Everett C. Hughes embarked on a study of French Canadian society. Focusing on the town of Drummondville (under the pseudonym Cantonville), Hughes sought to describe a society that he believed was undergoing monumental transformation that was undermining the traditional structures and culture of a folk society in favour of modern, urban structures and practices. Like Miner, Hughes (1943, 2) believed that French Canada, marked by "a rural cast of mind and ... close-knit traditions" that were largely due to the centrality of religion and the power of the church (10–11), was being rapidly drawn into modern, secular capitalist society.

According to Hughes (1943, 3), the French Canadian people were not wholly alien to capitalist relations but had "stabilized their way of life about the earlier and simpler institutions of the capitalistic system of production and exchange." Whereas other societies had modernized along with the expansion of industry, French Canada, as a result of its common will and unique historical circumstances, had succeeded in retaining a more primitive form of society. Hughes looked upon this survival as a heroic, although temporary, miracle in the face of the adversity of industrial "conquest" (Fournier 2001, 337; Hughes 1943, 2).

Hughes (1943, 2–3) argued that the irresistible expansion of the industrial economy not only changed economic arrangements but also had an effect on culture and transformed social structures:

> Again and again a few people, possessed of technical knowledge and capital, have gone to new regions and there brought about an

> industrial and social revolution among people accustomed to simpler modes of living. Such colonial expansion is more fateful than mere military conquest, for eventually it changes social structures, the ways of making a living, people's wants, and all those aspects of culture which have to do with creating and attaining ambitions.

Hughes believed that French Canadians, "bound by sentiment, tradition, and kinship," were at the mercy of "invading agents, armed with capital and techniques from older English and American centers of finance and industry" (2). In the face of the assimilatory power of industrial capitalism, the central elements of traditional French Canadian society, including its religious nature, would inevitably be replaced by the modern, foreign, and secular norms of modernity. Moreover, like Miner, he believed that the attachment of the French Canadian people to a traditional culture, foreign to the invading capitalists, put them at a distinct disadvantage, relegating them to the role of abundant, cheap labour.

As the work of Gérin, Barbeau, Miller, Montpetit, Miner, and Hughes demonstrates, the equation of French Canadian society with the premodern and the location of religion as central to this designation were not limited to advocates of clerico-nationalism but were elements within a shared discourse of concern regarding the future of the French Canadian nation.

As Tomoko Masuzawa's analysis in *The Invention of World Religions* (2005) demonstrates, the equation of religion with the premodern was not limited to the writings of the above-mentioned social scientists; rather, she suggests that such thinking was related to a vision of Europe as a harbinger of universal history, which emerged in the late nineteenth century. Masuzawa argues that at that time a questioning of the future of religion – brought about by a belief that religion was in a state of transformation or decline – turned the attention of scholars toward the origins of religion (12). Masuzawa locates this focus on origins in three seemingly independent fields of inquiry – philology, anthropology, and orientalism – each of which equated religious practices with particular historical forms of society.

As Masuzawa (2005) asserts, through its construction of language families, nineteenth-century philology allowed European scholars to closely associate their contemporary culture with pre-Christian antiquity (xii). The philological debates of that period eventually led to an association of the origins of Christianity with Greco-Aryan traditions rather than with the Hebrew Bible. Concurrent with this Aryanization of Christianity was the Semitization of Islam (xii). This racialization of religion served to particularize Islam as the religion of Arabs, whereas Christianity was able to maintain its universality. The universality of Christianity, which had previously been attributed to monotheism, was replaced by a Hellenic universality of reason. Nineteenth-century Hellenists argued that reason had allowed ancient Greeks to discern unity amid a plurality of Gods and phenomena (xiii). Christian Europe, with or without religion, came to be seen as the carrier and disseminator of this new universality.

At the same time, European anthropologists in their search for the origins and nature of religion engaged in analyses of what they deemed the most primitive forms of religion. These researchers engaged in systematic collection, cataloguing, and comparison of various beliefs and practices that they deemed to be religious in order to develop a model of the myths, rituals, and other practices that were common to tribal societies (Masuzawa 2005, 16). The characteristics of the "contemporary savage" were conflated with ancient and extinct traditions and were thought of as being on the brink of disappearance (4, 12). Not only were these societies seen as exhibiting the most elementary forms of religion, but religion was also considered to be pervasive in all aspects of life. It was this pervasiveness and the temporal connotations attached to it that most decisively distinguished these tribal societies from modern European society.

Masuzawa (2005) argues that religion was also a central feature in nineteenth-century Orientalist thought. Unlike the elementary tribal religions that appeared to be without history, the religions of the Orient were seen as arising out of specific historical circumstances (17). The pervasiveness of religion in Oriental societies was accounted for by the absence of events promoting or permitting the dissipation or privatization of religion. It was these historical events, acts, or figures that, in turn, accounted for the distinction between the Orient and the Occident. Thus, in nineteenth-century Europe, developments in the fields of philology, anthropology, and oriental studies "promoted and bolstered the presumption [among many Europeans] that this thing called 'religion' still held sway over all those who were unlike them: non-Europeans, Europeans of the premodern past, and among their own contemporary neighbors, the uncivilized and uneducated bucolic populace as well as the superstitious urban poor, all of whom were something of 'savages within'" (19). As a result, within a particular historical context, religion became associated with a series of others, all of whom were conflated with the historical other of the premodern.

As this chapter has demonstrated, in mid-nineteenth-century Québec, within a discourse concerning the nature and future of French Canadian society, the secular emerged as that which was proper to the modern, whereas religion was regarded as a key element of what was thought of as traditional French Canadian society. These objects appeared within various statements that, despite traversing fields, normative positions, and theoretical positions, shared a common discourse defining French Canadian society in opposition to the modern. Within this discourse, religion and the secular, like all objects within discourse, could never emerge in isolation. An object is always related to, and defined in reference to, other objects. Thus, as meaning cannot exist without reference to other objects, there was never a moment at which the secular emerged in isolation. The secular that emerged in mid-nineteenth-century French Canada was always related to, and defined in relation to, an understanding of religion that emerged concurrently. The secular, that which was proper to the modern, could not emerge without reference to religion, that which was proper to the premodern.

Unlike narratives of secularization and secularism, the secular is not an ahistorical entity waiting to be discovered or unveiled, nor is it the product of progressive historical forces of modernization; rather, the emergence of the secular and religion in nineteenth-century Québec was the result of various contingent events and struggles, namely rebellion, upheaval, and the emergence of a conception of modernization in which French Canadians, as carriers of particular ethno-cultural traits, were viewed as unable to make the transition to modernity.

By historicizing the emergence of the secular and the religious in a particular form, this chapter begins the work of denaturalizing and historicizing these categories, whose naturalization limits our way of being. By demonstrating the contingent and historical emergence of these categories, we can begin to challenge the limiting discourses and practices of secularization and secularism as well as the narratives of the nation that rely on them for a sense of continuity.

3 The Quiet Revolution and the State-Centred Nation: Immaturity, Abnormality, Autonomy, and Authenticity

With the death of Premier Maurice Duplessis in 1959 and the electoral victory of the Québec Liberal Party under Jean Lesage the following year, a period of intense social change and modernization known as the Quiet Revolution was inaugurated in Québec. During the period 1960-66, Québec undertook a series of reforms, including the development of a welfare state, the passage of the Hospital Insurance Act (1961), the creation of the Ministries of Cultural Affairs (1961) and Education (1964), the establishment of the Société générale de financement (1962), the Québec Pension Plan (1965), the Caisse de dépôt et placement du Québec (1965), and the Société québécoise d'exploration minière (1965), the nationalization of all private hydroelectric facilities (1963), and the introduction of a series of other social and electoral reforms.

According to most historical narratives, these measures were accompanied by profound cultural and social transformations. In taking control of institutions previously administered or regulated by the church, the Québec government was said to have initiated a redefinition of what it meant to be French Canadian. Sophie Therrien (2004) argues that, as a result of the Quiet Revolution, the "ethnic and religious anchorings of identity began to lose their relevance." First, rejecting the anti-statism of clerico-nationalism, the Québec state emerged as the only tool through which the realization of a "normal" modern society could be achieved.

The religious pillar of the French Canadian nation, and with it the entire edifice of clerico-nationalism, had been undermined. With the emergence of the centrality of the state, "the 'French Canadians' disappeared, [and were] replaced by the 'Québécois'" (15).

Second, the identification of the state as "the embodiment of the French nation in Canada" (Guindon 1988, 104) also meant a marginalization of the Catholic Church. Whereas the Duplessis government had declared Québec officially Catholic, supported the dominance of the church in the provision of social and educational services to the French Canadian people, and promoted a morality dictated by church authorities, the Liberal government pursued a policy of deconfessionalization and state control of many educational, health, and social welfare institutions while seeking to create a pluralist society guided by secular values (Gauvreau 2000, Seljak 1996, 109–10).

Accompanying the privatization of the Catholic Church was a marked decline in interest and participation in religious practice, an abandonment of religious orders by many members of the clergy, and "a rapid erosion of the church's social and cultural authority" (Gauvreau 2000, 803). As Peter Gzowski remarked in 1963, the "French and Catholic people of Quebec ... are changing faster than any group of people on the continent. What they are changing from, as much as anything else, is their consent to domination by the Catholic Church and clergy of their schools, their social ideas, and in some ways even their politics" (Magnuson 1963, 43).

Thus most accounts of the Quiet Revolution describe it as a period of rapid secularization. This transformation is thought of not merely as an institutional secularization brought about by the privatization of religious power but also as a revolution in mentalities. The French Canadian people, once described predominantly on the basis of their deep religiosity, were said to have become secular. However, this secularization was not seen as the death knell of the French Canadian nation but as a feature of its maturation, modernization, and normalization.

Prior to the 1980s, explanations of the Quiet Revolution generally followed the narrative supplied by what Michael Gauvreau (2000, 806) labels the heroic school of the Quiet Revolution. According to this perspective, as evident in the work of Michael Behiels (1985) and Léon

Dion (1993), the Quiet Revolution was the product of the heroic labour of a small group of generally foreign-trained intellectuals. Whether liberal or neonationalist, they sought to awaken the French Canadian people to the errors of traditional nationalism by combating the corruption of the Duplessis regime and the all-pervasive repressive power of the clerical authorities (Gauvreau 2000, 806). Freed from the shackles of tradition, the French Canadian people would be able to begin their entry into modernity.

Historical analyses since the late 1970s have offered an alternative account of the Quiet Revolution (e.g., Linteau, Durocher, and Robert 1979; Young 1994). In these studies, the Quiet Revolution appears as the culmination of a long historical process of the unfolding of the forces of economic liberalization, capitalization, and modernization. It is the advancement of these long-term economic processes that is said to account for the political, cultural, and social transformations of Québec in the early 1960s.

As Gauvreau (2000) argues, within both of these accounts, "Roman Catholicism and Catholic values loom as shadowy, elusive presences." Religion is portrayed as "a repository of 'tradition,' an institution mired in a rural, utopian past and thus inevitably destined to melt away in the face of the march of secular ideologies and cultural practices" (804). Religion appears as an object acted upon by external secular forces rather than as a dynamic force within the modernization of French Canadian society. In an important intervention, Gauvreau (2000, 2005) argues that a nuanced understanding of the Quiet Revolution must account for the role of Catholicism in the promotion of modernization in Québec. In attempting to do so, he locates the "roots" of the Quiet Revolution not in a group of dedicated secular intellectuals or in the forces of economic liberalization and modernization but in the efforts of the church to formulate a solution to the catastrophe of the Great Depression.

Although Gauvreau's analysis provides a crucial critique of dominant narratives of secularization in Québec, it too falls into the historiographic trap of a search for origins. The positing of Catholicism as the origin of the secularization of Québec – a position also advocated by David Seljak (1996) – serves a parodic function (Foucault 1971, 93–94) by mocking the venerated identification of secularization with enlightenment and of religion with tradition. It can, however, as seen in the next chapter, also promote the notion of the exceptionalism of Judeo-Christian civilization. Moreover, it fails to acknowledge the multiplicity of forces at play in, and making possible, the emergence of what it deems an origin.

Thus, although this chapter follows Gauvreau in asserting the importance of reinterpreting the role of Catholic practices and theology in the transformation of the definition of national identity in Québec, it does not conceive of them as origins; rather, they are treated as moments within a series of moments in which forces engaged in a battle of interpretations sought to take control of, and to define, the secular and the French Canadian nation. In other words, the practices and discourses associated with the Quiet Revolution are not treated as the end product of enlightenment or modernization but as state forces attempting to take control of the secular.

This chapter first analyzes Québec in the 1930s, where Gauvreau locates the origins of the Quiet Revolution. During this decade, various projects, guided by corporatist and personalist thought, attempted to Christianize what were referred to as the secular intermediary realms, those existing between the church, the state, and the economy. Second, the chapter investigates the emergence of statements associated with personalism, liberalism, and neonationalism, which saw modernization not as the death knell of religion but as that which could permit individual and societal normalization and maturation and even the development of authentic religiosity. This modernization involved a freeing of the individual from the structures of traditional authority.

Finally, this chapter describes the redefinition of that which was proper to the state and that which was proper to the church. In other words, it attends to the formation of the notion of a public sphere that included institutions previously controlled by the church and a privatization of religious authority. In this discourse, the secular appears as the realm of autonomy from the traditional authority of the Catholic Church, an autonomy necessary for the normalization and maturation of the French Canadian nation. Central to this discourse is a delineation of the proper place of religion in a "normal," modern, democratic, pluralist society as well as a vision of the secular as a realm of autonomy. The secular here is not depicted as opposed to religion but as the sphere in which there is sufficient autonomy for one to become either authentically religious or nonreligious. As a result, this transformation in understandings of the secular and the religious laid the grounds for the dominance of a new state-based, secular conception of the québécois nation.

According to Gauvreau (2000), and to a somewhat lesser extent Behiels (1985), Ferretti (1999), and E.-Martin Meunier and Jean-Philippe Warren (2002), the Great Depression propelled Québec toward the secularization and modernization of the Quiet Revolution. For these authors, it was the reaction of the church and various other social actors to the social and economic devastation of the 1930s that necessitated an increased role for the state. Although the church responded to the Great Depression by expanding its role in the administration of health, educational, and social welfare institutions, as well as by increasing the number of religious civil society organizations, it came to increasingly rely on the state to finance these institutions. The increased financial control of the state over institutions of the secular realm, along with the growing independence of civil society organizations from the church, allowed the role of the church to eventually be marginalized.

Such an understanding of the role of the Great Depression in the secularization of Québec, however, problematically imparts an essential identity to the Great Depression and then declares this event to be a causal factor. In contrast to such an understanding, genealogical analysis must consider the relationship between an event and its interpretation. It is the interpretation of an event that allows it to arrive in a certain way. An event such as the Great Depression, although singular and one-off, should not be conceived of as occurring in isolation. First, although events must not be folded into the past and the future, they cannot be temporally divorced from either. An event is always implicated in the present and, therefore, in both the past and the future. Second, and consequently, as the act is not isolated from the future, its interpretation is also one of its constitutive elements. In other words, once an interpretation of an event is made, it becomes part of the event itself, enabling the event to arrive in a particular form.

Historical analysis, therefore, should seek to delineate the forces that permit an event to arrive in a particular form. Consequently, what is of significance for this analysis is the manner in which the event of the Great Depression was interpreted and thus arrived in discourse and practices in Québec in the 1930s. It is this interpretation, made possible by various forces – which themselves enabled a series of other interpretations and practices – that is described in the following section.

Re-Christianization and Social Catholicism

In Québec the economic collapse of the Great Depression had widespread and deep ramifications. The rapid industrial expansion and investment of the 1920s ground to a halt, leaving millions in destitution and misery. Mills were shut down in the Saguenay region, declining demand for manufactured goods led to widespread unemployment in Québec City and Montréal, and the falling prices for hay and cod undermined the farming and fishing industries in the Eastern Townships and the Gaspé region. In single-industry towns, as much as half of the populations were unemployed, resulting in the closure of shops, services, and suppliers. Many rural school commissions were forced to close since they were unable to pay the $200 annual salaries of their headmistresses (Mann Trofimenkoff 1982, 233–35).

Those wishing to escape economic destitution found the traditional escape hatch of migration bolted shut. Emigration to the United States was halted by an American prohibition on immigration. A lack of available capital and arable land made rural colonization, despite its continued promotion by clerical authorities, an unrealistic enterprise. Cities also began instituting impediments on rural migrants. Fearing that these migrants would add to the pool of the unemployed, all municipalities in Québec instituted residency requirements of up to two years for all who wished to avail themselves of financial assistance and services (Mann Trofimenkoff 1982, 235).

As Henri Bourassa declared in the House of Commons, the economic crisis had led to 75,000 residents of Montréal living in conditions unfit even for animals (Mann Trofimenkoff 1982, 235). By 1933, the worst year of the Great Depression, 300,000 people in Montréal (approximately one-third of the population) relied on handouts to survive. Rat- and disease-infested shantytowns sprouted up on the outskirts of Hull and Valleyfield, and towns were not only full of itinerant young men but also home to entire families wandering the streets in search of temporary work, a hostel, or a soup kitchen (236).

With more than one-third of the labour force out of work and the destruction of rural life, there arose a significant fear of social disorder and collapse. This social and economic catastrophe came to be seen as a threat to traditional society and as a possible breeding ground for irreligion and communism. Consequently, various actors began to provide analyses of the roots of the Great Depression and to propose solutions. The dominant interpretation of the Great Depression in Québec in the years following the stock market's crash in 1929 was that it was a failure of liberal capitalism. The turmoil resulting from the economic collapse was not seen as merely the result of the economic machinations of capitalism; rather, it was largely attributed to the anomie of liberal capitalist society. Although the Catholic Church and clerico-nationalists continued to promote a policy of rural colonization, the misery of the Great Depression and the resulting fear of instability promoted, above all, the invigoration of a program of social Catholicism in Québec.

In 1891 Pope Leo XIII published the encyclical *Rerum novarum*. This document, meant to serve as the social charter of the church in the industrial era, argued for the necessity of developing a stable corporatist social order that promoted the dignity of all members as brothers in God. The rich and the poor, "as the head and arms of a single body," were to avoid conflict, workers were to denounce class struggle, and capitalists were to avoid dishonest exploitation (Ferretti 1999, 126). Instead of the individualism and inherent class conflict of liberal capitalism, a Catholic corporatism was presented as the basis of a modern, industrial, yet still Catholic society.

Although the Catholic Church in Québec undertook a series of actions in line with the teachings of social Catholicism – including the formation of the Association catholique de la jeunesse canadienne-française (Catholic Association of French Canadian Youth) in 1903, the think tanks École sociale populaire (ÉSP) and Sémaines sociales du Canada in 1919 and 1920, and the Confédération des travailleurs catholiques du Canada (Confederation of Catholic Workers of Canada) (CTCC) in 1921 – it was not until the Great Depression and the realization of the permanency of industrialism and the immediacy of the threat of economic liberalism that the church embarked on a significant program to re-Christianize society.

In 1933, generally following the model of re-Christianization through the "Catholic action" of Pope Pius XI's 1931 encyclical *Quadragesimo anno,* a group of clerics – including Joseph-Papin Archambault, head of the ÉSP – devised the Program of Social Restoration, which outlined the church's vision of corporatism. It depicted a society structured around professional organizations comprising workers and capitalists in each sector of the economy, a social order based on respect for private property balanced by the interests of society as a whole, a respect for capitalism tempered by the principle of a just family wage, and support for a form of federalism in which the rights of provinces and the two founding peoples would be respected (Ferretti 1999, 137). The Program of Social Restoration was endorsed by the bishops, nationalist intellectuals, and the CTCC.

Above all, the program was a critique of liberal capitalism. It attributed the excesses of capitalism to the introduction of liberal ideas into the realm of economics, which had resulted in the pre-eminence of material values. Consequently, a new economic vision was required, one with a human face (Lacombe 2003, 44–45). As cleric Georges-Henri Lévesque argued in 1934, the economy must be mastered not for the benefit of individuals but in order to serve the common good of society: "There are two factors, human needs and material needs, and we must put each one in its proper place. Are we the servants of wealth [*richesses*] or should wealth [*richesses*] serve us?" (45).

As Sylvie Lacombe (2003, 45) argues, the primary enemy in the battle against liberalism was actually communism. Liberal capitalism was seen as instituting a system of conflicting class interests, which if left unchecked could lead to communism and the irreligion of the Soviet Union. In *Quadragesimo anno,* Pius XI invoked the need for a holy war against this materialist and atheist "incarnation of the Demon." In Québec, Archambault organized anti-communist rallies in towns across the province, engaged the ÉSP in the printing of anti-communist signs and brochures, and transmitted his anti-communist message in radio programs and sermons (Ferretti 1999, 135). It was for this reason that the church and its lay supporters rejected social credit as a response to the crisis of the Great Depression. According to the church, creditism was merely a monetary reform that failed to profoundly transform society in line with the teachings of Pius XI. Invoking the words of St. Paul, church officials deemed creditism, like all "profane novelties," a heresy. They denounced creditism as "charlatanism," deeming it a "hazardous system" whose exponents exhibited revolutionary passion (Dupuis 2003, 35).

A second enemy of those championing corporatism in 1930s Québec was the Liberal government of Premier Louis-Alexandre Taschereau. The Taschereau government was seen not only as corrupt but also as having allowed, through its lax policies, the conquest of the province by Anglo-Canadian, British, and American finance (Mann Trofimenkoff 1982, 234; Quinn 1938). The corporatists sought to achieve a resolution of the economic inferiority of French Canadians by humanizing the economy and subordinating it to the needs of society (Lacombe 2003, 45).

To oppose the Taschereau government, the church briefly openly engaged in electoral politics, supporting the Union Nationale party, made up of the Duplessis Conservatives and the breakaway Action libérale nationale party of Paul Gouin. However, with the electoral victory of the Union Nationale in 1936, and the subsequent rupture of the party, the church returned to the anti-statist, apolitical position described in the previous chapter.

Despite both the concerns aired outside of Québec during this period and the common historical interpretation of corporatist movements in Québec during the 1930s, the vast majority of movements did not advocate fascism. Fascist voices did exist, primarily in the form of the National Christian Socialist Party of Adrien Arcand, evoking critiques of communism, socialism, liberalism, and finance capitalism. The position of these marginal voices, however, must be carefully distinguished from the corporatism espoused by the clerico-nationalists, the church, and the Catholic Action movements. Although Arcand and his supporters wished to establish a corporatist state in Canada based on the Italian and German models, the "professional" or "social" corporatism of the church in the 1930s aimed to "short-circuit" the state (Lacombe 2003, 47; Quinn 1938). Rather than instituting a corporatist state, the dominant corporatist vision placed the church between civil society and the state. By serving as an intermediary, the church could limit the state's involvement in social affairs instead of promoting its predominance.

Among the most important facets of the Catholic corporatist vision were the Catholic Action movements. The activities of these movements primarily involved large-scale projects of popular education. According to Archambault, popular education was necessary in order to promote "a Catholic sense," which was achieved by "lead[ing] the intelligence to think, conceive, and judge – naturally, spontaneously – in a Catholic way, according to the spirit of the Church, following the doctrine of its teachers and the directives of its leaders" (Gauvreau 2000, 807–8).

Exemplary of these movements in Québec was the Jeunesse ouvrière chrétienne (JOC). Formed by cleric Joseph Cadijn in Belgium and officially launched by Pius XI in 1924, the JOC first appeared in Québec in the early 1930s. Led by cleric Henri Roy, the goal of the JOC was to "embody the social Catholic vision in the milieu of the working class itself" (Cole-Arnal 1997, 512). Its members sought, through the education and activities of Catholic proletarian youth, to protect traditional Catholic life and piety against the misery and temptations of urban life. To do so, Roy argued in *Un problème et une solution* (A Problem and a Solution) (1934), "the young must always be Christians, not only at church ... but always, at the factory, in the family and on the street" (Cole-Arnal 1997, 513).

In its periodicals, the JOC invoked the desire for the "workplace to be Christian" by following the example of "Jesus the Worker" (Cole-Arnal 1997, 514). It offered staunch support for Catholic unions and denounced nonconfessional unions, which they saw as a threat to social stability. Adhering to the dominant corporatist message of the church, the JOC, like the CTCC, repudiated all class struggle. Primacy was placed on industrial peace and social order. Workers' grievances were to be resolved only "according to the regulations of morality and judgement of religion" (518).

Not only did the JOC provide courses for young Catholic workers to prepare them for the workplace, but it also offered extensive preparation for marriage and family life. This was undertaken in order to promote the nuclear, Christian, patriarchal family. Such activities culminated in the mass marriage of 106 couples at the 1939 JOC Congress, which came to be known as the Congress of the Hundred Marriages (Cole-Arnal 1997, 521). The continual struggle to Christianize all aspects of life, Roy declared, brought with it the possibility of "a spiritual revolution which would renovate individuals, families and societies" (519).

In the late 1930s, social Catholicism in Québec underwent an important transformation as a result of the dominance of personalist theology, particularly the left personalism of Jacques Maritain and Emmanuel Mounier. Personalism offered a critique of both "the faceless automatism of totalitarianism and the atomization of liberal capitalism by asserting the value of the human person" (Gauvreau 2000, 808). This critique, however, did not entail a reassertion of individuality; rather, personalism asserted that human potential could be realized only through membership in a wider community. As a result, the emphasis on ritual, personal piety, and individual redemption, which came to be seen as part of the inauthentic religiosity of traditional, folk, or popular religion, was replaced by a focus on modern spiritual authenticity.

As Gauvreau (2000, 809) correctly asserts, with the rise of personalism, the corporatism of the 1930s was "not so much swept away as reinterpreted." Like the earlier corporatism, personalism offered a compelling critique not only of the individualism, materialism, and hedonism of liberalism but also of the three dictatorial statisms of communism, fascism, and monopoly capitalism. Rather than the nation, the church, or the state, personalism sought, in the words of Jesuit cleric François Hertel, to affirm the human being as "the centre of the universe" around which society and the state must converge (813). A corporatist, "pluralist social order" based on "the freedoms of individuals, of families, and professional bodies" was seen as the form of social order proper to a modern civilization (813–14). Personalist organizations such as the Jeunesse étudiante catholique (Young Catholic Students) and periodicals such as *La Relève* began to refrain from directly political and nationalist discourse and attempted to apply the principles of personalism to the specific problems of French Canadian society. Unlike the earlier activities of the Catholic Action movements, which focused on the Christianization of individuals within secular social realms, personalism argued that genuine Catholic social action should be undertaken to find solutions to collective problems (Behiels 1985, 21).

Not only was social Catholicism applied to concrete collective social problems, but a collectivist conception of salvation was also asserted.

It was this collectivist mentality that was said to differentiate modern, authentic religiosity from the traditional practices of the church. As Alex Pelletier and Gérard Pelletier (1944), two prominent members of the Jeunesse étudiante catholique argued, according to the traditional teachings and practices of the church, "holiness seems too much like an individual adventure, this *solitary* voyage *on a path bordered with thorns* ... On the contrary we see all humanity, like a river, marching towards the Kingdom. We are a small drop of water in this river. We are the limbs of the mystical Body, members of an immense people comprising sinners and saints, in solidarity with all these people."

In 1943, in response to the church's proclamation of the doctrine of the Mystical Body of Christ – which in Québec was interpreted as a rejection of the notion of individual salvation – cleric Maurice Lafond asserted that Christ came to earth not to save souls but to attack injustice. According to Lafond, traditional Catholicism, which had argued that a Christian society could be realized by working outward from the salvation of the individual, had been proven incorrect by the conditions of the modern world. For personalism, a Christian society could be realized only through the institution of its proper conditions of possibility: "In today's society, institutions are too often a permanent occasion of sin and evasion of the divine. We must seize hold of these institutions. Through them we can prepare the Christian social climate that, with the aid of God's grace, will assure the reign of virtue" (Lafond 1943).

Within personalist thought and practice, therefore, primacy was given to the social. It was not the holy individual who would create a Christian society but rather a Christian society that would enable the authentic religiosity of the individual. The fulfilment of the human being was seen not only as the product of the cultivation of individual qualities but, more importantly, also as the product of the relationships that grouped humans together as a society (Gauvreau 2000, 815).

According to future Canadian prime minister Pierre Elliott Trudeau, personalism as lived Christianity was the only modern ideology that "offers true freedom to the human spirit ... the only one that gives an answer to all problems." In opposition to liberalism, within which each individual sought his own liberty at the expense of others, and Marxism, which sought to promote "the liberty of all by removing liberty," personalist Christianity, where all were equal brothers in Christ, was the source of true freedom (Gauvreau 2000, 817). It was through lived Christianity that the personalist Catholic Action movements believed they could achieve a truly social democracy, comprising the economic democracy promised by Marxism but without the loss of personal freedoms. They argued that by severing notions of class from the struggle for economic justice, "Christianity would find its role in the modern world" (818).

As with the earlier corporatism, central to this personalist vision of social democracy were the intermediary bodies of the secular realm: municipalities, parishes, trade unions, and political and charitable bodies. It was these intermediary bodies that served as the terrain of Christianization. It was in this intermediate realm that class antagonisms could be reconciled. As argued by Claude Ryan, the national secretary of Catholic Action, who would later serve as the editor of *Le Devoir* and the leader of the Québec Liberal Party, Catholicism accepted class division as essential to the functioning of a healthy society (Gauvreau 2000, 819). By fostering a communitarian spirit within intermediary bodies, personalist social Catholicism could overcome class conflict without undermining the social function of the division of classes. Therefore, the primary focus of Catholic social action should be in the spiritual and cultural realms, where it was required to combat the depersonalization of industrial relations and their reduction of individuals to "a conformist mass, incapable of participation in civic life." It was through engagement in the secular realm that, in the words of Catholic Action student leader Camille Laurin, social Catholicism could resist these trends and forge "the democratic union of all citizens" (820).

It was also through participation in the intermediary realm that Christians could achieve self-fulfilment and authenticity. It was in this realm, rather than in the private realm of individual piety, that one could engage with the social whole. As Gauvreau (2000, 820) argues, personalism rested on the notion of an "unbridgeable gulf" between traditional and modern religious attitudes and practices, and it depended on a radical break with clerico-nationalism, which required believing that "Québec's past contained nothing of value for modern Christians." Popular religious practices were dismissed as "relics of a medieval age, traditions that could offer humans no guidance in framing modern values and institutions" (821).

Personalism, therefore, marked an important retranslation of the concept of the secular as described in the previous chapter. No longer was religion defined as that which was proper to premodern or traditional society and incompatible with modern society. Instead, it was *traditional* religion that was associated with the premodern and deemed incompatible with modernity. Religion could be compatible with the modern world if it took a personalist form. Thus there was no longer a simple distinction between religion and modernity but a division between modern and premodern religion. Not only was popular religion assigned to the past and placed in opposition to the modern world, but it was also seen as problematic, an obstacle to maturity, normality, and authenticity. It was traditional religion that many personalists declared to be the source of Québec's "inferiority" (Gauvreau 2000). In the words of Ryan, traditional religion was "a devirilized religion ... A timid religion ... A religion where the questions of the day and fundamental issues of faith cannot be addressed without seekers of truth being immediately silenced by authority. A religion where vigorous theological reasoning ... is no longer found ... In sum, a religion where, for many generations, intellectual life was stunted" (821). Traditional religion was seen as one of submission and rigidity rather than engagement and dynamism. Instead of a passive, anti-intellectual, routinized religion guided and prompted by authority, modern religion – the religion proper to an educated, economically prosperous, industrial civilization – was seen as an active religion whose practices were the result of authentic personal initiative and faith. According to Hertel, traditional religion in Québec was merely "a habit to which the mass of the people simply conforms" (823).

Invoking the notion of folk society developed by the Chicago School, the studies produced by the personalist Catholic Action movements of the 1950s described traditional religion as characterized by the childish superstitions of primitive societies, "a question of prayers, rosaries, of devotions ... It is a question of passive acceptance, of obedience in everything, not of profound understanding ... There is often nothing positive or active" (Gauvreau 2000). It was merely a "sociological religion," a series of moral laws and practices "devoid of spirituality" (825). This past-oriented, passive religion had produced in Québec "an immobilized people, a nation turned to the past more than the future" (823).

Particularly after 1945, traditional Catholic thought came to be seen as divorced from the reality of human life. It was perceived to be oriented toward the needs of a rural rather than urban society. This rural orientation, combined with its orientation toward the past, meant that traditional religion could not play a creative role in promoting social solidarity and personal self-fulfilment. Consequently, it was unable to offer an alternative to the threats of liberalism and Marxism. Instead, the detachment of traditional religion from modern life risked promoting these ideologies by creating what Ryan described as "a gulf between religion and life that works at the level of the daily life of ordinary people, opening it to diverse manifestations of a decadent civilization" (Gauvreau 2000, 824).

Perhaps most important to the adherents of personalism in Québec was the sense that the incompatibility of traditional religion with modern society had created a spiritual crisis in the province. This crisis was perceived to be manifested in an intergenerational conflict of values that resulted from a feeling of disconnection among members of the younger generation from the religion of their parents. The ossified and rural nature of traditional religion meant that it was unable to adapt to the rapidly changing values, customs, and practices of modern society. Personalists feared that due to the contradictions between traditional Catholicism and modernity, religion "would ultimately be overwhelmed and discarded" (Gauvreau 2000, 825). It was only through the diffusion of modern personalist values into all aspects of French Canadian life that this risk could be averted. Personalists believed that by engaging in the secular realm in an active, authentically religious fashion, rather than retreating to the private realm of clerical authority, religion could be renewed in a modern, authentic form.

Liberalism and Neonationalism

Consistent with the position of personalist theology, the two intellectual and political currents that, according to most observers, dominated postwar Québec also shared a belief in the detrimental effects of traditional religion. Known alternatively as liberalism and neonationalism (Behiels

1985), neoliberalism and neonationalism (Roy 1993), or melancholy nationalism and anti-nationalist liberalism (Létourneau 1998a, 1998b, 2000; Maclure 2003), the dominance of these two discourses was such that Maclure argues that "in their different shades and variants," they have "saturated – besieged ... representations of identity ... coming to regard each other as both mutually limiting and exhaustive of society's political space" (11–12).

Maclure (2003) asserts that these two discourses in their various manifestations have served as the limits for thinking and being Québécois and thus have posed an obstacle to instituting alternative conceptions of the nation, community, and belonging in Québec. These postwar discourses are considered by many to be the generative origin of the Quiet Revolution and secularization in Québec. Behiels (1985), for instance, argues that it is in the challenge that these two competing ideological movements mounted to traditional nationalism in postwar Québec that one can locate the intellectual origins of the Quiet Revolution. Fernand Roy (1993, 98) suggests that, in their common rejection of traditional nationalism and their desire to create a new modern Québec, postwar liberalism and neonationalism, rather than being two separate social projects, were variants of a single project of modernization.

Consistent with the analytical treatment of historical discourses throughout this book, in engaging with the discourses of liberalism and neonationalism, I am not attempting to either assess their validity or provide an exhaustive account of the statements made within these discursive groupings. Instead, I describe the common manner in which the objects of religion and the secular appear across this apparent discursive divide. Despite offering importantly distinct historical narratives and political solutions, both liberal and neonationalist statements conceive of traditional religion as a crucial factor in the historical development of abnormal, immature, pathological individuals and societies. In contrast, it is in the secular realm, with the absence of clerical authority, that individual, national, and societal maturation, normality, and health can be achieved.

Given the dominance of personalism in Québec during the period under consideration, the importance of the Catholic Action movements, and the fact that many of the figures associated with liberalism and neonationalism emerged from these personalist movements, their critique of traditional society, practices, and ideas should not be surprising. In the late 1930s, following the dictates of the Vatican, the Québec church had attempted to sever the ties between nationalism and Catholicism, articulating instead a more universalistic interpretation of Catholicism (Gauvreau 2000). The lay leaders of the Catholic Action youth movements in the 1940s – Claude Ryan, Camille Laurin, Pierre Elliott Trudeau, and Gérard Pelletier – who would come to be important figures in the liberal and neonationalist movements, sought to maintain the sense of community and belonging necessary for individual and collective self-fulfilment while avoiding what they considered the excesses of clerico-nationalism (827).

Despite rejecting the clerico-nationalist equation of church and nation, these leaders did not seek to abandon the connection between religion and the Québec nation. In fact, they believed that in a period of rapid social change, religion as a cohesive force remained necessary to the survival of the French Canadian people. Rather than dissociate religion from nationalism, the Catholic Action movements sought to "rejuvenate the creative synthesis of Catholicism and French Canadian nationalism by uncoupling Catholic values from their identification with qualities derived from a more static, poor rural society that perpetuated psychological immaturity and inferiority" (Gauvreau 2000, 827).

It was this perceived inferiority of the French Canadian people that both neonationalists and liberals sought to understand and remedy. In the years following the Second World War, the economy of Québec continued to be marked by an ethnic division of labour. The primary and secondary sectors of the Québec economy were directed and controlled by British, Anglo-Canadian, and American corporations. Whereas Anglo-Canadians generally filled managerial positions, French Canadians made up the bulk of the working class. Thus, despite the modernization of the economy, French Canadians remained an economically inferior group. The question of why French Canadian society had failed to produce its own entrepreneurial and managerial class was fundamental to both liberal and neonationalist thought. Although these two postwar intellectual currents differed in their conclusions regarding the causes of, and the solutions to, French Canadian inferiority, both considered traditional nationalism an obstacle to its resolution.

The neonationalist discourse that emerged in postwar Québec involved a critique of the national and clerical elite, as well as the traditional nationalism that they promoted. Neonationalists believed that the actions of the elite had served to undermine nationalism and nationalist sentiment, particularly in the eyes of the urban population. They pointed, above all, to the gap between the rhetoric and promises of politicians and political parties and their actions once elected. Such a critique resulted in a split in the nationalist movement in Québec in the years following the return to power of Duplessis's Union Nationale government in 1945. During the 1945 electoral campaign, the Union Nationale party championed the cause of provincial autonomy. Consequently, it received the backing of the traditional nationalist elite, including Lionel Groulx and Henri Bourassa, who saw the party as a force to combat the centralization policies of the federal government of Louis St. Laurent.

However, younger nationalists, such as Gérard Fillion, the director of *Le Devoir,* and André Laurendeau, the editor-in-chief of *Le Devoir* and *L'Action nationale,* were highly critical of the policies and corruption of the Duplessis government. In particular, they believed that its policies were insufficient to protect provincial autonomy. They argued that its economic liberalism had promoted a conquest of Québec by foreign capital and had failed to address the economic inferiority of French Canadians. Moreover, these neonationalists (as they came to be known) were critical of the government's lack of a coherent program of socio-economic reforms aimed at modernizing Québec's social welfare and educational institutions. Rejecting centralized federal policies, they believed that Québec had to develop its own policies. Modern industrial society was seen as requiring an interventionist state (Behiels 1985, 22, 44).

The neonationalists were also critical of what they perceived as the church's abandonment of French Canadian nationalism. The shift in the 1930s away from strong support for groups, institutions, and programs promoting French Canadian nationalism and toward the promotion of Catholic Action movements, which lacked a particular nationalist emphasis, was considered especially problematic (Behiels 1985, 45).

Neonationalists argued that the marginalization of nationalism by these groups meant that the church was denying "the national dimension of the milieu they wished to conquer" (45). Laurendeau (1953, 21) asserted that in their attempt to establish a more universalistic conception of Catholicism, the clerical elite had mistaken universality with "the will to uproot oneself, as if one had to cease actively belonging to a national community in order to be a Catholic and in some cases had to deny a prior solidarity with that community."

More significant than the criticism of the national and clerical elite was the neonationalist call for the development of a new nationalism. Such a rethinking of nationalism was considered necessary due primarily to the rapid industrialization of Québec, a process whose significance, neonationalists argued, had been underappreciated by traditional nationalism. The most important aspect of industrialization was the rapid growth of the "fourth estate of the nation": the French Canadian urban proletariat (Laurendeau 1947). It was believed that this class, as the largest in French Canadian society, would increasingly come to dictate its future.

According to the neonationalists, this development required urgent action. The working class was seen as constituting, "along with big business, the group of men least influenced by the national question, and consequently the least prepared to accept sacrifices for the collective good" (Laurendeau 1947, 88). Having been removed from rural life, the working class was perceived as having a weaker attachment to the nation's traditions and culture. Moreover, placed in the materialist world of industrial capitalism, these workers tended to give prominence to their own economic interests rather than to national concerns (Behiels 1985, 40).

This most recent conquest of Québec was not seen simply in economic terms; rather, for neonationalists, it was also a traumatic cultural conquest. As workers were drawn to urban centres in search of employment, their traditional, rural French Canadian culture was undermined in the urban, working-class milieu. According to early neonationalist thought, this culture was not replaced by one indigenous to the French Canadian working class but by American and Anglo-Canadian popular culture (Behiels 1985, 42).

For some of the early neonationalists, the most prominent aspect of this foreign culture was its irreligiosity. It was believed that although the majority of French Canadians continued to practise the rites of Catholicism, their daily life was dominated by nonreligious activities and values. Neonationalists, like Ryan (1957), believed that as the lives of working-class French Canadians became removed from religious and national values and traditions and as faith became increasingly divorced from religious practice, even routine practices would eventually be discarded (Behiels 1985, 42). Thus, in the face of industrialization, a renewal of nationalism was required in order to maintain the religiosity of the population and a sense of the common good.

According to the neonationalists, traditional nationalism was unable to combat the process of denationalization that they saw occurring among the urban working class. As argued by cleric Gérard Dion and fellow professor Joseph Pelchat at Laval University as well as by members of the Équipe des recherches sociales at the University of Montréal, including Camille Laurin, Jean-Marc Léger, D'Iberville Fortier, and Pierre Lefebvre, traditional nationalism's focus on the rural led it to largely overlook the realities of the largest social class in Québec, namely the urban proletariat. Traditional nationalism, "ignorant of the working-class milieu and barely aware of the extraordinary economic evolution ... could not make people hear its message because they no longer spoke the same language" (Behiels 1985, 43).

In opposition to this static conception of the nation and its identification with rural society, neonationalists sought to develop a nationalism reflective of the urban, industrial experience of the bulk of the French Canadian population. In the words of Laurendeau, the task facing the neonationalists was to overcome the division of nationalism from lived experience by seeking to "bring together the national and the social, or more exactly to allow their synthesis" (Roy 1993, 99).

Central to neonationalism was a reinterpretation of the history of French Canada, one that by the mid-1950s had become the officially sanctioned position of the Saint-Jean-Baptiste Society (Behiels 1985, 106). Beginning in the late 1940s, a group of historians at the University of Montréal began to articulate a vision of Québec history that challenged the dominant view of New France as an agricultural, Catholic society. The major figures within what would come to be known as the Montréal School – Michel Brunet, Guy Frégault, and Maurice Séguin – all argued that until 1760 New France had been a "normal" colonial society, similar to British America.

In the words of Frégault (1954, 100), they "had lived through, and were living through, the same collective experiences. They were colonial societies and they had the same attitudes toward their respective mother countries. They belonged to the same age and cherished the same basic aspirations." The economy of New France was not one dominated by agriculture but was a mixed economy in which "devout farmers were joined by merchants and fur trappers, among others" (Rudin 1997, 99). If anything, New France was a nation of merchants, who were dominated by a dynamic commercial bourgeoisie.

With the Conquest of New France in 1760, a cataclysmic event whose effects the Montréal historians believed were still being felt in Québec in the 1950s, the normality of this society was derailed. According to Séguin (1995, 15), this "catastrophic disaster ... tore the young colony out of its protective, nurturing environment, impairing its organization as a society and a budding nation, condemning it to annexation, to political and economic subordination." The immediate consequence of the Conquest was the emigration of New France's administrative, military, and entrepreneurial elite (Brunet 1958). The remaining members of the commercial class were unable to compete with British merchants, who were the recipients of most government contracts and had advantageous ties to the new metropole of England. Within thirty years of the Conquest, French Canadians found themselves almost completely excluded from significant commercial activities. As a result, forced "to rely on its own resources," French Canada was "doomed to an anaemic collective survival" (111).

According to the Montréal School, rural agriculturalism was not the natural form of French Canadian society but a socio-economic form imposed on it by the catastrophe of the Conquest. The traditional nationalism of *survivance,* in the form of the myths of agriculturalism, anti-statism, and messianism, was declared to be a direct result of the Conquest. In order to rationalize the economic superiority of the English conquerors, the clerical elite developed a nationalism emphasizing non-economic objectives. This clerical nationalism, in naturalizing the form of post-Conquest French Canadian society, obscured the true source of economic inferiority. In the words of Brunet (1954, 138), "incapable of continuing the commercial and industrial traditions of the founders of the French empire in North America, [they] convinced themselves that they were an agricultural people. Obliged to take refuge on the land, they concluded – or rather their conquerors concluded for them – that they had an agricultural mission to fulfil."

In sum, both the inferiority of the French Canadian people – not only in terms of their economic position but also in terms of the retrograde nature of their institutions – and their reliance on clerical authority were perceived by the Montréal School to be the result of the English Conquest, which "severed" the nation from normal historical progress (Lamarre 1993, 19). As Maclure (2003, 24–25) explains, since 1760 French Canada had been faced with the "tragic existence of ... [a] perpetual dilemma of subsistence or assimilation." The task established by the Montréal historians for nationalists hoping to overcome French Canadian inferiority, therefore, was the rectification of two centuries of history (Séguin 1995, 210).

According to Brunet (1954, 1957), this task involved overcoming the myths of clerico-nationalism. First, nationalism had to be divorced from agriculturalism, which impeded French Canadians from recognizing that their arrested development was not the consequence of a divine mission but was a disaster precipitated by the Conquest. Second, in contrast to anti-statism, neonationalists asserted that the state was not something to be avoided but the instrument through which inferiority could be overcome and normality achieved. Rectifying the disaster of the Conquest and overcoming anglophone domination required the creation of an interventionist state.

The entrenchment of ethnic discrimination, coupled with a lack of technical expertise and capital, meant that a penetration of French Canadians into the top echelon of industry could not be accomplished by individual initiative alone. Neonationalists argued that it could be realized only through the development of a welfare state (Behiels 1985, 108). As Fillion asserted, "French Canadians will remain drawers of water and hewers of wood, small shopkeepers and small-time investors, with a few millionaires here and there, as long as they do not learn to use the only government at their disposal to elaborate and carry out a grand economic strategy" (97). There were, he argued, "a certain number of accomplishments that only a modern state can fulfill, especially when it has the responsibility of seeing to the common good of an undeveloped community" (108–9).

No industrial society could rely on the private sector to meet the socio-economic and cultural needs of its members, as French Canadian society had attempted to do. The state, rather than being a threat to French Canada, could be put to use for the promotion of individual and national self-fulfilment. Thus, within neonationalist discourse, nationalism became closely associated with socio-economic transformation and national normalization, a project intimately linked to the state. As a result, within this discourse, the secular, which had earlier been defined as the realm of authenticity, was conquered by the state. It was the state, rather than the church or the Catholic Action movements, that was to be the active force ushering in normality and authenticity.

The importance accorded to the state in québécois thought in the years following the Second World War was not limited to neonationalism but was also a central theme within liberalism. Like neonationalism, a particular historical perspective was central to québécois liberal thought. This perspective – associated with the Laval School of historians, including Marcel Trudel, Jean Hamelin, and Fernand Ouellet, and with historical sociologists and economists based at Laval University, including Jean-Charles Falardeau, Albert Faucher, Maurice Lamontagne, and Maurice Tremblay – offered an explanation of French Canadian economic inferiority distinct from that of the Montréal School. Rather than placing the blame for the second-class status of French Canadians solely on the English Conquest and occupation, it portrayed the French Canadians as "the architects of their own difficulties" (Rudin 1997, 131).

By showing hostility toward all those things deemed to be outside influences, French Canadians had developed institutions ill-suited for the modern world and had readily accepted petit-bourgeois and authoritarian socio-economic ideas (Trudeau 1956). Ouellet, for one, believed that the neonationalism of the 1950s was continuing on this same path by focusing on "externally induced problems instead of tending to [its] own house, which was badly in need of repair" (Rudin 1997, 150).

Rather than the normal society depicted by the Montréal historians, the Laval School portrayed New France as an immature, underdeveloped colonial society (Trudel 1957). Hamelin (1960) argued that prior to the Conquest, New France was not a vibrant merchant society but "no more than a shadow of the commercial colony imagined by Champlain in 1618." New France was a colony controlled by the metropole and continually faced with shortages of capital and skilled labour. The French bourgeoisie exploited the colony and transferred nearly all profits back to France. Hamelin concluded that the lack of a significant French Canadian entrepreneurial class in the aftermath of the Conquest was "a consequence of the French regime, and not ... of the Conquest" (13).

Echoing these sentiments, Ouellet (1956) suggested that the values of the *ancien régime,* together with exploitation by the French state, had impeded the creation of a strong French Canadian middle class imbued with a proper bourgeois mentality. French Canadian nationalism, according to Ouellet, was simply an outgrowth of the *ancien régime* mentality and clericalism that had not been overcome in French Canada. It was the prevalence of these ideas, promoted by a conservative middle class dominated by professionals rather than by the bourgeoisie, that prevented the restructuring of the society's institutions in accordance with the imperatives of industrialization. As the petit bourgeoisie and the peasants were "reared in the same milieu," both were unable to adapt to the changing economic circumstances (Rudin 1997, 150–51).

Ouellet located the inferiority of the French Canadian people in the development of what he deemed the pathological familial form of seventeenth-century New France. He argued that as a result of the fur trade, the institution of the patriarchal family had been decimated in New France and replaced by a family under the direction of women. Generalizing from the historical example of Julie Bruneau-Papineau, Ouellet asserted that women were unable to cope with this role. Consequently, they "came to depend on [their] family and to strike out against everything outside the family circle" (Ouellet 1958, 49). For children socialized in such an environment, individual achievement was not something to be valued. Consequently, Ouellet argued, they were incapable of functioning in a liberal society (49–51). For Ouellet, this pathology of French Canadian society was another example of the need to contend with internally generated problems.

Economists such as Faucher and Lamontagne also argued that inferiority was the product of internal rather than external factors. Through historical analysis, they sought, like the Montréal historians, to determine why "industrialization had not been a realization of the main ethnic group of the province" (Faucher and Lamontagne 1964, 271). Unlike neonationalists, however, Faucher and Lamontagne concluded that "Québec's industrialization had nothing specific to do with, and was not fundamentally influenced by, its cultural environment," namely that of a conquered people (268). They suggested, rather, that the social institutions developed by French Canadians had been unable "to go ahead or keep abreast of industrial change" (271).

Faucher and Lamontagne argued that it was the weakness of these institutions that caused the inability of French Canadians to achieve positions of economic leadership. In order to overcome this institutional gap, Lamontagne (1954) advocated for an increasingly centralized interventionist federal state. He believed that French Canadians had to overcome their apparent inability to bear responsibility for their inferiority and that, instead of simply complaining about the misdeeds of the English, they had to set out to engage with the federal state and the capitalist economy. More importantly, they had to transform their own institutions in order to make them compatible with the needs of the modern economy. If they failed to do so, Lamontagne contended, they had only themselves to blame (Rudin 1997, 133).

For the Laval sociologists, namely Falardeau and Tremblay, it was not the Conquest but the dominance of the Catholic Church that was largely responsible for the plight of French Canadians. A colleague of Everett C. Hughes, Falardeau employed many of the ideas of the Chicago School, seeing French Canada as a folk society in the process of transition (Rudin 1997, 131). Falardeau argued that it was the very structure of French Canadian society, originating in New France, that discouraged individual initiative. He contended that since the time of colonization, the Catholic Church had sought to develop "much less an active enterprising citizen than a submissive and faithful parishioner." French Canadians had failed to challenge the dominance of clerical authority and in the postwar period remained reluctant to "express [their] opposition to the ideas or actions of a priest" (132). This failure to resist clerical authority was seen as a failing of the French Canadians themselves rather than as something imposed from without.

Like Brunet, Tremblay argued that much of French Canadian inferiority was the consequence of the ideology of agriculturalism espoused by the clerico-nationalist elite. However, unlike his neonationalist contemporary, Tremblay did not equate the emergence of agriculturalism with the English Conquest but instead argued that agriculturalism was an internally generated phenomenon, unrelated to the events of 1760. It was the failure of French Canadians to engage with and develop a strong state that enabled the dominance of the Catholic Church and its vision of a rural, Christian society. In the absence of an active state, the Catholic Church became the dominant institution in French Canada. Through the institutions it directed – the parish, classical colleges, colonization societies, and the family – it was able to institutionalize the notion of a French Canadian agricultural mission (Behiels 1985). Tremblay further argued that the fusion of the idealism of *ancien régime* French thought and the Catholic prioritization of contemplation over activity in New France meant that even educated French Canadians lacked the initiative necessary for capitalist enterprise. He suggested, in sum, that the dominance of Catholicism had made it nearly impossible for French Canadians "to compete on an equal footing in the higher echelons of economic activity with our Anglo-Protestant fellow citizens" (117). In order to overcome their inferiority, French Canadians had to develop a new mentality and infuse this mentality into modern institutions.

Ideas consistent with those advocated by the Laval School were also evident outside the academic environment. In Montréal in the early 1950s, a group of intellectuals and activists centred on the journal *Cité libre* – including Falardeau, Trudeau, Gérard Pelletier, Charles Lussier, Maurice Blain, Guy Cormier, Réginald Boisvert, Jean-Paul Geoffroy, Pierre Juneau, Roger Rolland, Jean Le Moyne, Pierre Vadeboncoeur, Marcel Rioux, Fernand Dumont, Léon Dion, and Jean Pellerin – began to promote a liberal and humanist ethos. In doing so, they sought to achieve what they referred to as the revolution of mentalities necessary to overcome the apparent spiritual and religious crisis confronting their generation (Behiels 1985, 62).

Many of these *citélibrists* pointed to the 1949 asbestos strike as the turning point in their social and political outlook. It was the behaviour of the government and the clerical elite during the strike that confirmed for them the irredeemably undemocratic and oppressive nature of the Duplessis regime, as well as the limitations on Catholic unions and the Catholic Action movement owing to clerical oversight. They took as their task the ideological continuance of the struggle of the asbestos miners against the repressive nature of the Union Nationale government. Doing so, they asserted, required a careful examination of French Canadian society, particularly its ideological foundations. The true threats facing the French Canadian people had to be distinguished from those that were merely ideological distortions. In the inaugural issue of *Cité libre,* Trudeau (1950, 21) outlined what this undertaking would require:

> We want to bear witness to the Christian and French fact in America. Agreed; but we must throw everything else overboard. We must systematically question all political categories bequeathed to us by the intervening generation. The strategy of resistance is no longer useful for the growth and maturation of the City. The time has arrived for us to ... cast aside the thousands of past prejudices that encumber the present and to build for the new man. Overthrow all totems, transgress all taboos. Better still, consider them dead ends. Without passion, let us be intelligent.

It was the dominance of an unquestioned traditionalism and a siege mentality long manifest in clerico-nationalism that posed the greatest obstacle to the modernization of French Canadian society. The liberals argued for the need to engage in a rationalist and scientific questioning of the unquestioned values and institutions of clerico-nationalism (Behiels 1985, 69, 85).

Nationalism was depicted by liberals as a historical anachronism, a doctrine that had outlived its historical function (Behiels 1985, 85). According to Trudeau, the system of security that had been developed after the Conquest to protect French Canadian society had become "overdeveloped." As a result, anything that differentiated French Canadians from the outside world was positively valued, and all change perceived as coming from without was scorned. The nationalism of survival had resulted in a rejection of everything associated with the English conquerors, including democracy and modern economic relations (Rudin 1997, 130–31; Trudeau 1956, 90).

Particularly with the infusion of clericalism, nationalism had held French Canada in a state if immaturity, preventing the development of a dynamic, creative French Canadian society and identity. As Rioux (1955, 12) argued, nationalism had in fact promoted a certain form of misrecognition, for it "has always had the tendency to define a French Canadian not on his own terms but by what he is in relation to other groups." As a result, French Canadian nationalism was said to be marked by a "cult of differences and the past" in which the present appeared only in relation to an idealized past (14). Defining the nation in terms of the past and its difference from others made adaptation to the modern industrial world impossible. As a result, the *citélibrists* argued that French Canadians needed to carry out a cultural self-critique in order to narrow the gap between their collective self-image and the realities of their modern existence. As Boisvert (1950, 19) stated, it was only through such a process that French Canadians and French Canadian society could mature into adulthood.

For the contributors to *Cité libre,* questioning the authority of the Catholic Church and traditional Catholicism was central to a project of progress. As dedicated Catholics, they saw this reappraisal of Catholicism in Québec as necessary in order to reinvigorate rather than undermine Catholicism. Despite agreeing with traditional nationalists that the survival of French Canada following the Conquest was due in large part to the efforts of the clergy, they asserted that the emergence of the church as the only institution capable of assuming this role had produced the negative long-term consequence of stunting the development and maturation of French Canada. As Le Moyne (1955, 3) stated, "It is a fact that the church constituted everything. It is another fact that we owe it everything, and the church does not know how terrible this reality is for it."

The *citélibrists* believed that the centrality and overwhelming authority of the church had resulted in a crisis of religiosity among their generation. They argued that this was due to two factors. First, the Catholicism espoused by the Québec church was dogmatic. As Rolland (1951, 33) asserted, in Québec, "Catholicism is not proposed or taught but rather imposed, inflicted, and driven home. God, that all-loving being who must be approached in the full freedom of one's heart, is injected like a serum ... If before the divine mystery anyone hesitates slightly, trembles, or dares to think, he is declared guilty of acting in collusion with Satan." This dogmatism was seen as engendering devastating psychological consequences. It stifled intellectual curiosity and promoted fear, guilt, and confusion among those who found it difficult to reconcile the demands of faith and reason, or religion and the modern world (Behiels 1985, 74). Moreover, the identification of Catholicism with the French Canadian nation meant that "nonbelievers [were] considered errants who have abandoned their caravan" (Pelletier 1955, 7). Second, as Gérard Pelletier (1952, 6–7) argued, the church's wealth and substantial involvement in the provision of services in the secular realm – education, health, and social welfare – threatened to compromise its spiritual mission and independence. An increasing need for funds to support its immense administrative bureaucracy had led religious officials to increasingly involve themselves in backroom politics.

The contributors to *Cité libre* proposed four measures intended to limit the power of clerical authority and thereby renew Catholicism in Québec: (1) cultural and intellectual thought had to be made autonomous from religious authority, (2) French Canadians must be provided with the rights of freedom of thought and religion, (3) Catholic laypeople should be accorded a more significant role within the church, and (4) the church had to be withdrawn from the administration of services in the secular realm (Behiels 1985, 79). These measures were, for Blain (1952, 213), the scandal that "must occur, the scandal of a Catholicism renewing the traditions of liberal humanism and an autonomous culture. The scandal of a church in which the real distinction between the spiritual and temporal spheres is re-established. The scandal of a spiritual freedom without any other condition but respect from the individual conscience."

Although the liberals of *Cité libre* wished to wait until the defeat of the Duplessis government and the institutionalization of democratic values, they too advocated the creation of an interventionist state (Behiels

1985, 115–16.) As Trudeau (1953) asserted, the retreat of the church to the private realm of spirituality did not mean that clerics should turn away from affairs of the secular realm. However, their engagement in such affairs must be as common citizens divested of clerical authority. The clergy, Trudeau argued, must be willing to accept

> that to solve purely temporal problems, a cassock did not ... provide any immunity before the law or public opinion, and that a doctorate in theology was not a certificate of universal or infallible competence. If it was well understood that a priest who chooses to serve secular forces has no more knowledge or authority than any other citizen, then clerics and laymen might be able to collaborate more serenely in the building of a church and a society that are truly Christian. (37)

It was not theology but rationalism and secular knowledge that could provide answers or guide action within the secular realm. As a result, it was not the church and clerical authority but the state, guided by such knowledge, that was the institution proper to the secular realm.

It was not the establishment of the collection of policies and institutional arrangements commonly referred to as the institutional secularization of the Quiet Revolution that marked the radical transformation of the secular in postwar Québec. These initiatives were instead the material manifestations of a victory of forces of the state that were already present within the discursive realm. As this chapter demonstrates, the secular in its essential form was not that which was proper to the state or separate from theology, religion, or the church; rather, it was only through various historical circumstances, emergences, disappearances, and transformations that, within various discourses in postwar Québec and later in practice, the secular came to appear as that which was proper to the state.

In Québec in the 1930s, in the face of the Great Depression and the doctrine of social Catholicism authorized by the Vatican, the Catholic Church undertook the re-Christianization of this secular sphere through the promotion of corporatism. By promoting social stability, its role as interclass mediator, and the evangelical practices of various Catholic Action movements, it sought to create a truly Catholic society.

The infusion of personalist thought into the Catholic Action movements in the late 1930s transformed this project of re-Christianization in two significant ways. First, instead of attempting to promote salvation through individual piety, personalism sought to transform the institutions of society in order to allow for a more Christian existence. Second, it was this active practice of Catholicism that was defined as authentic. Thus the secular realm became the realm of authenticity. It was through the transformation of this realm and through one's activity within it that authentic religiosity was possible.

In postwar Québec, the secular was once again reinterpreted. Within both neonationalist and liberal discourses, traditional clerico-nationalism came to be seen as an obstacle to overcoming the social and economic inferiority of French Canadians. Both the equation of the French Canadian nation with a rural mission guided by a clerical elite and the authority of the church appeared as key factors hindering modernization. As a result, a redefinition of the nation was necessary.

Liberals and neonationalists asserted that a healthy, modern French Canada required the development of a new outlook, one in which French Canadian identity was more closely in line with the actual reality of French Canada. Moreover, overcoming inferiority necessitated the development of an interventionist state, one that could protect the rights and promote the welfare of French Canadians. Within both neonationalist and liberal discourse, this project necessitated the withdrawal of the church from secular administrative functions and its replacement by the state. Thus, by the 1950s, the secular had been conquered by forces of the state.

The narrative of the conquering of the secular by forces of the state is not a narrative of secularization. It does not refer to a singular secular. What it describes is not the development of ideas about the secular nor a realization of its essence. Instead, it is a narrative of the coming into being and becoming dominant of various seculars. Consequently, as part of a historical ontology of ourselves, this chapter challenges the dominant and often immediately contemporary appearance of the secular as the domain proper to the state. It simultaneously challenges the dominant identification of the private as the realm of religion. In opposition to the naturalization of the relationships between the secular and the state and between religion and the private, these relationships are depicted as historical and contingent. The chapter, therefore, challenges the view that the presence of religion in the secular realm is an aberration.

4 The Construction of the Secular Québécois Citizen and the Problem of the Religious Subject

With the territorialization of identity and the formation of a Québec nation-state, the Québec nation not only faced questions of its relation to the Canadian state – leading to a number of constitutional crises, two failed referendums on independence, and the development of a prominent sovereigntist movement – but also was presented with two possible archetypes of national identity within the conceptual and legal framework of a nation-state. These two ideal archetypes were posed as distinct ethnic and civic conceptions of the nation. The former would maintain an ethno-cultural conception of the nation as a people who had simply territorialized their identity. Within this model, the Québécois, as the French Canadian residents of Québec, would appear as a majority nation within the territory of Québec residing alongside various minorities who were not French Canadian. These minorities would be accorded equal rights and protections by the Québec nation-state but would exist outside of the nation. Within the latter, civic conception of the nation, the Québécois would comprise all who resided in Québec. Within this model, the Québec nation-state would serve as the instrument through which all residents of Québec, not only the majority French Canadian ethnic group, would be represented as Québécois and would realize their freedom and potential.

The Problem of the Presence of Religion in the Public Sphere in Québec

Toward the end of the twentieth century, within the context of an ongoing restructuring of the nature of citizenship in Québec, religion re-emerged within public discourse as an object of concern for the nation. The emergence of religion as a problem for conceptions and practices of belonging and community in recent times is, of course, not unique to Québec. Various struggles have taken place in a number of states concerning the presence of religion, particularly Islam, in the public sphere and the threat that it is said to pose to identity and governance. Although the processes through which the assemblage of phenomena that have been labelled religious and problematic in Québec may differ from those of other contexts, an analysis of Québec demonstrates the constructed nature of those categories and ways of being that are taken for granted elsewhere. Thus, although the particular manner in which religion has come to appear as problematic in Québec is specific to Québec, we should not see Québec as an isolated case. The emergence of religion as a problem in Québec should not be reduced to the product of factors unique to Québec, such as a certain national mentality. Unique in the manner in which it emerges in Québec, the problem of religion is simultaneously reflective of a broader equation of the secular and the political.

The first recent manifestation of the concern with the public presence of religion in Québec occurred in 1988 when a group of parents of students attending Henri-Bourassa High School in Montréal organized to protest the potential establishment of Arabic language courses in their children's school. Despite the fact that most of the parents who had requested the introduction of these courses were Christian Arabs, the opponents, equating the Arabic language with Islam, argued that the instruction of Arabic was part of a broader process of Islamization (McAndrew 2002b, 137). In their words, "the teaching of Arabic is only the first step in a larger strategy, the next will be the Quran" (Helly 2005).

In 1992 another controversy arose in Québec concerning religion. This time religion appeared as an object of concern within a debate regarding the requirement of female teachers to don the hijab in some Muslim private schools. Critics argued that this regulation was a violation of the religious freedom of non-Muslim teachers (Ciceri 1998, 49).

The requirement for teachers to wear the hijab was interpreted as much more than a workplace regulation or imposition. Unlike other requirements or restrictions on dress in the workplace, this demand was seen as a religious imposition and, therefore, as particularly problematic. The ostensibly religious nature of the hijab provoked concerns about infringements on individual rights and autonomy. The response incited by this requirement was of a nature and intensity that were very different from those associated with other workplace uniform regulations. In 1995, on the basis of a ruling by the Commission des droits de la personne (CDP) and public pressure, the schools in question changed their policies, making the hijab optional.

Alhough these incidents provoked some public interest and media coverage, it was not until the autumn of 1994 that the issue of the presence of religion in the public sphere became what McAndrew has labelled a discursive "social happening" (Clément 1994) – a topic that in the years to come would be debated "ad nauseum" (McAndrew 2006, 1).

On September 7, 1994, thirteen-year-old Émilie Ouimet arrived for the first day of the school year at École Louis-Riel in Montréal wearing a hijab. That same day, after refusing to remove her headscarf, Ouimet was expelled by the school's principal, Norman Doré, who justified his act by likening the hijab to neo-Nazi regalia (Kutty 1994; Todd 1998, 438). Over the next year, the case of Ouimet and eleven other students who were removed from the classroom for wearing the hijab became a point of societal contestation concerning the nature of citizenship in contemporary Québec. The largest teachers' union in the province, the Centrale de l'enseignement du Québec, voted to support a ban on the hijab in schools. The CDP and the Conseil du statut de la femme (CSF) conducted inquiries into the issue of accommodations for religious minorities and, with reservations, supported the right of students to choose to wear the hijab. Numerous conferences and public hearings were held by community and academic organizations in order to debate the issue. Furthermore, dozens of editorials and news articles appeared in Québec's newspapers – including at least forty-three articles in the four major Montréal dailies in the three months immediately following Ouimet's expulsion (Lenk 2000, 75) – that offered various positions concerning the accommodation of the practices of religious minorities and the permissibility of religious clothing and practices in the public sphere.

At question in each of these events was the place of the religious in the public sphere. Grounding the concern over the public appearance of religious dress, practices, and language as well as over claims made in the name of religion is the problem of the publicity of the religious subject. It is the presence of this subject, as the bearer of the aforementioned symbols, that is seen as requiring attention and for which arrangements must be made. As a result, in two respects, this recent emergence of religion as a problem is not merely a reinvocation of the other historical discourses in which religion appeared problematic. First, unlike the discourse of modernization and secularization described in Chapter 2, this new discourse is not concerned with the ability of French Canada, as a religious society, to survive contact with modern social arrangements; rather, the public appearance of religion is regarded as a phenomenon whose presence in an already secularized Québec society provokes concern and requires attention. This is not to suggest that an equation of religion with the premodern and an equation of the secular with the modern disappear; instead, what appear as problematic, abnormal, and even incompatible with modern social and political arrangements are the publicity of religion and the presence of the religious, particularly the Islamic subject, in the public sphere. What is problematic is not religion itself but manifestations of religion that escape their modern relegation to the private realm.

Second, unlike the discourse described in Chapter 3, this recent discourse is not concerned with religious control over the institutions of the public sphere. Although anxiety about the control over public institutions remains present in this discourse, as evident in repeated allusions to the Algerian Civil War, Afghanistan, and political Islamism, its focus is the nature of subjects within public spaces. Primarily at issue, therefore, is the proper mode of public conduct. What is at issue is not primarily whether religious subjects wish to take control of the public sphere but what measures need to be taken in order to ensure that their presence does not corrupt the functioning of this sphere. As discussed later in the chapter, at issue is whether and how the religious subject is able to engage properly as a citizen and political subject.

Whereas the discourse outlined in Chapter 3 established the necessity of limiting the influence of religious authority in social and political matters as a prerequisite of the emergence of a mature, pluralist society, the recent discourse questions the parameters of pluralism and the dangers that pluralism poses for the nation. It includes calls for a narrowing of the scope of pluralism in order to protect universal, secular values. As mentioned in the Introduction, what is posited in the recent discourse is a paradoxical need to limit pluralism in order to protect pluralism.

Unconstrained multiculturalism and cultural relativism are constructed as potential threats to core universal and national values and to secular society itself. The universal is seen as requiring protection from the particular, especially the inassimilable particular. Not only must universal rights and freedoms be protected from particularist religious doctrine, but the universal and natural public/political subject must also be maintained in the face of the divisive influence of particularist religious identities on public conduct.

The recent problematization of religion can be differentiated from the discourse outlined in the previous chapters in another crucial way: whereas the discourses of the mid-twentieth century involved a critique of the role of the Catholic Church in Québec, itself conceived of as an endogenous religious institution, the recent problematization of religion has focused on religion, and constructed the threat that it poses, as exogenous. Within this most recent emergence of religion as a problem, a focus is placed on the protection of an already secularized nation from infiltration and corruption by exogenous religious threats, particularly those associated with Islam. The religious practices of immigrants are seen as an impediment to their full integration into the Québec nation and, therefore, as a threat to social cohesion.

In sum, at issue in the recent discourse and in each of the above-mentioned events is the presence of the religious in the public sphere. The focus of the recent discourse is the question of how one must present oneself and behave in this sphere. In other words, the debates surrounding these recent events involve attempts to determine the parameters of the acceptable and desirable way of being in public and the limits of membership in the nation. As this chapter demonstrates, the reasons for the concern over, and the solutions offered to contend with, the presence of the religious within the public sphere are not uniform across the discourse. Common to all statements, however, is the notion that the presence of the religious within the public sphere is an issue requiring attention. In short, common to this recent discourse is the public presence of the religious subject as an object of concern.

This recent concern with religion and the religious should not be seen as merely a resurgence of the ideology and movement of secularism. As Asad (2003, 16) argues, the secular is conceptually prior to the doctrine of secularism. In order to understand the functioning of a particular discourse of secularism, it is necessary to understand the force of the concepts that it employs. Secularism invokes the secular as an object or phenomenon with a stable, transhistorical essence. However, as Chapters 2 and 3 have demonstrated, the secular has not been historically stable. Over the course of history, various seculars have emerged and become dominant in relation to national identity in Québec. The secular in its historical variants always precedes, and permits the appearance of, secularism in its various forms. Therefore, in order to understand the recent problematization of religion and its role in the crisis of identity in Québec, it is necessary to treat it as a manifestation of the secular's emergence and dominance in a particular historical form as the normal way of being in public.

It is the emergence of the public presence of the religious subject as a problem that affords an opportunity to investigate the secular as a historically emergent phenomenon. The emergence of an object or phenomenon as problematic and abnormal is simultaneously the exposure of that which is constructed as normal. Thus the emergence of the public presence of the religious subject as problematic is also the exposure of the secular as the normal way of being in public. This exposure of the normal through the abnormal, and thus the secular through the problematization of the religious, occurs in two related ways. First, the secular is illuminated. The emergence of religion as a problem is also the illumination of the presence of the secular as unproblematic. In asserting itself, the secular, which may have operated at a low level of visibility, is moved from the shadows of the background into the foreground. With the emergence of the religious subject as a problem, the assumptions related to the secular are articulated.

This articulation permits the second way that the secular is exposed. Once the presence of the secular as the norm is articulated, an interrogative spotlight can be shone on it, enabling a questioning of these assumptions and a denaturalizing of that which is presented as natural. As a result, the emergence of the religious subject as an object of concern provides an opening through which it is possible to glimpse the parameters of our historical way of being. It permits a disclosure of the limits imposed by the dominance of the secular and a disclosure of the categories that appear as natural and given as a consequence of this dominance. Moreover, it presents an opportunity to explore these limits and, in denaturalizing that which is given, opens the possibility of re-evaluating these values. This assessment in turn makes possible an understanding of its relation to, and the problems it creates for, certain formations of national identity.

Through an analysis of the recent emergence of the presence of the religious in the public sphere in Québec as a problem, this chapter engages in an exposure of the dominance of the secular. First, through an examination of the discourse in which the public presence of the religious subject emerged as a problem in Québec in the mid-1990s, a description of the manner in which the secular is articulated is made possible. After exposing the presence of the secular, the chapter engages in an interrogation of the assumptions and narratives upon which it relies. To do so, this chapter details and critically engages with the dominant narrative of citizenship in Québec, that of the attempted abandonment of an exclusionary ethnic nationalism and the development of an inclusive, universalist *citoyenneté québécoise*. Second, the problem of the religious subject and the normalization of the secular subject are related to two other historical discourses of citizenship: synoecism, grounded in the emergence of the abstract secular human being, and orientalism. Through this interrogation, the chapter describes both the manner in which the secular came to be naturalized as the normal way of being public and how its dominance delimits and governs the political.

The expulsion of Émilie Ouimet in 1994 sparked a widespread debate in Québec over the public presence of religious clothing, symbols, and practices as well as over the parameters of "reasonable accommodation" for religious minorities. Not only was the *affaire du foulard* the subject of intense debate in Québec's francophone media, but it also became the subject of numerous academic papers and conferences, public hearings led by various civil society groups, and judgments rendered by quasi-governmental bodies. Although often overlooked in accounts provided by media in other Canadian provinces, by the mainstream anglophone media in Québec, and by some academic articles (Lenk 2000; Todd 1998), the debate in Québec concerning the permissibility of religious symbols and practices in the public sphere has involved numerous, often conflicting, positions. Moreover, although some media articles have taken the form of reactionary polemics, the issue has also often been the subject of careful, nuanced examination. In the statements consistent with the latter form of analysis, religion is not something that is included or excluded but something whose presence in society must be managed. Thus, despite a variety of approaches to the issue, the presence of religion in the public sphere is viewed as problematic, as something requiring consideration, and for which solutions much be developed.

Within the debates concerning the permissibility of religious symbols and practices in public space in Québec, two themes have regularly emerged: first, the debate has been couched in terms of fundamental rights and values; and second, the issue has been framed as one of social cohesion and integration. In relation to the first theme, the prohibition of the hijab in the classroom was viewed, by both the opponents and the proponents of the measure, as an issue of rights. As Coryse Ciceri (1998, 103–4) notes in her detailed discourse analysis of the debate in the francophone media in Québec, what she labels the "juridico-political arguments" of both the opponents and the proponents of the prohibition of the hijab commonly involved an invocation of the fundamental rights and freedoms granted to all citizens of Québec. Not only did these arguments refer to the valorization and protection of the freedoms of religion, expression, and association present in both the Canadian Charter of Rights and Freedoms and the Québec Charter of Human Rights and Freedoms as well as in international intiatives such as the International Convention on Civil and Political Rights, but they also proclaimed the need to protect these rights as fundamental human rights. In Canadian, québécois, and international law, religious rights are defined as the right both to belong to a religious group and to engage in religious rites and practices, including practices related to clothing (CDP 1995, 9).

According to the Québec Charter of Human Rights and Freedoms, an individual cannot be discriminated against on the basis of religion. The Québec Charter defines and prohibits two forms of discrimination: it can be direct, such as a policy that bars members of a particular religion from obtaining services or employment, and it can be indirect, such as the adoption of an ostensibly neutral, universal policy whose effects are prejudicial to particular individuals on the basis of their religion. Examples of indirect discrimination, as outlined by the Commission des droits de la personne, include the establishment of a strict dress code or work schedule that conflicts with the religious beliefs of individual employees or students (CDP 1995, 9). In the face of such conflicts, the employer or service provider has the legal obligation – as outlined in various legal rulings and governmental documents (CCCI 1993; CDP 1995; CRI 1997, 2004a) – to modify the rule or, if it can be demonstrated to be essential to the institution's mandate, correct its discriminatory effects (McAndrew 2007).

Statements opposing the prohibition of the headscarf argued that this measure was a violation of fundamental rights and contrary to the values of Québec society. First, it was argued that proscribing the hijab was tantamount to direct religious discrimination since it targeted a particular religious practice, unjustly impeding the right of Muslim women to freely enact their faith (Bourret 1994; CDP 1995; Ciceri 1998, 103; Gagnon 1994b; Gruda 1994). As a religious symbol and an article of faith, the hijab could not be prohibited without infringing on freedoms of religion and expression. Second, prohibiting veiled students from attending public schools was portrayed as a restriction of access to free, public schooling and thus as a contravention of the right to education (Bourret 1994; Ciceri 1998; CDP 1995; CSF 1995; Gruda 1994). Students who, due to familial or community pressures, were unwilling or unable to remove their headscarf would either be forced to attend private Islamic schools or be completely excluded from organized education. Third, it was argued that a ban on the hijab, as it targeted and affected particular groups, was contrary to the enshrined equality of all citizens.

Critics of the measure also asserted that it contravened state neutrality toward different religions since symbols associated with Christianity and Judaism, such as the cross and the kippa, were permitted, whereas an Islamic symbol was proscribed (Gagnon 1994b). Consequently, they argued, the ban on the headscarf had nothing to do with secularism, as it did not seek to remove religion in all its forms from the public sphere, but unjustly targeted particular religious subjects. Moreover, it was argued that as the prohibition concerned only a symbol worn by women, they would unduly feel the effect of the measure.

Opponents of the prohibition on the presence of religious symbols were not alone in the invocation of fundamental rights and values in their arguments. In explaining their support for prohibitive measures, proponents also commonly made reference to rights, freedoms, and the equality of citizens. According to Ciceri (1998, 97), in the debate concerning the hijab, the arguments of proponents involved two main assertions with regard to rights and freedoms: first, that the wearing of the headscarf was itself an infringement on fundamental rights and equalities; and second, that the right to wear a hijab had to be balanced against other rights and values. As a result, proponents pointed to the need, in some instances, to limit certain rights and freedoms in order to protect other rights and the welfare of the nation. They argued that permitting the hijab in schools afforded privileges to certain groups but not others. As argued in the pages of the magazine *L'actualité*, toleration of the headscarf accorded particular privileges to girls and was therefore discriminatory toward boys. The author asked, assuming that the latter would be unthinkable, "if we accept a veiled girl, do we accept a boy in a cassock?" (Paré 1994). Other newspaper articles asserted that permitting the hijab meant affording it a status superior to that of other signs of belonging that were prohibited (Bastien 1995; Geadah 1995). As Yolande Geadah (1995), a researcher for the CSF argued, "if one admits that a public institution such as a school has a right to prohibit the wearing of a hat or studded leather clothing ... what obliges us to modify our internal regulations in favour of the wearing of the hijab in school?"

According to proponents of the ban, permitting the wearing of the hijab not only affords privileges to a certain group but is also injurious to particular groups and individuals. Among the most vociferous of such arguments were those related to suggestions that the Islamic headscarf is a symbol of religious fundamentalism and the repression of women. Within these arguments, the hijab was portrayed as a symbol of the inferiority and submission of women (Ciceri 1998, 100). The hijab was described as "a symbol of servitude" (Verstraelen 1995), as "an emblem ... of the subservience of women 'enslaved' by their own husband, their father, the '*malitude*' of males" (Auclair 1995), and as a testament to the reduction of "women to simply guardians of the household, good for procreating and above all, for obeying their master" (Bensalem 1994a).

Moreover, the hijab was framed as an imposition. Due to the strong pressure of religious authorities, the Muslim community, and the family, women were said to be either forced or manipulated into wearing the hijab. As a result, it marks a restriction of the rights and autonomy of women. Although in some cases "the persecuted adopt[ed] the point of view of their persecutors" and chose to wear the hijab (Vaillancourt 1994), women who wore the hijab generally did so as a result of pressure and threats. Women did not complain, whether because of their youth – "women that wear it will not complain mostly because they are primary school students" (Côté 1995) – or because of the fear that they "are constrained in publicly affirming that it is their choice" (Geadah 1995). Consequently, it was argued that it was necessary and justifiable to contravene religious freedoms in order to protect other fundamental rights. As Geadah (1995) argued, the "freedom of women to refuse to wear [the hijab] is infinitely more threatened than that of the young women who insist on wearing it."

Furthermore, as a "particularly strong symbol of Muslim fundamentalism" (Baillargeon 1995) and thus an emblem "of the bloody fanatics of Algeria – or elsewhere – of terrorizing women, slitting the throats of women and little girls" (Auclair 1995), the hijab was deemed a threat to Québec society. In such arguments, toleration of the hijab was viewed as "the infamous peak of the iceberg" (Bensalem 1994b) and a harbinger of practices such as "the excision of little girls" (Geadah 1995). As suggested in an article in *Le Devoir*, "if one pushes the logic of tolerance to its end point, one will ultimately arrive at accepting polygamy, the stoning of adulterous women, and the sharia for our Muslim fellow citizens" (Garnier 1995).

In 1995, in the pages of the alternative weekly *Voir,* Richard Martineau (1995) instructed readers to learn from the "lessons of Algeria" in considering the limits of tolerance in Québec:

> Imagine ...
>
> It is October 26 and Marjo[1] is giving a concert at the Capitole. After the first encore, she leaves the stage and begins to walk toward her dressing room. In a corner, two men are waiting, a notebook for autographs in hand. As she signs her name, one of the men pulls a revolver from his pocket and shoots her twice in the head. Reason for the attack: the singer has offended proper morality.
>
> It is November 4 and Pierre Foglia[2] hops on his bicycle outside of *La Presse.* He is cruising leisurely on Boulevard Saint-Laurent in Montréal when a truck, springing out from Rue Notre-Dame, strikes him with full force and leaves the scene rapidly. Twenty minutes later, at the hospital, Foglia succumbs to his wounds. Reason for the attack: the journalist was overly critical of the religious authorities.
>
> It is November 16 and a high school student is removed from the classroom in front of her teacher and classmates. The next day, the police find the young girl near the Saint Lawrence River underneath a bush with her throat slit. Reason: she refused to obey her older brother.
>
> Science fiction? For Québec, yes. But in Algeria such attacks are an everyday occurrence. Over the past eighteen months, Islamist fundamentalists have killed thirty-five Algerian journalists. They have murdered the director of the school of the arts, a singer, a playwright, writers, sociologists, the owner of a football team, women who dress in an overly Western fashion, and men who visit the library too often ... It is as if in Québec a death squad had decided to kidnap Richard Desjardins,[3] to kill Gilles Maheu,[4] to place a bomb in Laval University, to slit the throat of Lise Bissonnette[5] – in sum, to kill all who think, who create ...

1 Marjo is a famous singer-songwriter.

2 Foglia is a well-known newspaper columnist.

3 Desjardins is a folk singer and film director.

4 Maheu is an influential actor, director, choreographer, and playwright.

5 Bissonnette is a writer and journalist.

In order to arrest the possibility of the rise of fundamentalism, and the possibility of such practices becoming tolerated, one had to stand strong in the face of demands for accommodation related to the hijab.

Accommodations, therefore, were not to be granted for all religious differences but only when judged "reasonable." As argued by Bernard Landry, the Québec minister of immigration and cultural communities, "religious freedom must not ... permit the submission of women or inequality of the sexes" (Ciceri 1998, 90). Moreover, one must not allow an appeal to the Québec Charter by those who wish to use the rights they are accorded to restrict the rights of others (Geadah 1995). Québec must always be vigilant in the provision of tolerance and accommodation, as fundamentalism "does not cease to appeal to democratic values in order to penetrate the institutions at the heart of which they wish to work toward the destruction of these same values" (Baillargeon 1995). As François Brousseau stated, the openness of Québec and its willingness to accommodate diversity could not allow "the intolerant [to] demand freedom and tolerance to advance their positions" (Lenk 2000, 83).

Central to the debate concerning the assertion and limitation of the freedom of religion was the ability to define the nature of the hijab. The hijab became the site of a struggle of interpretation between advocates and opponents of its prohibition. As the Canadian and Québec Charters as well as international agreements legally protect religious practices, some opponents of the prohibition of the hijab attempted to define it as a religious symbol and the wearing of the hijab as a mandate of Islam. The Canadian Muslim Forum argued that "the veil is a divine obligation" (Ciceri 1998, 91). As "a Quranic commandment" (Boulanger 1994), the hijab was a symbol through which Muslim women marked their religious beliefs, identities, and convictions (Bourret 1994; Collectif de femme 1994; Lévesque 1995). Restricting the wearing of the hijab, as an important religious practice, would be a violation of religious freedoms and contrary to the pluralist nature of Québec.

To undermine the protection afforded to the hijab as an aspect of religious practice, some proponents of its prohibition argued that the hijab was not a religious symbol. First, it did not correspond to the privatized conception of religion as "the relation of man – and woman – with their creator" that they asserted was protected by the Québec Charter (Auclair 1995). Second, they argued that, as the Quran recommends only that men and women dress modestly, the wearing of the hijab is not a divine commandment (Ciceri 1998, 98; Geadah 1994, 1995). Rather than "a Quranic commandment" and, therefore, a divine revelation, the obligation to wear the hijab is the product of men, originating in the hadiths. As a result, there was no obligation to afford it legal protection.

Other proponents of the prohibition of the hijab did not seek to deny the religious nature of the hijab but to associate it with a particularly unacceptable form of religion: Islamic fundamentalism. According to Geadah, the hijab was not an essential aspect of the "Muslim uniform" but an aspect of the fundamentalist interpretation of Islam (Ciceri 1998, 92). As a symbol of fundamentalist religion, it was also a symbol of intolerance and the oppression of women. In the words of journalist David Emmanuel Roberge, "a simple piece of cloth does not bother me in the least ... On the contrary, when the veil is a vehicle of values affirming the oppression of women and the supremacy of men, then I am no longer in agreement with it" (Tahon 1996, 182). Moreover, the hijab was described as a political symbol, or more accurately, as a symbol of a form of religion that did not respect the separation of the religious and the political. To concretize the political nature of the hijab, repeated allusions were made to the atrocities occurring at the hands of Islamists in Algeria as well as to the brutality of sharia law (182–86).

Defined in this manner, the hijab appeared as a serious threat to Québec. To downplay the perceived threat of the religious nature of the hijab and its association with fundamentalism, some opponents of the ban on the hijab attempted to portray it as a cultural symbol and practice. They argued that, like all clothing, the headscarf was part of a culture, "like jeans are part of North American culture" (Dagenais 1995). As a result, the hijab acted as a marker of cultural identity. In wearing the hijab, young Muslim women were asserting their identity. This desire to publicly express one's identity was not described as particular to Muslim youth but as a common aspect of the adolescent experience (Ciceri 1998, 104). The wearing of the headscarf could simply be a provisional phenomenon, a manifestation of teenage rebellion against societal conformity, a rebellion that could later turn toward a rejection of the hijab (Gruda 1994). The hijab, therefore, may be only a "style" – an aspect of a "normal passing crisis of adolescence" (Gagnon 1994a). Through this definition, the hijab was both granted importance as a cultural marker and made banal as a passing phenomenon of youth rebellion. Defined in this manner, the headscarf's religious threat was downgraded. So too, however, were the legal protections afforded to it as a religious symbol.

The struggle to define the hijab in the process of balancing rights claims is particularly evident in the documents outlining the judgments rendered in 1995 by the Commission des droits de la personne and the Conseil du statut de la femme with regard to the presence of the hijab in schools. According to the CDP (1995, 12–13), although the veil had been used by extremists both to assure the submission of women and as a politico-religious symbol and although it had been the subject of various interpretations of the Quran, in the context of Québec, "we have to presume that the choice [to wear the hijab] constitutes a way of expressing belonging and religious convictions." It would be incorrect, then, either to assume that the hijab was a symbol of militantism or to banalize it by equating it with any other headwear. However, the CDP asserted that if the hijab became infused with political or sexist symbolism and thus placed the "public order or the equality of the sexes in peril," a school would be justified in proscribing it (13).

A further key consideration in this judgment was the issue of choice. For the hijab to be permitted in schools, the wearing of the hijab had to be the product of an individual's free will. The school was given the task of maintaining an environment free of the pressures of ostracism, one in which, it was made clear to young Muslim women, the hijab should be worn only if it was their choice to do so (CDP 1995, 13).

The issue of the nature of the hijab was given much more attention by the CSF. A significant portion of the document prepared by the CSF concerning the issue of the permissibility of the hijab also dealt with its definition. As this document noted, "the veil is not a simple piece of cloth; it is also a symbol" (CSF 1995, 5). As a religious symbol, it was protected by the Québec Charter. However, as a symbol of values contrary to those of Québec society, it was not protected. For the CSF, understanding the nature of the hijab was essential to determining its permissibility. To do so, first, the CSF posed the question of whether the headscarf was a "religious symbol or a symbol of the inequality of women" (8). In order to answer this question, it sought first to demonstrate both the pre-Islamic origins of the hijab and its presence in various religious traditions. Citing the work of Juliette Minces (1990), it argued that the veil first appeared in

Islam not for religious reasons but to differentiate Muhammad's female followers from slaves and to protect them from rape during a period of social and political upheaval in Medina. Second, the CSF addressed the issue of whether wearing the hijab was in fact a religious obligation for Muslims. Based on the theological interpretation of Jawad Sqalli, president of the Centre d'études arabes pour le développement, the CSF determined that wearing the veil was not a religious obligation. The only obligations present in the Quran, it asserted, were the five pillars of Islam: the profession of faith, prayer, alms to the poor, the hajj, and fasting. In relation to dress, there is only a recommendation that men and women dress modestly. According to the CSF, the notion that wearing the hijab is an authentically religious obligation was merely "the work of Muslim fundamentalists" (CSF 1995, 8).

Having dismissed the authentically religious nature of the hijab, the CSF proceeded to consider the question of whether the hijab was a symbol of the inequality of women. To answer this question, the document tracked the symbolism of the hijab in various contexts. In doing so, it noted that the equation between unveiling and women's autonomy was not always straightforward. First, as the document described, the veiled woman had been the focus of various colonial and anti-colonial projects. In the nineteenth century, the French colonial authorities had engaged in a campaign of deveiling in Algeria to eradicate a symbol of "backward" culture and assert the moral superiority of the French. It was in this context that a notion of the protection of the veil in the name of Islam emerged (CSF 1995, 20). Furthermore, the CSF argued that just as enforced veiling, as had occurred in Iran in the 1970s, was an imposition on women, legally prohibiting the wearing of the veil in public, as had occurred in Iran in the 1930s, resulted in a loss of autonomy for women. Barred from wearing the veil, women did not want to leave the house "naked," and parents refused to send their daughters to school (21).

As these cases demonstrate, in various political struggles the appearance of women became a marker of national, religious, or community identity. The unveiled woman became a symbol of modernization, and the veiled women became a symbol of Islam. As a result of these struggles, women became "depositories of Muslim identity." Consequently, it was very difficult for them to contest a particular element of identity without being seen as traitors to their community (CSF 1995, 21).

For the CSF, therefore, the hijab was essentially an instrument for the social control of women. Moreover, as it applied rules of modesty to women but not to men, it was a symbol of the inequality of men and women (CSF 1995, 21, 38). As a result, it was something that should be struggled against. In the words of the CSF, "as feminists ... [if] we critique the sexism of our culture, we should equally be able to critique it when manifested in other cultures or other religions in alliance with the women belonging to other cultures and religions" (38). However, the CSF concluded, struggling against the hijab should not involve a call for its prohibition. Such a measure would unfairly punish women and impair their autonomy. It was the public school that provided a place where children were protected from the influence of their parents and could learn to think for themselves. As a result, it was unfair that the struggle against sexism and fundamentalism should be placed "on the back (or more so on the head) of the girls who wear the veil" (40).

The second major theme within the debate concerning the hijab was that of social cohesion. For proponents of its prohibition, the wearing of the hijab was seen as a threat to social cohesion in two principal ways. First, as Ciceri (1998, 101) noted, the public donning of the headscarf was associated with a refusal of immigrants to integrate into Québec society. It was a defiant display of difference and a "refusal to adhere to a way of life, a way of thinking, a philosophy" (Paré 1994). Moreover, it was an exhibition of a perceived "superiority of the soul, of virtue, of vocation" (Paré 1994). As Micheline Milot argued, religious beliefs strongly influenced an individual's perception and valuation of the other. She asserted that for Muslims in Québec it was the Quran and Islamic moral values – rather than, and sometimes in opposition to, Occidental values – that served as referents in identity formation. It was the perceived superiority of Islamic values over those of Québec and a greater identification with the wider Islamic world than with their fellow citizens that retarded the integration of Muslims in Québec (CSF 1995, 31).

As a result, the refusal to integrate was related to the second major threat to social cohesion: an undermining of the common values, culture, and identity of Québec. Commentators voiced their concern that if Québec accommodated religious diversity, properly québécois values and culture as well as any shared values would become diluted. As Brousseau wrote, "modern societies all have a need for diversity, tolerance of multiplicity and difference. But they also have a need for cohesion and shared references ... in the negative face of lebanonization, balkanization, yugoslavization" (Lenk 2000, 84). It was these shared references that had to be protected. Some responded to the dilemma of religious diversity with common xenophobic refrains such as "when in Rome do as the Romans"; "when one arrives in a country, I feel they must adopt the customs of that country and not the inverse"; "they should conform to our social norms. If they are not happy they can return to their country"; "foreigners should adapt to the customs of Québec"; "if I was to go to their countries I would live like them" ("Êtes-vous" 1995).

Most, however, asserted that accommodations for religious diversity must be reasonable. To highlight the need to limit unreasonable accommodations, Landry registered his disagreement with modifying the scholarly calendar to take into account the holidays of religious minorities: "If the days off in Québec are determined on the basis of the Christian calendar, this is the natural order of things, taking account of our past" (Ciceri 1998, 90). He argued that "Québec is always ready to make 'reasonable accommodations' to aid in the integration of cultural communities" (Lessard 1995). Accommodations must be granted not simply to permit difference but also to foster the integration of minorities into broader québécois society, with its values, customs, and history. Accommodating religious differences without the aim of promoting integration into common Québec culture and values meant that, "in wanting too much to respect others," the Québécois risked "finishing by no longer respecting ourselves" (Garnier 1995).

If Québec allowed for the undermining or dilution of its culture, values, and traditions through accommodations, it would "soon have no culture to offer to immigrants" (Côté 1995). Thus opponents of the permissibility of the hijab saw the religious practices of minorities and their demands for the accommodation of difference as threats to social cohesion.

Those who opposed the prohibition of the hijab also framed their arguments in relation to the issue of social cohesion. In doing so, they raised the threat of Islamic fundamentalism for Québec society, a threat that would be heightened by exclusionary measures. Barring veiled Muslim girls from attending public schools would result in the creation of a marginalized group who would be denied "the same opportunity as all other Québécois" (Lavigne 1995). The consequences of exclusion were not simply a denial of economic opportunities but, more importantly, also the denial of the opportunity to be initiated into the common values of Québec. This integration was seen as necessary given the perception of Islamic fundamentalism as a "spreading disease" (Lenk 2000, 83) in Montréal and its suburbs, particularly in Brossard, where there are "families who occupy a space where one is in Iranian, Egyptian, Maghrebian, Pakistani, etc. territory." It is from such "neighbourhoods with a high density of immigrants that fundamentalists emerge" (Bensalem 1994b). Students excluded from public schools would be easy prey for fundamentalists. As Milot suggested (Ciceri 1998, 92) and as McAndrew (2006, 2–3) has emphasized, the public school had the responsibility to transmit the common civic values of Québec to its students. In doing so, it could be a space for the transformation of the student, as the teaching of common values contributes to the relativization of the values of the familial sphere (3).

The school serves as a place where the religious constraints of parents are relaxed and children are free to forge their own identity. In this space, students not only engage in an internalization of common values but also learn how to moderate their identity and how to put certain differences in parentheses when in the public sphere (McAndrew 2006, 12). In other words, they learn how to behave as secular citizens. Thus opponents of the prohibition of the hijab argued that such a measure, in blocking the access of Muslim girls to public education, would inhibit their ability to function as citizens.

Citoyenneté québécoise

In order to understand the importance accorded to issues of rights and social cohesion, it is necessary to locate the debate concerning the permissibility of the religious in the public sphere within recent transformations in concepts and practices of belonging and nationhood in Québec. Since the early 1990s, the Québec state has undertaken the "well-orchestrated and much publicized" project of the "construction and development of a *citoyenneté québécoise*" (Juteau 2002, 441). According to both government and academic discourse, this emergence of Québec citizenship is the culmination of a gradual process of the transformation of the boundaries of the Québec nation that began in the 1960s, marked by the shift from an ethnic to a civic conception of the nation. The de-ethnicization, secularization, and territorialization of national identity in Québec that are said to have occurred since the beginning of the Quiet Revolution are presented in official discourse as an expansion of the boundaries of the Québec nation, an opening toward otherness, and a progressive move from the particular to the universal.

According to the dominant narrative of this transformation, the origins of civic nationalism in Québec can be located in the Quiet Revolution (Bourque and Duchastel 2000; Bramadat 2005; CCCI 1993; CDP 1995; Ciceri 1998; CRI 2004b; Fontaine and Shiose 1991; Gouvernement du Québec 1990; Juteau 1996, 2002; Juteau and McAndrew 1992; Lamoureux 2000; Maclure 2003; Milot 2002, 2006; Plourde 1993). Consistent with the historical narratives outlined in Chapter 3, the measures undertaken by the Québec state during this period are seen as having initiated profound cultural and social transformations, including a redefinition of national identity.

The initiatives undertaken by the Québec state during the Quiet Revolution are said to have given "Québec the means to define itself as a political society founded on a territorial and linguistic base" (Ciceri 1998, 18). This project primarily involved the construction of a territorially based community. With the increasing centrality of the state, brought about by the expansion of state administration of social, educational, and healthcare institutions, the "ethnic and religious anchorings of identity began to lose their relevance" (Therrien 2004, 15). The emergence of the interventionist Québec state as the institution "defining and regulating the destiny" of francophones within Québec resulted in the dissolution of the pan-Canadian French Canadian nation and in the creation of two new identities: the Québécois and the francophones outside Québec (Juteau 2002, 443).

The policies of the interventionist Québec state were aimed at redressing the economic, social, political, and cultural inferiority of Québec's francophone community. One of the strategies advocated by nationalists to accomplish this goal was the legislation of French as the language of the public sphere. Doing so, it was hoped, would counter discrimination against ethnic Québécois and the French language. However, according to Diane Lamoureux (2000, 118), such legislation also resulted in a "fundamental rupture" in Québec nationalism.

In 1977, one year after its election, the Parti Québécois (PQ) passed Bill 101, the Charter of the French Language. Because Bill 101 made French the common public language of Québec, and thus de-ethnicized the *fait français* (French presence) in Québec, language and culture came to be dissociated. The French language was no longer portrayed solely as a characteristic of the culture of the majority ethnic group in Québec but also as a vehicle through which various cultural and ethnic groups formed a common community (Allor and Gagnon 1994, 16–17). This measure also recognized the plural nature of Québec society but stipulated that the public manifestation of pluralism was to be bounded by the common use of the French language (Lamoureux 2000, 118). Children of immigrants and of francophones coming to live in Québec from elsewhere in Canada were obligated to be educated in francophone schools, businesses were mandated to conduct business in French, and the French language was ordered to appear as predominant on all signage in public areas.

The following year, the Québec government sought to further delineate the nature of cultural pluralism in Québec by entering into the Cullen-Couture Agreement of 1978 with the Canadian government. This decision, in granting the Québec government full decision-making powers with respect to the selection of immigrants within the parameters of federal guidelines, furthered the autonomy previously granted to Québec vis-à-vis the federal government in relation to immigration by the Lang-Cloutier Accord of 1971 and the Andres-Bienvenue Accord of 1972. The former authorized Québec to engage in the recruitment of immigrants, and the latter required the federal government to take into account the position of representatives of the Québec government on the requirements for the admission of immigrants to Québec (Ciceri 1998, 18).

In the same year that the PQ entered into the Cullen-Couture Agreement, it furthered the institutionalization of the right of minorities to maintain and develop their cultural life – enshrined in 1975 in the Québec Charter of Human Rights and Freedoms – with the introduction of a white paper titled *La politique québécoise du développement culturel* (1978). This document outlined the importance of ethnic minorities to Québec culture, arguing that there could be no culture without minorities. It also stipulated that all ethnic minority groups had the right to demand that the state provide them with the cultural tools necessary to maintain and develop their cultures (Gouvernement du Québec 1978, 64; Juteau 1996, 49). The document outlined a notion of pluralism that rejected both the American model of an assimilationist melting pot and the Canadian model of multiculturalism in favour of a policy of integration. In the words of the Québec minister of immigration,

> The immigrant is ... an active member of an evolving québécois community; he adapts to and integrates into the francophone québécois community; the immigrant, carrier of an authentic culture, has contributed to enriching the cultural patrimony of the québécois collectivity; they belong, therefore, to *minority* branches of the québécois culture; they can be grouped according to country, nation, race, ethnicity, language, civilization, culture, religion, or other markers of identity. (Fontaine and Shiose 1991, 436)

Minority groups were further differentiated as immigrant minorities, colonial minorities (primarily the English), and Aboriginals.

In 1980 minority groups were again regrouped by the Québec state with the invention of the term "ethnic minority communities." This new group included all individuals who had a "maternal language ... other than French or were born outside of Canada" (Fontaine and Shiose 1991, 436). In April 1981 a new term – "cultural communities" – emerged in the document *Autant façons d'être québécois: Plan d'action du gouvernement du Québec à l'intention des communautés culturelles* (Many Ways of Being Québécois: Plan of Action of the Government of Québec with Regard to Cultural Communities) (Gouvernement du Québec 1981). According to the newly formed Ministry of Cultural Communities and Immigration, mandated to maintain and develop cultural communities, highlight the contribution made by members of these communities, and foster integration (Juteau 2002, 444), members of cultural communities could be identified by the following criteria:

> 1/ A place of birth outside of Canada, or place of birth of one of their parents outside of Canada and knowledge of the language of the community of origin or knowledge of a language (other than French) of the cultural community of origin; 2/ A maternal language other than French; 3/ Belonging to a visible community; 4/ Belonging to an ethnic or cultural group, the group being defined by common ethnic and cultural traits. (Fontaine and Shiose 1991, 437–38)

As Danielle Juteau (1996) argues, with the creation of cultural communities, those residing in Québec were divided into two mutually exclusive categories: the Québécois and the cultural communities. The introduction of these categories created a vision of Québec with "a central core of nationals surrounded at the periphery by smaller and culturally diverse circles" (50).

In 1990, with the introduction of the Québec Liberal Party's *Au Québec pour bâtir ensemble: Énoncé de politique sur l'immigration et l'intégration* (Let's Build Québec Together: Policy Statement on Immigration and Integration) (Gouvernement du Québec 1990), the opposition of these two mutually exclusive categories was replaced by the official redefinition of the québécois nation in more inclusive terms. Rather than maintaining a division of the Québécois from the cultural communities, all residents of Québec, regardless of ethnic origin, were defined as comprising the Québécois. In another example of what Louise Fontaine and Yuki Shiose (1991, 437) have called the incredible "lexical creativity" of the Québec state, this expansion of the nation involved the creation of another new category: the Québécois of cultural communities. Thus, beginning in 1990, all residents of Québec were designated as Québécois, though Québécois of different types.

This document also provided a clear articulation of the policy of interculturalism, through which the Québec state sought to foster social integration. Presented as "a desirable and specifically Québécois form of pluralism" (Juteau 2002), interculturalism was based on two main principles. First, integration was defined as a long-term process culminating in the ability of immigrants and their descendants to participate fully in Québec society and to develop a feeling of belonging to this society (Gouvernement du Québec 1990). Central to this process was a mastery of the French language, which enabled both the participation of all citizens in public life and the expectation of this participation. Second, interculturalism was to be guided by a moral contract that outlined the rights and responsibilities of Québécois of all origins and the relationship between immigrants and the host society in the development of a common public culture (Juteau 2002, 445; McAndrew 1995). As a result, the limits of pluralism were defined by the boundaries of the fundamental values of Québec society. As the document asserted,

> the Québec position on intercultural relations aims always to avoid extreme situations where different groups integrally and rigidly maintain their culture and their traditions of origin in reciprocal ignorance and isolation. In effect, the whole of our population places the greatest importance on the respect of all Québécois for democratic values defined by the [Québec] Charter, notably those relating to the equality of the sexes, to the status of children, and to rejection of all discrimination based on ethnic or racial origin. (Gouvernement du Québec 1990, 17).

In order to promote integration, Québec undertook measures to counter indirect discrimination. The primary tools utilized by the state were the development of "programs of access to equality" and the determination of reasonable accommodations, primarily for religious differences. Schools, social service providers, and other institutions were mandated to develop policies aimed at increasing inclusion and promoting access and equity for minority groups (CCCI 1993).

In contrast to the aims of multiculturalism, the goal of the Québec government in adopting practices that fostered inclusion and integration was neither to valorize and promote the maintenance of immigrant cultures nor to assimilate all citizens into an already present homogeneous québécois culture; rather, through accommodation of difference, the state sought to manage "a democratic space of deliberation" in which "holders of diverse traditions" could express diverse interests and develop consensual solutions (Ciceri 1998, 31).

At times, the Québec government appeared to be at great pains to differentiate this intercultural approach from that of multiculturalism. It argued, in the words of Landry, that it was "against multiculturalism" and "did not subsidize difference" (McAndrew 1996, 295). It argued, rather, that interculturalism, "without glorifying difference like multiculturalism, permits the expression of the particularities of each citizen" (293). As a result, all policies implemented by the government relating to pluralism, despite perhaps appearing to subsidize difference, were undertaken only with the objective of social integration, which meant bringing cultures together and transforming them rather than maintaining them intact (294).

Beginning in 1994, and coinciding with the Ouimet affair, the Québec government began the process of creating a universal québécois citizenship. Marking the first time that the term appeared in official discourse (Juteau 2002, 447), in 1995 the Conseil des communautés culturelles et de l'immigration (CCCI) was asked to determine the essential components of a *citoyenneté québécoise* (CRI 1997, 13). The first official manifestation of this new universal conception of citizenship emerged shortly thereafter with the replacement of the CCCI by a new advisory council called the Conseil des relations interculturelles (CRI). The term "cultural communities" began to disappear from the lexicon of government discourse in Québec.

This disappearance was also evident in the institution in 1996 of a Ministry of Relations with Citizens and Immigration, replacing the Ministry of International Affairs, Immigration and Cultural Communities, which had itself replaced the Ministry of Cultural Communities and Immigration in 1993. In announcing the creation of this new ministry, Premier Lucien Bouchard asserted that the Québec nation was constituted by a collection of equal citizens of various origins, languages, and political orientations. He suggested, moreover, that it was the responsibility of the Québec state to bring these citizens together and ensure the protection of their fundamental rights (Juteau 2000, 6–7).

This task was to be accomplished by the creation of common, rather than particularist, institutions and values. To that end, an increased emphasis was placed on the creation of civic links between various groups. The creation of particular institutions for cultural communities and the separation of citizens into the categories of cultural communities and host society were viewed as divisive rather than as aiding the process of integration (Juteau 2002, 448). André Boisclair, the PQ minister of relations with citizens and immigration, asserted that the key to managing cultural diversity was to reconcile "our" fundamental values with the right of immigrants to their cultural heritage (CRI 1997, 7–8). As Juteau (2002, 448) notes, with the introduction of these policies, "pluralism was not discarded ... [but] the recognition, and reconciliation, of differentiated categories and identities was replaced by the idea of equal citizens united by common attributes, attachments, and interests."

With the constitution of a universal québécois citizenship, a new distinction emerged in the québécois national imaginary. No longer were citizens differentiated on the basis of ethnicity. Instead, the categorization of individuals on the basis of "ethnicity or immigrant trajectory [was] discarded and replaced by the citizen, a status that transcends political, ethnic or ideological belongings" (Juteau 2002, 451). Within this new mode of belonging, citizens were differentiated on the basis of their capacity or willingness to abide by the common culture and fundamental values of Québec and to comport themselves properly in the public realm. In other words, a new division emerged between good and bad citizens.

The development of a *citoyenneté québécoise* took place in the context of a broader policy orientation in Québec and other states in reaction to what they perceived as the threats and opportunities of a new global economy and the related transformations in patterns of migration. The focus of these policies was to promote adjustment to the new globalized knowledge economy and to counteract the atomization and social and national dissolution perceived to be resulting from neoliberal socio-economic relations and intensified immigration. To contend with these concerns, policies were developed with the aim of fostering social cohesion through the inclusion and activation of marginalized groups and individuals. The inclusion and integration of all citizens were seen as the result of, and prerequisites to, a stable, secure, and prosperous society. Thus they were key to preventing both the development of an underclass of unemployed or underemployed individuals and the emergence of ethnic ghettos. In relation to social policy, measures were introduced that rejected both the social expenditure approach of the welfare state and the overreliance on market forces, the voluntary sector, the family, and the individual to generate the "life-chances" associated with neoliberalism. Although states articulated a belief that a reintroduction of the welfare state would render them uncompetitive in the global economy, they feared that neoliberal policies and austerity measures had led, and would increasingly lead, to an intensification of social exclusion. Consequently, the development of what was referred to as a social investment model or social investment state was promoted (Dufour and Morrison 2005; Jenson and Saint-Martin 2003, 78).

Although the specific methods to achieve inclusion and social cohesion differed between states, there existed a belief in many states that attending to these issues was an urgent task that could be accomplished only by state intervention. In general, the social investment model, which in Québec took the form of what was labelled the "social economy," involved the implementation of policies seeking to increase the life-chances of all citizens through a focus on training and early childhood education and development.

It was in line with this concern with social cohesion that the Québec government introduced the aforementioned measures to aid in the integration of members of cultural communities. Prior to the late 1980s, the immigration policies of Québec had been relatively restrictive, with immigration permitted mainly on the basis of family reunification or through special programs for asylum seekers from designated regions (e.g., Indochina and Haiti). At the beginning of the 1990s, as evident in *Énoncé de politique sur l'immigration et l'intégration* (Policy Statement on Immigration and Integration) (Gouvernement du Québec 1990), the Québec government began to develop an immigration policy involving the active recruitment of immigrants. The attraction of immigrants was seen as necessary for both demographic stability and the international economic competitiveness of Québec. With the signing of the Gagnon-Tremblay Accord in 1990, the Québec government was granted much greater responsibility for attracting and integrating immigrants to Québec. With the introduction of these measures, immigration increasingly came to be seen as an issue involving the management of new populations rather than simply as one of inclusion and exclusion. Immigration was necessary to, and beneficial for, the stability of Québec, and pluralism was an undeniable feature of Québec society. However, given the stakes associated with social cohesion, the immigrant also appeared as a potential threat to the stability of Québec. The immigrant thus became a figure who had to be acted upon by policies of integration. As is evident in both the debate concerning the hijab and the transformations in conceptions and practices of citizenship in Québec, carefully planned measures were needed to balance the integration of immigrants and the maintenance of the common values and institutions necessary for social cohesion.

Thus, in the early 1990s in Québec, the public presence of religion emerged as an object of concern both within a transformation of the conceptions and practices of citizenship and alongside the growing perception of pluralism as a threat to social cohesion. However, the reason why the publicity of religious practices and subjects came to be seen as particularly threatening requires further elaboration. To that end, it is necessary to outline how religion and the religious subject appear within discourses of Québec national identity as objects requiring governance.

The dominant narrative of the development of the *citoyenneté québécoise*, as described above, is one of a gradual opening, an expansion of national boundaries, a stripping away of categories of differentiation, and a radical shift from an ethnic to a civic nationalism. It is, in short, about the emergence of a way of belonging grounded in universal rights and values. Consequently, it appears as a project divorced from relations of power. However, as Juteau (2002) argues, despite the move away from overtly ethnic boundaries, the recently formed community of citizens in Québec is anchored in another "homogenized notion of cultural belonging." The universal character of Québec citizenship is not the result of the passive unveiling of that which is present in the absence of particularities and categories of differentiation but is the product of an active "attempt by the Québec state to define a universal national identity that would subordinate all others. The national model of citizenship is preferred over the postnational ... the undifferentiated over the differentiated" (442).

As Isin's (2002a, 4) genealogies of citizenship demonstrate, citizenship "does not exist as an immutable and given fact"; on the contrary, the construction of the citizen, although often masked in a language of universality, is possible only on the basis of relations of exclusion and alterity. Citizenship and noncitizenship, even when formulated in universal terms, always emerge through particular strategies and technologies, such as affiliation, identification, dissociation, and misrecognition (25).

Universalization through the apparent inclusion of all despite racial, ethnic, religious, or other particularities obfuscates the arbitrary mechanisms through which it includes, excludes, and governs. Just as an ethnically bounded regime of citizenship permits the exclusion of ethnic others on the basis of an identity that is portrayed as naturally constituted, so too do liberal conceptions of citizenship allow for subordination and domination by reference to universal and natural rights and values and to a particular conception of the human. Both forms of citizenship function through a naturalization and normalization of a certain subject, making those who are excluded seem abnormal and naturally excluded.

Moreover, as Isin (2002a, 5) argues, in the construction of narratives of citizenship, dominant groups have always defined themselves in relation to transitive and distant others: barbarians, Orientals, and the historical self. In focusing on these others, they mask the domination and stigmatization of various immanent others, such as migrants, women, the differently abled, the mentally ill, children, and racial, ethnic, sexual, or religious "minorities." The focus on the equal status of all citizens and on universal human rights in liberal discourses and practices of citizenship makes them particularly effective in masking the manner in which citizenship is constructed in relation to various others and, consequently, the arbitrariness of the methods it employs to govern immanent others.

As Asad and John Milbank argue, liberalism is grounded in the invention and naturalization of the figure of the abstract human (Asad 2003, 144) and in the assertion that "we are all instances of such a species" (Milbank 2004). According to Milbank, the human that appears in liberal thought "is the pure individual, thought of in abstraction from his or her gender, birth, associations, beliefs" (213). What is, however, essential to the pure individual is a free will, the capacity to break with any ascribed nature, and even the ability to will against oneself (Asad 2003, 133–34; Milbank 2004, 213). As free will is the essence of the human, it serves as the basis of the modern notion of human rights, conceived of as natural and inalienable (Asad 2003, 134).

Within this discourse of human rights, the state asserts itself as the only institution that, through the delegation of individual rights to the people, can enforce and protect human rights. Consequently, as suggested by Asad (2003, 135), echoing Arendt (1951), human rights come to depend on national rights. In order to protect their human rights, the state claims the right to punish and otherwise coerce its national citizens. Thus, despite the universal and abstract character of the rights-bearing person, the discourse of human rights positions each state as responsible for the protection, care, and governance of a limited population of such individuals. Therefore, within the discourse of human rights, there remains "an unresolved tension ... between the moral invocation of 'universal humanity' and the power of the state to identify, apply, and maintain the law" (Asad 2003, 138).

This tension is particularly evident within the doctrine and practices of secularism. Among the most crucial and earliest acknowledgments of individual freedom within the discourse of natural and human rights is the right to freedom of religion. The doctrine of secularism promotes itself as an answer to the dilemma of how the individual right to religious belief can be recognized within, and protected from, the authority of the state. Secularism asserts that only a strong, secular state can enforce human rights and enable individuals to exercise their free will and thus their humanity. However, as Saba Mahmood (2008) notes, the discourses and practices of modern secular democratic states in relation to religion must be distinguished from those of secular totalitarian states. Although both forms of the secular state regulate religion, the secular democratic state must engage in a calculus of freedom and coercion in doing so. As freedom of religion is protected as a human right, it cannot easily be abrogated by the liberal state.

All citizens can appeal to the state to curtail or extend their ability to practise religion. Thus any regulation of religion must be enacted as a limitation instituted to permit the exercise of other freedoms. As evident in the judgments of the CSF and the CDP, this consideration has often involved the state entering into theological debates to serve as the arbiter of that which is essentially or authentically religious and thus worthy of state protections. As a result, for the modern democratic state, religion appears as a phenomenon that requires careful management and governance rather than ignorance or elimination.

The emergence of both the notion of the abstract individual and the notion of the political community as the collection of equal abstract citizens involved a critique of the religious inequality of the post-Reformation absolutist state. With the abandonment of the doctrine of *cuius regio, eius religio* (whose realm, his religion) and the acceptance of religious minorities, members of minority groups arose as a particular problem for the democratic state based on the notion of the abstract citizen (Asad 2003, 174). Minorities were officially equal to all other citizens, whose rights to religious difference were viewed as inalienable. However, they also required particular rights and protections. Moreover, the political inclusion of minorities, with different beliefs, identities, and potential loyalties, was seen as a threat to the cohesion of the nation-state. Thus the practices of the liberal state with regard to religion could not amount to ignoring religion but had to include "its ongoing regulation through a variety of state and civic institutions" (Mahmood 2008).

In order to promote the cohesion of the community of equal citizens belonging to various minority and majority groups, the state had to develop a common national identity in each of its citizens (Asad 2005). To be a citizen was "to reflect, as an individual, the collective personality [of the nation-state] ... embodied in [its] laws and conventional practices." Although this personality "may not be regarded as eternal and unchangeable," it is always considered a precondition of citizenship. As a result, the citizen is never only identical with himself or herself but must also represent "an abstract quality that can be separated from his or her social identity" (Asad 2003, 176). In this light, Juteau's assertion that the development of a *citoyenneté québécoise* was a project of both the homogenization and subordinization of identities appears less as a critique of the nature of québécois civic nationalism and more as a statement about the technologies of governance proper to the modern state.

Among the strategies employed in the construction of a universal citizen identity is a division between public and private identities and ways of being. Whereas all identities constructed as particularities, such as gender, religion, and ethnicity, are located in the private sphere, the public sphere is portrayed as the space in which one is able to escape the force of these ascriptive and particularist identities. The public sphere appears as a neutral space of freedom. This seeming neutrality disguises the manner in which the liberal public sphere has always been a site of exclusion. As Juteau (2002, 450) argues, under the cover of universalism, the specificities of particular groups come to be associated with the normal way of being in public.

However, a focus on the public sphere as an exclusionary, non-neutral space still remains within the bounds of the discourse of secular liberalism. The progressive inclusion of various excluded subjects in the liberal public sphere – women, those without property, and members of religious minorities – has not, and will not, render it free of power. Power is not present in the public sphere because certain groups or individuals have attained control of it or because it has not reached a particular stage of progress; rather, "the public space is a space necessarily (not just contingently) articulated by power" (Asad 2003, 184).

The secular public sphere is not simply the neutral space where individuals can emancipate themselves from the coercion of religious force but also a space in which the self is constantly disposed to power in the constitution of itself as a secular citizen proper to this sphere. In its very constitution, the public sphere is a space that requires one to comport oneself on the basis of a particular abstract identity and is therefore always a site of power. The public sphere, as the site proper to the universal, abstract, secular subject, is always a site of the foreclosure of possible ways of being.

In order to understand the effects and stakes of this naturalization, it is crucial to attend to the manner in which the naturalization of the secular as the way of being proper to the public sphere serves to limit the political. To do so, it is useful to address Jacques Rancière's (2001, Thesis 1) critique of what he calls the "vicious circle" of political philosophy. I invoke Rancière's work not to champion his ontology of the political but because it illustrates the manner in which certain ontologies of the political can serve to depoliticize, marginalize, and consequently silence various struggles and subjects (Morrison 2013b). Crucial to this limitation of the political has been the recent inclination to institute and/or preserve what Rancière (2004, 302) refers to as "the realm of pure politics."

According to Rancière (2001, Thesis 1), these conceptions of the political are based on an interpretation of Aristotle's partition of the political and domestic and on his definition of the citizen – the subject proper to politics – as "he who partakes in the fact of ruling and being ruled." Through the lens of Arendtian and Straussian political thought, these definitions come to demarcate the political as the public sphere through a series of oppositions differentiating the way of life proper to the political from that proper to the private. The political is identified with "eu zen" (a conception of the good life), praxis, and the life of "public action, speech and appearance," whereas the private is identified with "zen" (the order of mere living and individual interest), poiesis, and a "deprived" life "entrapped in idiocy" (Thesis 1, Thesis 2; 2004, 298). Within such an understanding, the political is not only defined as a particular realm or form of relationship but also "deduced from the properties of a specific way of being and is explained in terms of the existence of a character who possesses a good or specific universality, as opposed to the private or domestic world of needs or interests" (2001, Thesis 1). Politics is thus defined as a mode of being proper to those who possess the characteristics proper to it. Consequently, the origins or the relationships that are considered to be definitive of politics are located in the characteristics of particular subjects and in the conditions of their coming together (Thesis 1).

The secular, then, has come to be seen both as the condition of possibility for the political – since the secular public sphere is seen as a necessary condition for the vital political interaction of citizens – and as that which defines the political subject, the one who can put aside private religious beliefs and interests and engage rationally in a determination of the common good. Consequently, in the absence of either a secular public sphere or secular subjects, the relationship definitive of the political appears impossible. Moreover, following the logic of those who argue for the necessity of a purification of the political, in order for this relationship to be possible, it is necessary to purify the universalism and autonomy of the public realm of any contamination from the particularism and coercion of the private sphere – that is, from any way of being driven by interest, necessity, irrationalism, or religious belief. Thus, in this conception of the political, not only are realms and ways of being, such as the religious, associated with the private and differentiated from the political, but they are also seen as requiring separation.

This is the closed or "vicious" circle to which Rancière refers. The political appears as a closed space whose subjects are always predetermined. However, as Rancière suggests, political subjects, such as man and citizen, are not definite collectivities but are designations open to constant interpretation, what he calls "surplus names," which call into question who is to be included in their count (Rancière 2004, 302). However, the ability to make claims and possess rights – and thus the qualities that must be attributed to an individual in order to do so – are not fixed but are instead the site of constant struggle (Isin 2002a).

For Rancière (2001, Thesis 7, Thesis 8; 2004, 305), such struggles, which he refers to as politics, are always opposed to what he denotes as police. Police, according to Rancière, is the ongoing process of the "partition of the sensible, whose principle is the absence of a void and of a supplement"; it is a perpetual attempt to unambiguously separate the political realm and political subject from other spheres and subjects (305). This partition seeks to separate society into distinct spheres with corresponding ways of being. In doing so, it attempts to eliminate any void or overlap on the map of society by articulating the realm of each phenomenon and form of subjectivity.

The naturalization of such clean divisions makes possible the silencing of various voices. As Rancière (2001, Thesis 8) argues, police permits the depoliticization of subjects to be accomplished through the clear distinction between the public and private and through the impossibility of any overlap between the public life of equals, in which rights can be claimed, and the private realm, "from which only groans or cries expressing suffering, hunger, or anger could emerge, but not actual speeches demonstrating a shared aesthesis." By challenging the givenness of the secular, the religious, and their relation to each other and to the public sphere, this history of the nation engages in the formation of what Rancière terms a "dissensus." In other words, in denaturalizing these categories, it aims to "distance the sensible from itself" (Thesis 8) by disturbing the map formulated through the process of police. It exposes the power relations through which certain phenomena are constructed as secular or religious, modern or premodern, national or foreign, and consequently as politicized, depoliticized, or anti-political. In doing so, it provides an opening for a reinterpretation and revaluation of the religious, the political, and the national.

Just as Rancière attends to the manner in which particular conceptions of the political marginalize and obfuscate struggles through depoliticization, Mahmood's (2005, 8, 32–34) analysis of women's involvement in the mosque movement in Egypt demonstrates the manner in which liberal conceptions of the political and agency, which locate agency in the political and moral autonomy of the subject, conceal ways of being political and marginalize and depoliticize certain struggles and modes of comportment. To continue in the language of Rancière, through the operation of police – the division of society into hermetically sealed realms, each with phenomena proper to it – certain acts, struggles, and issues associated with ethics, morality, or religion, and thus deemed proper to the private realm, can be dismissed as nonpolitical, and their constitutive role or influence on politics, even in its "purified" form, can be concealed or discounted.

As Mahmood argues, in line with the liberal conception of agency, feminist analyses of women's participation in religious movements or their adoption of what are perceived to be conservative religious practices such as veiling generally take one of two positions. The first equates the actions of these women with subordination. Women's adoption of behaviours associated with religion is deemed to be either the result of direct or societal coercion or the result of false consciousness (Mahmood 2005, 1–2). In contrast, the second position considers the adoption of religious dress or other modes of comportment to be a form of agency or resistance to subordination. The focus of this position is "explaining resistance and finding resisters" (Abu-Lughod 1990, 43). Both the adoption of religious dress and practices and the support of religious movements are seen as being undertaken by women either to advance their social standing or, in the postcolonial context, to resist the dominance of Western norms (Mahmood 2005, 6–7).

Women's engagement with what is considered patriarchal religion is therefore seen either as an imposition on, and thus a limitation of, agency or as an expression of it. Common to both positions is the equation of agency and freedom with autonomy, understood as "the capacity to realize one's own interest against the weight of custom, tradition, transcendental will, or other obstacles" (Mahmood 2005, 8). As Mahmood notes, what is unique to liberalism is not the identification of freedom with self-realization, an idea that is also present in Platonic, Buddhist, Christian, and Islamic thought; rather, the distinctive aspect of the liberal conception of agency is the relationship it develops between self-realization and individual autonomy. Within liberal thought, the process of self-realization is equated with the ability to realize one's own will. Individuals are free only if their actions are the product of their own will rather than the result of custom, tradition, or coercion. These notions of freedom and agency are consistent with arguments that equate the veil both with women's unfreedom, as an imposition, and with their freedom, as "a product of free choice and evidence of their liberation from the hegemony of Western cultural codes" (11, 195).

As Mahmood (2005, 16) suggests, analyses of the motivations of veiled women through the concepts of coercion and resistance ignore or dismiss as a product of subordination or strategy the discourses of morality, divinity, and virtue that the women of the mosque movement invoked. In her analysis of these women, Mahmood argues that although their activities placed them in conflict with several structures of authority, the rationale they offered was not an assertion of gender equality and resistance to male authority, a form of identity politics, or a reinscription of traditional roles. The mosque movement was neither "a case of deplorable passivity and docility" nor a deliberate act of resistance (15). Following Judith Butler (1993, 1997), Mahmood (2005, 15) argues that permitting only two categories of behaviours – those who passively abide by norms and those who engage in active resistance – obfuscates the multiplicity of ways of being in which norms are differently inhabited. She argues that the women did not passively accept and abide by religious norms but sought through the adoption of pious behaviour and dress to engage in a form of ethical self-formation.

Both within liberal theories of agency and within liberal conceptions of the political, such behaviour appears as inherently nonpolitical. Seen through the lens of a compartmentalization of the ethical and the political, the actions of the women of the mosque movement can appear only ethical/religious. Mahmood (2005, 34–35) argues that although the ethical activities of the mosque movement have not engaged with those institutions and practices associated with the realm of politics, such as the electoral process, claims making, and the judiciary, they have challenged the norms of secular-liberal governance and, in doing so, have been unsettling to both the state and Islamist political parties. Thus "the political efficacy of these movements is ... a function of the work they perform in the ethical realm" (35). However, in the case of the mosque movement and other religious movements, the relegation of their activities to the ethical realm makes any effect they may have on the already constituted, purified political realm appear as a danger – either a contamination or an attempt to take over and dissolve the political into the ethico-religious and thus into the object of state discipline. The possibility of acts or phenomena being at once ethical/religious and political is incongruous with the operations of police and the purification of the political.

Orientalism and Divided Loyalties

Not only do religious subjects appear in opposition to the neutral, abstract citizens of the public sphere, but their ability to wholly and authentically adopt this neutral persona is also an issue that causes concern for social cohesion. As Michael McConnell (2000, 91) argues, "the essential problem is that religious believers have an allegiance to an authority outside of the commonwealth." The divided loyalties and obligations of religious subjects create a phenomenon that has been alternatively referred to as the "partial citizen" (Spinner-Halev 2000) or "citizenship ambiguity" (McConnell 2000).

As McConnell (2000, 92) notes, the problem of the divided loyalties of religious subjects is not a new concern but has been present in the work of theorists of democratic citizenship since at least the time of Jean-Jacques Rousseau. In *The Social Contract* (1762), Rousseau asserts the incompatibility of being "at the same time both churchman and citizen," as religious subjects "have never known whether they ought to obey the civil ruler or the priest ... [They have] two rulers, two homelands ... two contradictory obligations" (179).

Recognizing this dilemma, John Locke offered a solution. According to Locke, the problem of divided loyalties is not inherent to the presence of religious subjects but is derived from a lack of clearly articulated and delineated jurisdictions for the government and religion. So long as both religion and the state recognize that the sources of their authority are separate and belong to separate realms, the religious subject can, as McConnell suggests, "be a citizen of both sacred and secular realms – he could enjoy dual citizenship – with no conflict of obligations." Thus, for Locke, it is "above all things necessary to distinguish exactly the business of civil government from that of religion and settle the just bounds that lie between one and the other" (McConnell 2000, 93). The dilemma of the partial citizen can be overcome only if there is a clear demarcation of the civil and religious spheres and only if religious subjects conduct themselves in a manner appropriate to each sphere.

What appears of concern in recent discourse is the ability of the Muslim subject to overcome such divided loyalties by recognizing the necessary distinction between the religious and public spheres and behaving according to the standards of each. As Cécile Laborde (2005) articulates, one concern in this regard is related to the apparent absence of a separation of civil and religious spheres in Islam. Islam is seen as all-embracing and thus a system of belief in which "everything pertains to religion" (321). Even the oft-cited proponent of multiculturalism Charles Taylor asserts that Islam poses a particular problem for pluralist society, as "for mainstream Islam, there is no question of separating politics and religion the way we have come to expect in Western liberal society" (Werbner 2000, 309).

A second concern is that the loyalty of Muslims to the democratic state is apparently compromised by an overriding allegiance to the global *ummah* (community) (Laborde 2005, 321). It is asserted, consequently, that Muslims find it difficult, if not impossible, to bracket their religious identity, values, obligations, and loyalties in order to adopt the persona of the universal citizen proper to the public sphere. It is in this sense that the hijab appears as particularly problematic in relation to social cohesion. As Laborde asserts, the hijab symbolizes the primacy of the believer over the citizen. In refusing to remove the hijab in the public sphere and articulating their refusal in terms of religious obligation,

Muslim women are also refusing to separate their identity and obligations as citizens from their private religious obligations and identity (327).

As Casanova (2004) has observed with regard to the different responses to the bids by Poland and Turkey to join the European Union, Islam appears as a specific threat to the clear division of the civic and religious realms, a division perceived as necessary for the stability of pluralist democratic society. During the negotiation process leading up to Poland's admittance to the European Union, the Polish episcopate "embraced European integration as a great apostolic assignment." This public call for Poland to serve as the vanguard in a project to "restore Europe for Christianity" prompted little concern, as secular Europeans were confident in "their ability to assimilate Catholic Poland on their own terms," whereas the prospect of Turkey entering the European Union generated significant anxiety (2, 3). This anxiety was present despite Turkey's willingness to meet the same conditions of membership as all other prospective members and despite the fundamentalist secularism practised by the Kemalist Turkish state. Thus, as Casanova articulates, the concern over the presence of Islamic practices in the public sphere cannot simply be the result of their religious nature but must also be the result of the status of Islam itself "as the other of European secularity" (7).

In order to understand the particular anxieties provoked by the public appearance of the Muslim subject, it is necessary to briefly address the relationship between what Isin (2002b) refers to as the two fundamental and interrelated perspectives within the dominant Western conception of the citizen: synoecism and orientalism. Synoecism, which sees "the polity as embodying spatial and political unification" and "the citizen as a secular and universal being without tribal loyalties," has been discussed at length above. What is significant here is the manner in which orientalism, as a discourse that portrays citizenship as "a unique occidental invention that oriental cultures lacked and the citizen as a virtuous and rational being without kinship ties," enables the recent emergence of the Muslim subject as an object of concern in liberal democracies (117).

Within Orientalist discourses of citizenship, epitomized by the writings of Max Weber, the development and presence of citizenship in the Occident is juxtaposed with its absence in the Orient. According to Weber, the failure of citizenship to develop in the Orient can be attributed to a common feature of Oriental societies, namely the absence of autonomous cities (Weber 1927, 318). In the Occident, the development of the autonomous city can be traced back to the establishment of juristic forms of fraternity, forged in antiquity (synoecism) and the communes of the Middle Ages in response to struggles and conflicts with external enemies. In both instances, leaders within the city grouped a selected portion of the population together under an oath obliging them to administer and protect the city (319). The bonds formed by this group were said to take the form of a rational recognition of common interest. Thus, for Weber, the polis is not merely the consequence of "common settlement in proximity" but is also "always the product of such a confraternity or synoecism ... a definite oath of brotherhood which signified that a common ritualistic meal is established and a ritualistic union formed and that only those had a part in this ritualistic group" (320).

In the Orient, in contrast, the development of such confraternity did not emerge for two main reasons. First, the Oriental city was unable to attain from the king the autonomy necessary to forge a brotherhood in arms. The army that formed in these societies was not the army of the city but the army of the king (Weber 1927, 320–21). Owing to "the water problem" and the subsequent need for large-scale irrigation projects, a large centralized bureaucracy developed in the Orient. Consequently, cities were reliant on the king and the bureaucracy for their survival (321–22). Thus the development of a polis was stifled.

A second factor inhibiting the development of a common identity based on bonds other than kinship was the persistence of magic in Oriental religions. As Weber (1927) argues, the presence of religiously mandated barriers between groups, such as castes within Hinduism, did not permit the formation of rational communities based on common interest. In the Occident, in contrast, "the magical barriers between clans, tribes, and peoples, which were still known in the ancient *polis* to a considerable degree, were ... set aside" (322–23). According to Weber, the dissolution of magical bonds in the Occidental city can be attributed largely to certain elements of Christian theology. He points specifically to the Pentecostal miracle, in which Jesus' disciples were divinely bestowed with multilingual abilities and an evangelical mission, one that was furthered by Paul's espousal of the need for "fellowship with the uncircumcised" (322). The Pentecostal miracle articulated a notion of community based on a commonality of faith rather than blood. In the words of Turner (2002, 266), "the Church was a non-coercive community or a corporation, not of kinship, but of common ends." As such, it undermined and permitted a transcendence of kinship associations.

Weber further argued that the institutional form of Christianity acted as a check on the centralized power of the king. The church, as an independent hierarchical power, developed a systematic theology and practices, as well as a substantial bureaucracy assigned to the task of administration and training. Due to its size and scope, it could not "be easily uprooted and act[ed] as a check on political power" (Turner 2002, 262). Both through its transcendence of magical kinship bonds and through its role as a check on centralized political power, Christianity permitted the development of civic bonds within the medieval Occidental city that, in its absence, were not possible in Oriental societies. Thus, within the dominant Western conception of citizenship, the Orient, which has come increasingly to be associated with Islam (Said 1978), appears as the other of citizenship.

It is these intertwining discourses of orientalism and a synoecism, based on the concept of the abstract human, that have permitted the emergence in recent years of the presence of the Muslim subject in public space as a focus of concern for the nation. The Muslim is positioned within debates about national identity, security, and social integration as one who is unable to comport him or herself in the manner necessary to be the secular subject proper to the public, political sphere. Inherently unable to overcome the divided loyalties of religion and citizenship, Muslims become perceived as a threat to social cohesion and to the fabric of the secular democratic nation-state. Confined to what Samuel Huntington (1993, 35) refers to as their "bloody boundaries," these troubling features of Islamic society and the Islamic subject need not be of immediate concern to liberal governance. However, as writers such as Bhabha (1990b) and Seyla Benhabib (2002) have noted, in the era of globalization, migration has meant that the exoticized other is no longer necessarily distant. In the "diaspora space" (Brah 1996, 16), the racialized, exoticized, primitivized, and stigmatized other exists side by side with the dominant group and becomes the target of various techniques of alterity: alienation, agonism, and/or selective affinity.

By merely engaging in the logics of inclusion and exclusion, and thus attempting to expand the population of citizens, we overlook the manner in which the public sphere is always a site of power. In doing so, we fail to acknowledge the manner in which the naturalization of equating the space and subject proper to the political with the secular limits the possibilities of citizenship, community, and belonging. Merely shifting or expanding the boundaries of public space, without addressing the unquestioned assumptions present in its very constitution, fails to provide a means to challenge these limitations and develop alternative modes of belonging.

5 Migration and the Crisis of Identity: From the Hérouxville Code to the Charter of Québécois Values

In the years following the controversy over the presence of the Islamic headscarf in Québec schools, several other incidents maintained the public presence of religion as a locus of debate and concern in Québec. The question of national identity and the place of migrants within the national imaginary had been a topic of utmost importance since the beginning of attempts to institutionalize a civic conception of the Québec nation in the early 1990s, particularly in the wake of the failed independence referendum of 1995, but within the reactions to a series of incidents in 2006 and 2007 (see Heinrich and Dufour 2008, Appendix), migration, pluralism, and the accommodation of religious and cultural practices in the Québec public sphere came to be increasingly framed in terms of a threat to québécois identity.

In the first of these incidents, on March 2, 2006, the Supreme Court of Canada upheld a 2002 decision of the Québec Superior Court that permitted Sikh students to wear a ceremonial dagger, or kirpan, to school. Ninety-four percent of French-speaking residents of Québec opposed the 2002 decision (Fine 2013). When he was eleven years old, the student at the centre of this incident, Gurbaj Singh Multani, was kept out of his Laval school for the five months that the decision was before Québec's courts. When Multani returned to school, he was greeted by 300 adults shouting at him to "Go home, Paki" (Fine 2013). In rendering its decision, the Supreme Court asserted that, in order not to infringe on freedom of religion, the kirpan must be permitted in schools so long as it was sown into a student's clothing.

One week later, a separate controversy concerning Sikh religious clothing emerged in Québec. This incident related to a report in *La Presse* (Perreault 2006) that revealed that the Maritime Employers Association of Québec was planning to accommodate Sikh truck drivers who, unless they removed their turbans, were unable to wear the safety helmets required when the trucks were being unloaded. The revelation that the association had offered to allow Sikh truck drivers to remain in their trucks during the unloading process provoked cries that this amounted to unfair, differential treatment of port workers. Commentators ridiculed the arrangement, stating that other drivers may claim that their religions do not require them to keep their tires properly inflated, follow speed limits, or abide by other legal requirements.

On May 4, 2006, news of an incident involving seven-year-old Luc Cagadoc began to spread throughout the Montréal media. Eventually gaining international attention, reports recounted how Cagadoc, a student born in the Philippines, had been repeatedly reprimanded by a teacher at Lalande High School in Roxboro for using a fork to push his food onto a spoon in the traditional Filipino style. He was called a "pig," and his manner of eating was labelled "disgusting." When his mother complained to the school's principal, Normand Bergeron, she was told, "Madame, you are in Canada. Here in Canada you should eat the way Canadians eat." If Luc continued to "eat like a pig," he would have to be separated from the other students (CTV 2006).

Three months later, the Commission des droits de la personne (CDP) announced a ruling in favour of the École de technologie supérieure (ÉTS) in relation to a complaint launched by a group of more than a hundred Muslim students. Two years earlier, students had been denied their request to rent space within the school to use as a Muslim prayer room. Instead of a dedicated prayer space, the school suggested that students could pray in empty classrooms. A second Montréal postsecondary institution, École polytechnique, followed suit, stating that "we are a secular institution and our mission doesn't include religion. It's education and research" (CBC 2004). The CDP ruled that the position of the ÉTS was reasonable.

Within three months, two additional incidents had gained significant attention, this time involving members of Montréal's Hassidic Jewish community. In the first incident, at the request of members of the community, the Parc Avenue YMCA agreed to obscure its windows with frosted glass so that Hassidic men in the neighbourhood would not be faced with the sight of women exercising. The second incident concerned the revelation of contents of a Police Service of Montréal brochure recommending that female officers not intervene in incidents involving male members of the Hassidic community in order to respect Hassidic regulations regarding gender roles and interactions.

On November 16, 2006, *Le Journal de Montréal* published a story stating that the Centre local de services communautaires (CLSC) of Parc-Extension in Montréal had stopped allowing male employees to assist with prenatal courses. This measure had apparently been taken in order to accommodate female Muslims, Hindus, and Sikhs, who it was thought would feel uncomfortable in the presence of male employees.

Two months later, a poll by Léger Marketing, commissioned by *Le Journal de Montréal,* the television station TVA, and the radio station 98.5 FM, revealed that 59 percent of Québécois saw themselves as racist.

The Hérouxville Code

In January 2007, the small town of Hérouxville (pop. 1,300), located in the rural Mauricie region, introduced a ten-page Code of Life. Despite the town being nearly universally white, francophone, and nominally Catholic, without any Muslim residents (Stasiulis 2013, 184) and little prospect of immigration, the code seemed to be addressed to immigrant practitioners of minority religions, particularly Muslims. The Hérouxville Code, like similar codes introduced in several other towns in Québec, forbade covering one's face in public, the accommodation of prayer and carrying weapons in schools, and practices such as stoning, burning people alive, dousing them with acid, female genital mutilation, and other barbaric and ostensibly Islamic acts against women (for the full text, see Drouin 2017).

The response to the Hérouxville Code was both heated and immediate. It nearly monopolized headlines and opinion columns for several months, serving as a focal point for the growing debates concerning the accommodation of cultural and religious practices. Whereas Hérouxville had been mentioned in only ten stories in the *Montréal Gazette* in the two decades prior to the introduction of the code, it was the focus of more than 150 articles in 2007 (Hamilton 2007).

Within media and academic circles, the Hérouxville Code and the support it received were explained to be less the result of hostility toward immigrants and more the result of "a small town expression of revolt against the big city of Montréal, its lifestyle and passive acceptance of cultural diversity" (Stasiulis 2013, 187 n7). Rather than being seen as representative of a general xenophobia at play in Québec nationalism, the code and the negative reaction to the other controversies surrounding accommodation listed above were portrayed as revelatory of a split between urban and rural conceptions of the nature of Québec's national identity. Some academics, including Tim Nieguth and Aurélie Lacassagne (2009) and Guy Chiasson and Junichiro Koji (2011), argued that the code was a manifestation of the emergence of two Québecs with conflicting conceptions of the nation.[1] The first Québec, made up of the ethnically, linguistically, and religiously pluralist urban centres, which received approximately 87 percent of international immigrants, viewed québécois identity as plural and cosmopolitan (155). The second Québec, consisting of near-homogeneous rural and small urban communities, was said to hold protectionist and assimilationist notions of the nation. As the prominent journalist Alain Dubuc suggested, "Hérouxville was angered by the tolerance of Montrealers, by their passivity towards the changes brought about by immigration, by their multi-ethnic culture, their rejection of religion, their 'gay village' and arrogant elites. What happened in Hérouxville is the ultimate expression of the fracture between the metropolis and the regions" (Stasiulis 2013, 187 n7).

---

1 Others, particularly those within Montréal's artistic community and, to some degree, academics such as Maclure (2003), have posed this bifurcation of identity as one of a generational divide, with the younger generation of Québécois more open to difference than the older generation, for whom identity is something that needs to be protected.

The view of opposing urban and rural national imaginaries is supported by studies examining the province's education system. As McAndrew (2010) and Marilyn Steinbach (2010) have observed, regions of Québec that receive few immigrant students are rarely exposed to cultural difference and pluralism in their lessons, even when mandated by the province's intercultural curricula. Thus, according to this view of two coexisting Québecs, in the regions of the province where residents are rarely exposed to ethnic, cultural, linguistic, and religious difference in their day-to-day experiences, these differences are perceived as distant and alien to proper québécois culture. In contrast, for residents of urban centres, who encounter these differences on a daily basis and have notions of pluralism reinforced through intercultural education, pluralism appears as part of what it means to be québécois.

Others, such as Stasiulis (2013, 188), have argued that the rise of debates in Québec concerning pluralism and the nature of national identity in Québec is the product of "a host of processes ... [that] have combined to jeopardize more inclusive forms of citizenship." Stasiulis contends that in response to these processes – including neoliberal globalization, the slowing of economic growth in central Canada, a decline in Canadian governmental discourses that link citizenship to social provisions, the global war on terror, Islamophobia, and securitization of immigration and citizenship – the Québec state has introduced a "refurbished" (6) version of earlier discourses of what Ghassan Hage (2000, 9–11) has labelled a "worrier nation." In this discourse, rather than the external anglophone threat to the nation of earlier nationalism, the "current object of worry is internal to the nation – its growing immigrant population from perceived nonliberal cultures" (Stasiulis 2013, 188).

Stasiulis asserts that since the 1960s Québec nationalism has involved a struggle to modernize yet retain core cultural values in order to forge what McAndrew (2010, 290) paradoxically labels "a traditional but modern francophone culture." The traditional aspect of this identity is grounded in an "atavistic and congenital sentiment of inferiority ... felt by every new generation of Quebecer[s]" (Maclure 2004, 38). As a result, it involves the adoption and generational transmission of a "victim status," a sense of being a member of an oppressed minority that, since at least the English Conquest, has been under threat of assimilation (Stasiulis 2013, 191). Through family, school, and popular culture, this self-identity is passed onto younger generations of white French Canadians, who have never had direct experience of "second-class citizenship" within Québec (McAndrew 2002a). Moreover, such a historical memory poses a unitary – white and francophone – national subject, in turn rendering problematic the possibility of an alternative form of community inclusive of those who do not bear such markers of identity (Beauchemin 2004; Maclure 2004, Stasiulis 2013, 192).

According to Stasiulis (2013, 192), the modern aspect of Québec national identity concerns its status as a society that underwent "late" and "rapid" modernization and secularization during the Quiet Revolution. Owing to the social and economic measures instituted during the Quiet Revolution, Québec was viewed as relatively socially and culturally progressive in contrast to the rest of Canada until the last decade of the twentieth century. In comparison to the other provinces, Québec offered, and to many extents still offers, greater social welfare benefits as well as more rights for women, organized labour, and sexual minorities. These rights and benefits are seen as the hard-won product of historical struggles against conservative elites (both English and French) and the dominance of the Catholic Church.

Within contemporary nationalist discourse, these recently emergent rights and values have been repositioned as traditional québécois values. For example, as Stasiulis (2013, 192) argues, the popular support in Québec for measures banning the niqab, or veil, depicted as a mark of Islamic subordination of women, is "triggered by a specific historical narrative of casting off the Roman Catholic patriarchal subordination of women in Quebec." Rather than portraying this aspect of Catholicism as a traditional value against which modern values can be defined, the more recent advocacy represents women's rights as an aspect of a traditionally egalitarian québécois culture to which migrants must conform (10).

The Hérouxville Code and other similar documents developed in Québec municipalities provide a list of such properly québécois values, against which the culture of migrants are implicitly positioned. The Hérouxville Code is divided into eleven sections, each related to a particular aspect of society. The first, "Regarding Women," which articulates that "we consider that men and women have the same value," lists actions and activities in which women are permitted to engage in Québec, such as voting, expressing themselves, driving, working, attending school, dancing, owning property, and dressing in a manner of their own choice.

It also lists prohibited actions, such as stoning women in public, burning them alive or with acid, female circumcision, and slavery. Similarly, the second section, "Regarding Children," states that "our children are required to attend schools recognized by the Québec Ministry of Education to assure their social development and aid in their integration into our society" (Drouin 2017, 7). It also declares that all forms of violence against children are prohibited.

As many commentators have noted, although some elements of these codes, such as the Hérouxville Code's bizarre inclusion of a description of the meaning of Christmas trees in Québec, serve the purpose of describing what the authors deem to be québécois culture, most of the rights and possible violations of rights that appear in these documents are already clearly dealt with in the human rights and criminal codes of Canada and Québec. As a result, the aim of the various codes of conduct is not simply to describe the laws and values to which citizens of Québec must adhere but also to reposition these laws and values as particular to Québec national identity. As Stasiulis (2013, 201) asserts in regard to the place of the figure of the child within such codes, "defining the value given to children as a national or civilizational rather than universal value ... suggests that some cultures are wittingly or unwittingly barbaric or cruel to children." Stasiulis's point regarding children can equally be applied to the place of women and sexual minorities in these documents.

In this sense, within the various codes of conduct, migrants or cultural minorities are portrayed as figures whose cultures, practices, and mentalities threaten progressive québécois society. However, they also bolster Québec national identity through their position of otherness. The listing of properly québécois values, portrayed as national and thus particular rather than universal, reasserts difference and, therefore, the boundaries of belonging and identity. However, unlike past boundary constructions, the articulation of difference in the Hérouxville Code does not refer to groups historically positioned as outside the nation but to those that, within a civic conception of the nation, are or could become officially recognized as québécois. Thus, beyond an urban-rural or generational divide concerning the nature of being québécois, what is revealed by the codes of the late 2000s is a dissonance between a legalistic, formal conception of national identity and one grounded in what are constructed as national values.

As mentioned in the previous chapter, attempts to institutionalize a civic national identity in Québec coincided with economic and social reforms responding to the growing hegemony of neoliberal globalization. The previous chapter addressed the manner in which the atomization and social dissolution resulting from neoliberal policy created a problem for the nation in the form of challenges to social integration. However, by undermining the state's capacity to provide social welfare benefits, and therefore social citizenship, neoliberal globalization also threatened many of the economic and social characteristics of what Stasiulis (2013) deems the modern aspect of Québec national identity. Compelled by the logic of austerity and international competitiveness, the retrenchment of the welfare state and its replacement by a neoliberal and later social investment model of governance required a reduction, if not reversal, of many of the progressive social and economic policies seen as central to the identity of Québec.

For some in Québec, such retrenchment was a betrayal of the nation. Many continue to identify with progressive state welfare provisions, such as universal healthcare, education, and childcare, as important markers of "being québécois." Like other modern (or newly traditional) characteristics of national identity, egalitarian economic policies resonate strongly with the people of Québec as the product of historical struggles. Events such as the 1949 asbestos strike and the 1959 Radio-Canada strike, during which intellectuals and workers joined together in struggles that combined industrial grievances with nationalist goals and visions, are seen by many observers as significant heroic moments in the history of the nation.

Such feelings were expressed clearly during the 2012 student strikes in Québec, known as the Maple Spring. During the strikes, launched to protest increased tuition fees and a perceived decline in the quality of education, strikers and their supporters often invoked nationalist themes and the promises of the Quiet Revolution. One of the major initiatives of the Quiet Revolution had been the creation of a publicly funded system of postsecondary education, as well as the promise that education would be made available to all, regardless of income. Education was declared a tool to modernize Québec society and aid in undoing the second-class citizenship of French Canadians. Transformations within the postsecondary education system, particularly tuition increases, were therefore perceived by students and many nationalists as a betrayal of earlier struggles and the promises of the Quiet Revolution.

Concurrently, austerity and market and labour reforms increasingly began to appear in mainstream economic and political discourse as both necessary and important markers of modernization in opposition to the perceived "backwardness" of state interventionism. As in many other states, such conceptions of modernization became, to different degrees, key elements of both state policy and the platforms of most political parties, including the once, at least nominally, social democratic Parti Québécois (PQ). However, the emergence of a new definition of modernization as marketization and its incorporation within the conception of national identity has remained incomplete.

Thus neoliberal globalization posed a basic problem for national identity in Québec. The modern aspect, in the form of economic and social provisions, became more difficult to maintain, and thus a key element of differentiation was destabilized. Consequently, the universalizing forces of neoliberalism made it increasingly difficult to distinguish Québec from the rest of Canada in terms of social and economic policy. At the same time, an entrepreneurial or capitalist identity was unable to replace state intervention as a marker of modernization or progressiveness. As a result, it was unable to serve as an adequate marker of difference. A vision of progressiveness remained as a key element of identity but one that seemed increasingly precarious.

The Hérouxville Code and the debates surrounding it must therefore be seen in the context of the destabilization of traditional markers of national identity owing to the increasing hegemony of neoliberalism and a reconceptualization of the nature of "traditional" québécois values. First, neoliberal globalization restricted, or at least was widely accepted within political circles to have restricted, the capacity of the Québec state to continue to provide or extend traditional progressive socio-economic programs. Moreover, the force of neoliberalism made it appear that neoliberal or social investment models were the only options available within a competitive global economy. Thus socio-economic policies no longer appeared as an option through which Québec could assert its difference. Moreover, as rationalization and marketization increasingly became the prevailing language of the economic and political elite, the vision of a modern Québec increasingly became tied to the retrenchment of the welfare state. The only viable vision of a modern state was that of a state that operated through individualism, entrepreneurialism, and the activation and responsibilization of its citizens. As a result, not only was the welfare state scaled back, but the connection between its progressive socio-economic values and Québec identity also became loosened.

Second, the "modern" social values of the Quiet Revolution – secularism, the equality of women, the rights of sexual minorities, and democracy – were discursively transformed into "traditional" québécois values. In turn, their place in the Québec national imaginary became solidified. Rather than being seen as aspects of a particular national project, when placed in opposition to the values of traditional nationalism, they became an unquestioned part of what it meant to be québécois. In this way, although socio-economic policies became increasingly divorced from the definition of québécois nationalism, rights became increasingly central. It should not be surprising, therefore, that in this context questions of rights, such as the debates concerning reasonable accommodation, became not only increasingly contentious but also tied to concerns over national identity.

Immigration and the Crisis of National Identity

Within this context of the weakening boundaries of differentiation and the increasing centrality of rights to conceptions of national identity, migration became an increasingly important issue in Québec. Writing about the place of immigrants within the American national imaginary, Ali Behdad (1997, 175) argues that, always being "ambivalent," they occupy a place of undecidability. Although Americans consider themselves a nation of immigrants, they also identify themselves against "immigrants as we try to control them" (Honig 2001, 77). As Bonnie Honig argues, "American exceptionalists, from Tocqueville to Hartz to Walzer, treat immigrants as the agents of founding and renewal for a regime in which membership is supposed to be uniquely consent based, individualist, rational, and voluntarist rather than inherited and organic" (73–74) . Thus, although Americans identify with immigrants as agents of national renewal, they are also seen as a threat to the nation. For

Behdad (1997, 166–67), the American ambivalence toward immigrants is due to "contradictory stereotypes: on the one hand, the immigrant is weak and wretched, and, on the other, powerful and dangerous; on the one hand an opportunist who steals our jobs, and, on the other, a lazy parasite who abuses our social welfare funds." As a result, the ambivalence of the American nation toward immigrants "is marked by both knowledge and disavowal, control and defence, exclusion and amnesty, acceptance and rejection" (166).

In response, Honig (2001, 77) argues that Behdad's account fails to include a further stereotype of the immigrant, one that most clearly explains the ambivalence of the host nation to the immigrant, namely "the supercitizen immigrant." As an object of identification, this figure is "the screen onto which we project our idealized selves." In opposition to anti-immigrant sentiment, activists and political theorists often emphasize the gifts that the immigrant offers to the host nation: "He works harder than we do, he values his family and community more actively than we do, and he also fulfills our liberal fantasy of membership by way of consent" (78).

Honig (2001) warns against such an approach, suggesting that there are "intimate connections" between the xenophilia of this discourse and the xenophobia against which it is opposed. As a result, she asks whether in "deploying the supercitizen immigrant on behalf of a national ideal ... these xenophiles feed the fire they mean to fight" (78). In answering this question, Honig argues that the myth of the supercitizen immigrant "generates a sense of quite *anxious* dependence upon the kindness of strangers," an anxiety that can quite easily transform xenophilia into xenophobia (76).

In contrast to other social and political theorists, Honig (2001) does not consider the alteration between xenophilia and xenophobia to result from shifts in power between nativists and inclusionists or from changes in the labour market; rather, she identifies "a deeper logic at work," namely that "the foreigner who shores up and reinvigorates the regime also unsettles it at the same time." It is the very set of qualities that allows the immigrant to be portrayed as an agent of national renewal that, at the same time, "animates a suspicion of immigrant foreignness": "'Their' admirable hard work and boundless acquisition puts 'us' out of jobs. 'Their' good, reinvigorative communities also look like fragmentary ethnic enclaves. 'Their' traditional family values threaten to overturn our still new and fragile gains in gender equality. 'Their' voluntarist embrace of America ... works to reaffirm but also endangers 'our' way of life" (76).

Although the foundational myths of Québec nationalism are, of course, different from those of the United States, the manner in which the immigrant figures within Québec's nationalist imaginaries, particularly its civic variant, is similar in many ways to that described by Honig. Given the low birth rate in Québec and its shrinking population in relation to the rest of Canada, immigration has become a vital tool for the reproduction of the nation. Not only do immigrants appear necessary to the economic well-being of Québec, but they are also seen as necessary to maintaining Québec's demographic importance within the Canadian federation and, as mentioned in the previous chapter, to protecting the place of the French language in Québec's public sphere, which is made possible through the preferential selection of francophone immigrants.

At the same time, however, arguments in favour of the economic benefit of immigration are always open to critique on the basis of the social and economic cost of settlement and integration. Guy Chiasson and Junichiro Koji (2011, 148), for example, assert that the crisis in national identity, exemplified by the Hérouxville Code, can at least partially be seen as a product of the Québec government's attempts to use immigration as a means to increase regional economic development and to decrease the burden of settlement on Montréal by promoting migrant settlement outside of Montréal. Moreover, migration has created conceptual and practical problems for national identity. Over the past two decades, although the welcoming of migrants has undermined the perception of Québec as an insular society, the seemingly conservative culture of migrants has increasingly been portrayed as a threat to the nation given that rights and equality are now defined as traditional aspects of québécois national identity. Thus, even as migrants are deployed as a symbol of the openness, pluralism, and modernity of Québec, their cultures, particularly their religiosity (itself legally protected), are also depicted as a threat to openness and modernity. Migrants are, sometime by the same figures, both celebrated for their contribution to a vibrant, pluralist Québec and deemed a threat owing to their ostensibly regressive values or lack of loyalty to the nation.

In the wake of the narrow defeat of the 1995 referendum[1] on Québec's independence from Canada, the tenuous position of migrants within the national imaginary was made evident. The infamous remarks of Jacques Parizeau, then the premier of Québec, depicted a clear distinction between French Canadians and "ethnics" in terms of membership in the Québec nation, and portrayed non-French Canadians as a threat to the nation's ability to fulfil its dream of, and right to, sovereignty. Speaking to independence supporters in the immediate aftermath of the referendum defeat, and using "nous" (us) to refer solely to the French Canadian population of Québec, Parizeau stated, "If you allow me, we'll stop talking about Québec's francophones. We'll talk about us: at 60 percent, we voted for [independence] ... It's true we have been defeated, but by what basically? By money and the ethnic votes, essentially" (Bilge 2013, 9). Shortly afterward, Parizeau fulfilled a pre-referendum promise to resign if the referendum was defeated. He was replaced as premier by Lucien Bouchard.

Five years later, Bouchard himself resigned in the wake of another scandal that revealed the difficulty of the sovereigntist movement's attempt to move away from ethno-nationalism. On December 13, 2000, responding to the request of B'nai B'rith and other representatives of Québec's Jewish community for the removal of the name of Lionel Groulx from a metro station in Montréal due to his anti-Semitism, prominent PQ supporter Yves Michaud stated that "there is an ethnic vote against the sovereignty of the people of Québec," who "probably [wish to] replace it by the Mordecai Richler station, the Boulevard René Lévesque by, no doubt, Boulevard Ariel Sharon, the Place Jacques-Cartier by the Place Galganov ... There is an ethnic vote against the sovereignty of the people of Québec" ("Ce qu'Yves Michaud" 2000).

The leader of the opposition Québec Liberal Party, Jean Charest, immediately responded to Michaud's comments with a motion in the National Assembly condemning references to "an ethnic vote against the sovereignty of the people." The motion was unanimously adopted,

1 The referendum question was "Do you agree that Quebec should become sovereign, after having made a formal offer to Canada for a new economic and political partnership, within the scope of the bill respecting the future of Quebec and of the agreement signed on June 12, 1995?" The voter turnout was 93.52 percent (4,757,509 voters), with 50.58 percent (2,362,648 voters) choosing "No" and 49.42 percent (2,308,360 voters) choosing "Yes."

and Premier Bouchard publicly dissociated himself from Michaud's remarks: "I do not hesitate to state, in the name of my party, in the name of the government ... of all Québécois and Québécoises, that we reject [Michaud's] statement" (Assemblée nationale du Québec 2000a). On December 19 an open letter, signed by Parizeau, Mathieu Bock-Côté, and dozens of other prominent sovereigntists, political associations, and citizens, was published in Québec newspapers. The letter stated that the National Assembly, in "an act without true precedence in the parliamentary history of Québec (or apparently most of the parliaments of Western democratic states) ... condemned a private citizen and violated his right to free expression." Moreover, it asserted that Michaud merely "regretted the challenge of the integration of certain groups of immigrants and recalled the character of the 1995 referendum vote, when there were many voting offices where 'yes' votes were nonexistent ... we should not deny the painful reality of facts" (Assemblée nationale du Québec 2000b).

A few weeks later, a second open letter, signed by fifteen sovereigntists under the age of thirty-five, offered both support to the National Assembly's condemnation of Michaud's comments and an alternative conception of the québécois nation. The letter stated that Michaud's remarks "stand opposite to the Québec in which we want to live, based on respect, inclusion and openness ... [Separatists] must put aside, once and for all, this attitude of victimization and chase away intolerance, now embodied by French Canadian nationalists, toward other Quebecers" (Brooke 2001).

Three weeks after the publication of the first open letter, Bouchard resigned as premier and retired from politics. Although he stated the reason for his retirement as his failure to reignite the sovereigntist project, most commentators agree that the true reason was the persistence of xenophobia and ethno-nationalism within the sovereigntist movement. The persistence of comments such as those of Parizeau in the aftermath of the 1995 referendum and those of the poet Raymond Levesque, who in 2000 stated that independence referendums were "family disputes" that immigrants should stay out of (Brooke 2001), demonstrated that at least among the older generation of sovereigntists, there was a resistance to the civic, pluralist nation to which Bouchard aspired. When asked why Bouchard was resigning, Deputy Premier Bernard Landry cited

Bouchard's belief that "the Parti Québécois is not an ethnically based party" (Brooke 2001).

Consistent with Honig's (2001) analysis of the place of the foreigner in America, an account of the negative portrayals of immigrants and other foreign minorities both in the Hérouxville Code and in the xenophobic statements above should not explain them simply in terms of a rise in xenophobic factions and ideology; rather, they point to a deeper logic of relations between host and immigrant within the context of the nation-state.

Despite liberal dreams of unconditional refuge and a universal cosmopolitan community, hospitality is always conditional, a conditionality that is further complicated, both conceptually and affectively, when it concerns the welcoming of outsiders into a national community. As Honig (2001, 76) argues, the plight of immigrants is that, because they are judged on the basis of their "contribution to the restoration of the nation rather than ... to the nation's transformation and attenuation, nationalist xenophilia tends to feed and (re)produce nationalist xenophobia as its partner."

In xenophobic and xenophilic statements, the immigrant appears as a figure who either threatens or offers to renew a particular vision of the nation. In this sense, immigrants or ethnic outsiders appear for some as those whose difference undermines the nation's aspirations of sovereignty and "traditional" culture and for others as those whose difference is representative of, and makes possible, the pluralistic "Québec in which we want to live" (Brooke 2001). For ethno-nationalists, in failing to support Québec's independence from Canada, immigrants were seen as taking from the nation, despite being sought after, at least partially, to boost the francophone population and French as the language of the Québec public sphere. Conversely, for civic nationalists, the presence of immigrants and cultural minorities allows for the realization of their vision of a modern, open, pluralist Québec. However, as the debates about reasonable accommodation make evident, when the cultures of these groups are seen to disrupt this vision of society, the xenophilic image of immigrants and minority groups can easily be transformed into one of xenophobia. Thus immigrants and minority groups perpetually hold a place of suspicion within the national imaginary as givers who may become takers.

The Bouchard-Taylor Commission

Political discussion in Québec in early 2007 was also dominated by debates concerning the Hérouxville Code and reasonable accommodation. Premier Jean Charest tried to downplay the significance of the code, labelling it "extreme" and an "isolated case" (Stasiulis 2013, 184). In contrast, the code was lauded by former PQ premier Landry and by Mario Dumont, the leader of the populist Action démocratique du Québec (ADQ), with the latter calling the code "a heartfelt cry" (Hamilton 2007).

On February 8, faced with defections from his party and the ADQ's use of the reasonable accommodation controversy to garner increasing support, Charest announced that a commission would be formed to clarify the notion of reasonable accommodation. The commission, officially named the Consultation Committee on Accommodation Practices Related to Cultural Practices, was to be co-chaired by two prominent academics, Gérard Bouchard and Charles Taylor. The mandate of the commission, which became popularly known as the Bouchard-Taylor Commission, was to: "*a)* take stock of accommodation practices in Québec; *b)* analyze the attendant issues bearing in mind the experience of other societies; *c)* conduct an extensive consultation on this topic; and *d)* formulate recommendations to the government to ensure that accommodation practices conform to Québec's values as a pluralistic, democratic, egalitarian society" (Bouchard and Taylor 2008a, 17). Dumont and the ADQ immediately opposed the commission, describing accommodations as "special privileges" and positioning themselves "as opponents of concessions and defenders of the historic identity of French Québec" (Anctil 2011, 6).

Leading up to, and concurrent with, the start of the commission's public forums on September 10, the issue of reasonable accommodation, aided by a number of additional controversies,[1] remained a central feature of political, media, and popular discussions. Reflecting the importance of the issue, the commission, with a budget of $5 million, received

1 These controversies included Muslim girls who wore the hijab not being allowed to play in sporting events; accommodations for a group of Muslims visiting a *cabane à sucre;* a directive from Québec's director-general of elections banning women in niqabs from voting; publicity around the amount of kosher products on supermarket shelves; a demand by the Conseil du statut de la femme that equality of the sexes be given primacy over freedom of religion in the Québec Charter of Human Rights and Freedoms; and the decision of the Québec government to prohibit bureaucrats from wearing ostentatious religious symbols.

more than nine hundred briefs. Bouchard and Taylor travelled around the province, holding three months of public, televised consultations in all regions of Québec, including remote areas of the province where "immigration was not a current issue and would probably not be in the foreseeable future" (Anctil 2011, 6). Throughout the course of the commission, Bouchard and Taylor attempted to minimize the negative aspects of the discourse surrounding the issues of diversity and reasonable accommodation. They repeatedly accused the media of sensationalism and of creating the perception of a crisis. However, as Jeff Heinrich and Valérie Dufour (2008, 10) argue, the media "did not invent anything"; rather, they simply "preached to their parish."

More than 3,500 people attended these forums, invited by the commission to make themselves heard on the subject of "the nature and source of the conflict that is dividing Québec society in order to imagine the means of reconciliation" (Bouchard and Taylor 2007, vi). Most of the speakers came prepared with statements from which they read, but spontaneous interventions and dialogue with the commissioners were encouraged, although citizens were provided only two minutes each to speak (Heinrich and Dufour 2008, 9). Many of the participants' statements and many of the interactions between the commissioners and citizens fed into an atmosphere of what Heinrich and Dufour (2008) label a "Circus quebecus" – complete with, among other characters, Bouchard and Taylor as the masters of ceremony, members of the media as illusionists of disinformation, and knife throwers who state, "I am not racist, but"; however, the statements made by both citizens and the commissioners offer an important insight into the questions of identity at play in the debate concerning reasonable accommodation.

At the outset of the commission, Bouchard and Taylor (2007, v) made clear that its focus would not be legal issues of accommodation but rather "a more basic problem concerning the sociocultural integration model that has prevailed in Québec since the 1970s ... and the theme of Québec identity." In doing so, they framed the accommodation debate as merely a symptom of a deeper questioning of identity.

In the consultation document that launched the commission, *Accommodation and Differences: Seeking Common Ground: Quebecers Speak Out* (2007), Bouchard and Taylor "told Quebecers who they are ... by naming or interpellating the different constituencies that make up the collectivity," and despite asking the people of Québec "to imagine a means of reconciliation," they provided them with a ready-made solution (Toledo Freiwald 2011, 73). Speakers were asked to identify themselves within the categories that Bouchard and Taylor had introduced as encompassing all who resided in Québec: (1) those belonging to a nation or a people, limited to "Quebecers of French Canadian origin ... a founding people established for four centuries in this territory," and "aboriginal peoples"; (2) the "English-speaking minority;" and (3) "ethnic minorities" or "cultural communities" (Bouchard and Taylor 2007, 2–4, 14).

To contend with issues of integration and identity, the commissioners provided a list of five possible models – assimilation, the mixing of cultures, multi-ethnicity, the civic nation, and interculturalism – the latter of which they endorsed as the best option (Bouchard and Taylor 2007, 19).

From the start, this list ruled out some of the possible approaches that citizens wished to bring to the table. Moreover, it "not only set the stage but also the terms for the debate it invites," terms that Toledo Freiwald (2011, 73–74) deems "haunted by the spectre of the 'nation.'" In according "paramount importance to the issue of collective identity, understood as rooted in one's culture of origin," the commission restricted the collective imagining to solutions "premised on an acceptance of the hegemony of the majority group, in relation to whom all others are defined by the somewhat threatening demands they make to be accommodated, to be granted entry into the charmed circle of belonging" (70).

Given the parameters provided for the discussion, it should not be surprising that many of the briefs presented to the commission were framed in terms of ethnic identity and the primacy of the nation. Many of the contributors who defined themselves as ethnic Québécois, or Québécois *de souche*, spoke in a language of "us," a category exclusionary of nonethnic Québécois. Alain C. Paiement (2007, 1), a resident of Gatineau, for instance, testified: "You can call me a Québécois *de souche* ... My ancestors arrived during the early period of the French regime. At the Pointe-à-Caillière Museum, one can read, inscribed on a stone, that that was where, in 1658, Jacques Archambault would have dug ... the first well in Montréal. That Archambault is the ancestor of all the Archambaults. I am one of them." In his brief to the commission, Marcien Bisson (2007) of Sagüenay further articulated this importance accorded to blood descent in the determination of identity: "I belong to the founding people of this country. About 800 ancestors on my father's side and as many on my mother's. Eleven generations of Bisson, Tardiff, Pinard, Bourassa, Fréchette."

As Toledo Freiwald (2011) notes, within many of the briefs presented to the commission, "the writer's desire to foreground a universalistic civic character to the Québécois collectivity comes up against a profound attachment to the particularist identity of a people and the nation." As she argues, although many statements expounded upon the importance of what speakers deemed definitive québécois values, "this set of civic values is ultimately an *added value,* added on to something expressed as more primary yet often left unspecified: the 'heritage' of Québec society, 'its culture ... its traditions'" (78). Describing this heritage, André Godin (2007, 4), a resident of Sherbrooke, testified that identity is formed, first, in the family through the transmission of "language, religion and social culture." However, "this heritage also consists of founding values we consider non-negotiable, such as equality among people regardless of race, religion, or ethnicity; democracy; and freedom of expression and religion" (8). The manner in which pluralistic values are sometimes viewed as a threat to the nation defined through descent or cultural heritage is perhaps best articulated in a statement made to the commission by journalist and future PQ leader Jean-François Lisée (2007, 3):

> We must start by restoring the majoritarian reference points. What are they? Democracy, gender equality, the charter of rights, freedom of religion? Fine, that's understood. We've just expressed the common denominator of all democratic societies. No. I speak of the québécois difference. In bold strokes: Québec exists because its majority has experienced a singular history, speaks French, and carries a religious tradition. To evacuate them, to devalue them, could lead only to losing one's self-esteem and, in the long run, hating the other.

The attachment to a particularist national identity in the face of demands to respect diversity and universalist values had left many feeling, as one speaker articulated, like "abused orphans ... uprooted from a land I always believed was mine and that my people are losing to a globalization of diversity" (Émery 2007, 4–5). Moreover, as Paiement (2007, 4) avowed, the confusion between the seemingly incompatible imperatives of integration into québécois society and maintenance of diversity at play in interculturalism had created "a recipe that guarantees paralysis, confusion, the rotting of the social climate, and terminal failure."

Rather than simply deeming this resistance to diversity a product of individual or societal xenophobia, we should see the statements as manifestations of the conflictual forces at play not only in Québec's model of interculturalism but also in the nation and identity generally. At the outset of the commission, Bouchard and Taylor (2007, 19) admitted that interculturalism "seeks to combine on an equal footing two elements that are *a priori* hard to reconcile, i.e., respect for diversity and the imperatives of collective integration." Yet, as Toledo Freiwald (2011, 73) recounts, imagining a reconciliation between liberalism and nationalism was the very task that the commissioners set for the people of Québec.

In their discussion of this challenge, and in supporting interculturalism as the best model to address it, Bouchard and Taylor "conflate two current but rather conflicting meanings of 'nation': 'nation' in the sense of a distinct people characterized by a common language and culture; and 'nation' in the inclusive sense of the citizenry of a country or a state (which might be multinational)." In referring to the relationship between the Aboriginal peoples and Québec, "nation" represents a community of common descent. In contrast, when referring only to Québec, "nation" is used to represent those residing in a given political territory, regardless of descent. As Toledo Freiwald argues, "such slippages allow the commissioners to avoid addressing the crucial question regarding the relation – in the Québec context – between 'nation' as it figures in statements that align Québec with other 'Western nations' that are similarly pluralistic (nation as a country/state), and 'nation' understood in the narrower sense of a distinct people" (Toledo Freiwald 2011, 75).

Not only does this approach paper over the differences between two distinct conceptions of nation, but it also obfuscates the inherent conflictual forces at play within the categories of identity and nation. As a result, interculturalism is not merely a matter of "imagining" a form of belonging in which ideologically opposed civic and ethnic conceptualizations of the nation can be reconciled, nor is the crisis of national identity merely due to a lack of imagination in the face of the changing demographic face of Québec and an inability to conceive of an effective mode of integration; rather, the ever-present instability of these categories, brought to light in the context of societal changes, is what disrupted the narrative of the nation that had once allowed this instability to be repressed.

As many scholars of nationalism have noted (e.g., Brown 1999; Yack 1996), a clear distinction between civic and ethnic nationalism does not hold. Not only do civic nationalisms rely on secularized or de-ethnicized myths, but their foundational values contain implicit and explicit cultural references. The limits of a purely civic conception of the Québec nation are made clear in the Bouchard-Taylor Commission's consultation document, where interculturalism is defined as a mechanism of integration through which minority groups can maintain aspects of their culture. However, these cultural elements must be adapted to the national culture, "borrow from its basic values and customs, adopt the French language, and share the national heritage and the Québec identity" (Bouchard and Taylor 2007, 21). In the model of interculturalism that Bouchard and Taylor offer, "the space that is Québec is not inhabited by different cultures but rather by a nation and its others" (Toledo Freiwald 2011, 76). As a consequence, although Bouchard and Taylor (2008b, 88) speak of the development of a "citizen culture" characterized by shared values such as gender equality that all "Québécois must recognize themselves in ... and achieve fulfilment through," the model "includes the very elements that would inhibit" this process because it "keeps circling back to the core tenets of a nationalist discourse" (Toledo Freiwald 2011, 77).

The commissioners contend that a successful model of integration is needed in order to "reconcile the imperatives of pluralism stemming from the growing diversification of our society and the necessary integration of a small nation that constitutes a cultural minority in North America" (Bouchard and Taylor 2008b, 93). Here, the addressee is clearly not all those residing in Québec but the Québécois *de souche,* who the authors view as needing to understand the necessity of integration. As in the case of the place of children within the various municipal codes of conduct described earlier in this chapter, the importance conferred on integration policies is not their role in aiding the well-being of migrants but rather their capacity to serve as an immunitary mechanism in the effort to protect the nation from a potential, yet necessary, threat.

The vision of "integration through pluralism" that Bouchard and Taylor (2008b, 94) endorse is meant to "promote an identity, culture, and memory without creating either exclusion or division." However, the identity, memory, and culture to which they refer are always predefined. As a result, "'the others' are consistently grouped together as the anonymous 'growing diversity' [to which the nation must respond], whereas the majority is awarded the identitarian badge of honour of recognition as a nation, further legitimated in its identitarian mission by being characterized as a vulnerable small minority nation 'mistreated by history'" (Toledo Freiwald 2011, 76–77).

Cultural difference, then, is permitted so long as it corresponds to and does not disturb a predefined conception of national identity. In this sense, even within Bouchard and Taylor's conception of interculturalism, migrants are of value to the nation on the basis of their potentially restorative role, and measures are needed in order to limit their potentially transformative role.

Central to the vision of a *citoyenneté québécoise* is a linguistic model of national community, with language recognized as the "shared property" of a civic nation – "a common good and a heritage that belongs to all" (Juteau 2002, 452). Historically, language was the clearest marker of distinction between French Canadians and the English of both Canada and the earlier British colonial regime. Until recently in Québec, language was tied to ethnicity. Those in Canada for whom French was a mother tongue could also claim a common descent. However, due to the territorialization of national identity and the consequent presence of small French-speaking minorities in the rest of Canada who were no longer conceptualized as belonging to the nation, as well as the phenomenon of mass immigration and the preferred selection of francophone immigrants, the equation of language with descent was disrupted.

Whereas scholars such as Nafay Choudhury (2012) argue that further fostering the French language as the "key element of Quebec identity facilitates a common sense of citizenship in Quebec," thus limiting the divisiveness of debates about reasonable accommodation, others have pointed to limitations of language as the basis of national community. For the nation to have force, language must be complemented by ethnic referents. As Balibar (1991, 99) asserts, "for [language] to be tied down to the frontiers of a particular people, it ... needs an extra degree [*un supplement*] of particularity, or a principle of closure, of exclusion." It is race – which Balibar defines as naturalized differences in culture and traditions rather than as biology or heredity – that provides such a supplement. Although racism is "always indispensable to its constitution," nationalism cannot be equated with racism, which is "always in excess" of nationalism and "always still insufficient to achieve its project" (54). Racism and nationalism cannot be reduced to one another, but race is always at play in the constitution of national identity.

Understanding race as a necessary principle of closure for the nation allows one to comprehend the continual deferral to ethnic referents within definitions of national identity. The xenophobia present in the Hérouxville Code and in many of the statements given to the Bouchard-Taylor Commission is not unique to Québec, nor is it, as Bouchard and Taylor (2008b, 75) would have us believe, that "French-speaking Québec [as] a minority culture ... needs a strong identity to allay its anxieties and behave like a serene majority." The reversion to an ethnic nationalism or to aspects of ethnic nationalism in the determination of the values upon which a civic nation can be founded is not merely ideological but also a revelation of the structure of the national identity. Despite the fantasy of the excision of race from nation, one cannot simply wish away race or develop institutional structures that can protect the nation from racism. The desire for a separation of nation from race, consistent with the structure of desire in general, is a desire for that which can never be realized but which is given force by the fantasy of its eventual realization. It is within this structure of desire and fantasy that the migrant in Québec has become the scapegoat for the lack of realization of national fulfilment.

From the Bouchard-Taylor Commission to the Law of Values

December 14, 2007, marked the end of the Bouchard-Taylor Commission's forums. At the press conference announcing the release of their final report, *Building the Future: A Time for Reconciliation*, Bouchard and Taylor continued to downplay the notion that Québec was facing a true crisis of identity. Rather, they argued that Québec was experiencing a crisis of representation and perception (Gagnon 2010, 15). In their final report, Bouchard and Taylor (2008a) offered thirty recommendations, with four given priority: (1) tabling a white paper on secularism that would provide guidance for new definitions and policies regarding interculturalism; (2) aiding the integration of immigrants through the introduction or improvement of programs to recognize their credentials and skills, increase their capacity in the French language, regionalize immigration, and coordinate the integration programs offered by different government departments; (3) promoting knowledge of interculturalism within all civil society institutions; and (4) intensifying the fight against discrimination.

On the day the report was released, Charest immediately rejected one of the commission's recommendations, namely that the crucifix above the chair of the president of the National Assembly be removed. In the following months, Charest did little to implement any of the recommendations or to support the report in the face of criticism. As Pierre Anctil (2011, 13) argues, "rather than take the matter into his own hands politically, and reaffirm the principles as the basis for current policies regarding diversity and immigrant integration, [he] preferred to win time and submit the question to an external body."

In political terms, this seems to have been a successful move in the short term, as on December 8 Charest was re-elected as the premier of Québec. Moreover, the election victory seemed to strike a death blow to the ADQ and Dumont. However, despite Anctil's prediction that, given the global economic collapse of 2008, there was "little likelihood that the debate on cultural diversity [would] resurface with such urgency in the near future," neither the debate nor its intensity have receded (Anctil 2011, 13).

The commission's recommendations were generally supported by organizations representing Québec's religious minorities, with the exception of the Canadian Jewish Congress's objection to the recommendation that state officials and judges be barred from wearing symbols of faith while conducting official duties. Critics of the commission's report focused on three issues. First, they argued that the proposals related to secularism and women's rights were insufficiently rigorous. Several labour unions argued that religious minorities would be able to use the right to religious freedom to undermine québécois values, particularly women's equality. Second, some nationalists, such as former PQ premiers Parizeau and Landry, attacked the commission on the basis that it did not do enough to promote the integration of immigrants into Québec society and that it placed the blame for the crisis on the French majority's lack of tolerance for difference (Anctil 2011, 14).

Third, within québécois intellectual circles, the report was coldly received (Gagnon 2010, 11). The principal objection of Québec's intellegentsia was that the commissioners accorded positive value to diversity without demonstrating the benefit of diversity for Québec (13). They argued that, in doing so, Bouchard and Taylor failed to distinguish between diversity and pluralism. Like the impetus for the creation of the commission, the assumption behind its report was not only that cultural and religious identity must be respected but also that the recognition of diversity was necessary for social cohesion. As a result, rather than addressing pluralism through institutional reforms that would equitably extend rights and freedoms for all regardless of their particularities, the focus on diversity required a rethinking of the fundamental characteristics of collective membership and common identity.

Rather than resolving the crisis of reasonable accommodation, the media's blanket coverage of the Bouchard-Taylor Commission over the course of several months not only maintained the presence of the issue in the popular imagination but, given the commission's focus on identity, also heightened the notion of cultural, particularly religious, difference as a potential threat to the nation. During its successful 2012 provincial election campaign, the opposition PQ, under the leadership of Pauline Marois, promised, if elected, to introduce a charter of secularism that would legally define and entrench Québec's secularity.

Once in power, details began to emerge in the Québec media regarding the plans of the new government to introduce what it was now calling a Charter of Québécois Values during the next sitting of the National Assembly. On September 10, 2013, Bernard Drainville, the minister of democratic institutions, held a press conference to officially introduce the Charter of Values. By the time it was tabled in the National Assembly on November 7, it had been officially renamed the *Charter Affirming the Values of State Secularism and Religious Neutrality and the Equality between Women and Men, and Providing a Framework for Accommodation Requests.*

The Charter of Values widened the scope of the earlier promised charter of secularism by legally defining the essential values of Québec society to which practices of accommodation of religious pluralism must conform. The government argued that such a legal definition of québécois values could, by setting limits on diversity based on core national values, protect Québec's national identity from the threat of religious migrants and unbridled pluralism.

The legislation included an amendment to the Québec Charter of Human Rights and Freedoms giving primacy to gender equality, secularism, and the French language over other rights, such as freedom of religion. Moreover, the Charter of Values prohibited employees of all provincial institutions, including even those working in provincially run liquor stores, from wearing ostentatious religious symbols. To explain what symbols would be considered ostentatious, the government distributed a poster with images of both those symbols that would be permitted (e.g., jewellery with small crucifixes, crescent moons, and the Star of David) and those that would not be permitted (e.g., hijabs, niqabs, turbans, kippas, and large crucifixes).

In terms of provincial politics, some have argued that the Charter of Values was merely a tool to allow the PQ government not only to distract the electorate from other social and economic problems in Québec but also to "manufacture a crisis" in order "to put sovereignty back at the top of the agenda" (Cooper 2013, 25). However, the debate concerning the Charter of Values also created problems for the PQ by further highlighting divisions both between Montréal and the rest of Québec and within the sovereigntist movement.

The Charter of Values was rejected by each of Montréal's fifteen municipalities, with all four main candidates for mayor of the city speaking out against it. Important figures within the sovereigntist movement, including even Parizeau and Jean Dorion, the former president of the Saint-Jean-Baptiste Society and deputy premier in the Bouchard government, argued against the Charter of Values, stating that it went too far. Maria Mouriani, a member of the Canadian Parliament for the sovereigntist Bloc Québécois and a Catholic of Lebanese origin who often wore a small crucifix, was expelled from her party for arguing on Radio-Canada that the Charter of Values "would be a slide backward into ethnic nationalism that risked excluding certain minority communities and women" and for wondering whether the sovereigntist movement would ever be able to move beyond what she labelled the "demons of populist intolerance" (Cooper 2013, 25).

The Charter of Québécois Values, then, rather than putting an end to two decades of debate about reasonable accommodation and the governance of cultural and religious difference in Québec, maintained – if not heightened – the tensions around these issues. Unlike the result hoped for by supporters of the Charter of Values, questions of the nature of québécois identity were reinvigorated rather than resolved once and for all. Faced with the instability of markers of identity and differentiation, such as progressive socio-economic policies and the French language, the Charter of Values was, on the surface, meant to serve an immunitary function, shoring up the national body in the face of external threats. It attempted to construct borders, clearly demarcating the self from its external other. Thus the immunitary task of law in the case of the Charter of Values, like that of the final report of the Bouchard-Taylor Commission and the Hérouxville Code, was to construct a definition of identity sufficiently strong to render the Québec nation impervious to external threats of assimilation. In this sense, the Charter of Values was responding to a crisis of borders.

However, the Charter of Québécois Values was also responding to a second crisis, one that was perpetual but was made manifest by an encounter with the otherness of migrants and other religious minorities. In this understanding of the events described above, what appears is, first, a crisis provoked by engagement with what was seen as an external threat and, second, an immunitary response to this crisis that sought to allay this threat by codifying the nature and limits of the national body. The task of law in this process was to overcome internal contradictions and the instability of markers of difference in order to establish a definition of the nation sufficiently strong to protect it from external threats.

The Charter of Values, then, was responding both in terms of immunization and in terms of overcoming internal differentiation. As a result, it attempted to deny the presence of any autoimmune reactions within the body. In contending with the external crisis, it attempted to paper over the perpetual crisis of all identity, namely that each identity contains a force that promotes its self-destruction. However, in doing so, rather than protecting identity, the Charter of Values effaced it by creating a closure and thus a nonidentity.

The Hérouxville Code, the final report of the Bouchard-Taylor Commission, and the Charter of Values each attempted to immunize québécois identity through definition. These attempts to define identity could not be undertaken simply in relation to a thin definition of identity – one based on universal values and rights, such as secularism, democracy, and equality of the sexes – because such a definition would fail to provide a particularism for québécois identity. At the same time, national identity could not be formulated solely on the basis of a thick (ethnic or racial) definition because such a definition would undermine the elements of the thin definition that were held to be definitive of the nation. In order to overcome the conflict between these two conceptions of québécois identity, it was necessary to make them identical to each other. To that end, not only did these documents ethnicize those aspects of civic national identity that would otherwise appear as universal values by reframing them as *traditional* or *foundational* québécois values, but they also redefined certain elements of an ethnic conception of national identity so that these elements would no longer appear threatening to Québec's modern rights and values.

Here, the place of Catholicism within the policies of the Marois government is instructive. In contrast to the recommendations of the Bouchard-Taylor Commission, the Charter of Values did not contain any legislation that would remove the crucifix from the National Assembly. Drainville justified this decision by arguing that rather than an ostentatious religious symbol, the crucifix was "an important part of Québec's Catholic history" (Cooper 2013, 25). The PQ government also reinforced the place of Catholicism as part of Québec's heritage by funding the restoration of churches in the name of "protecting our sacred heritage." In contrast to the portrayal of minority religions, the definition of Catholicism in terms of heritage, which rendered it a historical object within a narrative of secularization, made Catholicism nonthreatening to secular Québec. Moreover, such a definition made it possible to forge a common identity between Québec's religious past and its secular present.

Attempting to immunize identity is not, however, without risks. Immunization requires absorbing a small, hopefully nontoxic amount of that which one wishes to protect oneself against. In the case of Québec, this undertaking has entailed protecting the québécois values of openness, democracy, pluralism, and equality from the corrosive values associated with minority cultures, particularly Islam. Doing so, however, has required absorbing anti-pluralist, discriminatory, nondemocratic values and creating closure rather than openness – just those things that immunization through definition was meant to protect against. In other words, protecting ostensibly québécois values has resulted in the operationalization of just those values that Québec is said to need protection from.

Conclusion

On March 5, 2014, at the request of the Parti Québécois (PQ) government, Lieutenant Governor Pierre Duchesne dissolved the National Assembly and announced that an election would be held on April 7. As a consequence, Bill 60, the Charter of Québécois Values, which had been tabled earlier that year, died on the table. Premier Pauline Marois stated that the reason for calling the election was to form a majority government that would guarantee the passage of Bill 60. In what amounted to virtually a single-issue election, the PQ and the centre-right Coalition Avenir Québec ran in support of the Charter of Values, whereas the Québec Liberal Party (PLQ) and the sovereigntist, social democratic Québec solidaire opposed it.

The results of the election were devastating for the PQ, with the PLQ winning a majority government. With the Liberal's victory, there was hope that the issue of the Charter of Values in particular and the sometimes vicious debates about Québec's identity in general could be put to rest. However, that would not be the case. In the intervening years, identity and the issue of accommodation of religious symbols and practices have continued to be sources of controversy in Québec.

In October 2017, in yet another attempt to resolve the issue, the PLQ government passed Bill 62, *An Act to Foster State Adherence to Religious Neutrality,* which, similar to laws introduced in Austria, Belgium, and

France, prohibited women from receiving any provincial or municipal services while wearing a niqab or burqa, including riding the bus, visiting the library, meeting with their children's teachers, or speaking to a doctor. In supporting this bill, which was eventually overturned by the Supreme Court of Canada, Québec's minister of justice, Stéphanie Valée, argued that it did not target any particular religious group but was meant to contend with "a legitimate question of communication, identification and security" (Hamilton 2017). Even this measure, however, was opposed by the PQ and the Coalition Avenir Québec, which maintained that it did not go far enough in secularizing public space.

Desiring the National, Desiring the Secular

At the time of writing, questions of migration, religion, and national identity remain prominent within Québec without any indication that they will soon abate. This continuation of insecurity around issues of identity should be seen as the result of the failure of the development of a secularist civic nationalism to attain a hegemonic status as a national narrative sufficient to provide both markers of difference from its non-national others and a sense of historical continuity, one that could repress, at least for a time, the ever-present crisis of the nation and overcome the appeal of ethnic narratives of the nation.

Both those who imagine the nation in ethnic terms and those who do so in civic terms feel a deep attachment to their differently defined nations. This attachment to, and conflict over, the nation can be understood within the relationship between desire and the nation offered by Lacanian scholars of the nation and nationalism. As discussed in Chapter 1, Lacanian thought understands lack as that which produces desire. Desire is the fantasy of recapturing the lost enjoyment as a fullness that marks entry into the social/symbolic world. In terms of the nation, fantasy promises the possibility of identification with, and wholeness within, the nation. In this sense, it promises the possibility of overcoming social antagonism and providing a social form in which lack is covered over.

Despite the impossibility of ever attaining wholeness, desire is sustained by moments of temporary or partial enjoyment of victories in national sporting events and war or even by moments of crisis in which the identity of the nation has to be articulated and protected. These moments provide a glimpse of what the nation – as enjoyment, as fullness – could provide. It is the partiality of these experiences and the promise they hold that sustain desire for the nation.

In a similar manner to the fantasy of national wholeness, secularism also functions through a fantasy of the attainment of a good life and just society freed from the irrationality and coercion of religion and religious authority. However, as argued in Chapter 4, the secular public sphere, despite appearing as a neutral space of freedom, is always a site of exclusion and always articulated by power. As a result, it is always a site of the exclusion and foreclosure of possible ways of belonging and being political.

Some scholars, such as Mark Cauchi (2009), recognizing the limits of secularism as currently and historically imagined and instituted, hold that we should continue to invest ourselves in a "secular to come." Referring to the Derridian concepts of "democracy to come," "justice to come," and "Europe to come," as well as to Derrida's problematization of the binary between religious and nonreligious categories and identities, Cauchi contends that the secular, in a manner consistent with all categories and identities, contains no essential meaning and therefore cannot be closed. As a result, he leaves open the possibility of a secular that is open to its other, namely religion – a secular "that may welcome religion into itself without ceasing to be secular" (9). In this sense, secularism would not be equated with a realizable political system or form of society but with "a *decision* or an *identification*" (12). The secular that welcomes religion is something to strive toward, always with the knowledge that it will never arrive, that it is always to come.

Disrupting Cruel Attachment

The question then arises of whether the nation should be approached in a manner similar to how Derrida approaches democracy, justice, and Europe and how Cauchi suggests we should approach the secular. Should one orient one's hopes toward a nation to come? Although such an approach initially may appear promising and appeal to the desire for identification and wholeness at play in those who are usually skeptical of the nation as a form of belonging, community, and identity, it erases the devastating physical and psychological costs of the nation and nationalism. The desire for wholeness within and through the nation has repeatedly served as a motivating factor in social conflict, war, genocide, discrimination, misrecognition, and the denial of rights to non-nationals and the merely human, to name only some of its associated evils.

As mentioned in Chapter 5, one cannot simply wish away race or develop institutional structures that can protect the nation from racism. The existence and perpetuation of the nation requires the institution of principals of closure and thus a perpetual reversion to race and ethnicity. The fantasy of the excision of race from nation and the establishment of a purely civic nationalism in which all are welcomed and included is just that, a fantasy. Consistent with the structure of all desire, it can never be realized but is motivated by the wish for its eventual realization. Given the inevitable nonrealization of the fantasy of national wholeness, the nation, in moments of crisis, lashes out at scapegoats blamed for stealing its enjoyment.

Both during and since the announcement of the Charter of Québécois Values, the anti-immigrant discourse of talk radio in Québec has not only created what Dominique Payette has labelled a "climate of fear that has no place in democracy" (Woods 2017), but also contributed to a significant rise in hate crimes against Muslims (Gouvernement du Québec 2015). Québec has also seen an increase in, or at least an increase in the public openness of, extreme-right anti-immigrant groups, such as Patriotic Europeans against the Islamisation of the Occident (Pegida), Soldiers of Odin, and La Meute, which have engaged in public protests against immigration and the presence of Islam in Québec.

On January 29, 2017, Alexandre Bissonnette, a student at Laval University who had espoused support for extreme-right, anti-Muslim positions, opened fire in the Islamic Cultural Centre of Québec City, killing six and wounding nineteen. In the wake of the shooting, politicians and members of the media and public acknowledged the danger of heated discourse concerning immigration, religion, and identity, and they promised to tone down their rhetoric. However, within a short time, as evident in the debate surrounding Bill 62, this discourse returned with little moderation of the tone or substance of comments.

Rather than thinking in terms of hope for a nation to come, we need to rethink the nation in terms of what Berlant (2011) refers to as "cruel optimism." According to Berlant, "a relation of cruel optimism exists when something you desire is actually an obstacle to your flourishing." Although all attachments, whether a kind of love or a political project, are optimistic, "they become cruel only when the object that draws your attachment actively impedes the aim that brought you to it initially" (1). As in the Lacanian "that's not it" structure of the reproduction of desire, disappointment in the object's inability to realize the aim that one associates with it does not extinguish desire; rather, "the *affective* structure of an optimistic attachment involves a sustaining inclination to return to the scene of the fantasy that enables you to expect that *this* time, nearness to *this* thing will help you or a world to become different in just the right way" (2). Optimism, in this sense, functions in a manner similar to Hage's (2003) conception of the role of hope within Australian nationalism. For Hage, hope is an affect that circulates, is exchanged, and to which access is unequal (9).

Hope in the nation as an object that promises identification, wholeness, freedom, and authenticity is not shared equally by all, and the loss of the nation as a world would be much more traumatic for some groups than for others. Yet the nation, in failing to fulfil these promises, is not only an object that has disappointed, and will inevitably continue to disappoint, but also an object to which our attachment prohibits the imagination of other forms of community and belonging that may better serve us. Although the loss of the object of attachment may require a period of mourning, it is only through abandoning the nation that we can break the cycle both of disappointment and of recurrent destructiveness.

The chapters of this book examine moments in the history of Québec when national identity was faced with a crisis. In each of these moments, the nation reproduced itself through a transformation of that which was said to be definitive of its essence. In contrast to the dominant narrative of secularization, which provided a means to permit the historical continuity of the nation despite these transformations, the historical investigations present in each chapter demonstrate that what was defined as properly religious or secular and the relationship of these categories of beliefs, realms, institutions, and behaviours to national identity underwent radical transformations and reversals.

By examining these moments of crisis, this book provides an alternative historical narrative of the nation, one in which crisis is the locus of dissolution, transformation, and consolidation. By disrupting secularization as a narrative of transhistorical continuity and offering an alternative, discontinuous historical narrative of the nation, this book hopes to contribute to the possibility of breaking free from the nation as the only imaginable form of belonging and, thereby, to provide an opening and impetus for discussions of the challenges and possibilities of developing new frameworks of community, belonging, and identity.

References

Abu-Lughod, Lila. 1990. "The Romance of Resistance: Tracing Boundaries of Power through Bedouin Women." *American Ethnologist* 17, 1: 41–55. https://doi.org/10.1525/ae.1990.17.1.02a00030.

Agamben, Giorgio. 2000. "Beyond Human Rights." In *Means without End: Notes on Politics,* 14–26. Minneapolis: University of Minnesota Press.

Allor, Martin, and Michelle Gagnon. 1994. *L'état de culture*. Montréal: GRECC.

Anctil, Pierre. 2011. "Introduction." In *Religion, Culture, and the State,* ed. Howard Adelman and Pierre Anctil, 3–15. Toronto: University of Toronto Press.

Anderson, Benedict R. 1983. *Imagined Communities: Reflections on the Origin and Spread of Nationalism*. London: Verso.

Arendt, Hannah. 1951. "The Decline of the Nation-State and the End of the Rights of Man." In *The Origins of Totalitarianism,* 267–302. New York: Harcourt Brace.

Armstrong, John. 1982. *Nations before Nationalism*. Chapel Hill: University of North Carolina Press.

Asad, Talal. 1993. *Genealogies of Religion: Discipline and Reasons of Power in Christianity and Islam*. Baltimore, MD: Johns Hopkins University Press.

–. 2003. *Formations of the Secular: Christianity, Islam, Modernity*. Stanford, CA: Stanford University Press.

–. 2005. "Reflection on Laïcité and the Public Sphere." *Items and Issues* 5, 3. https://issuu.com/ssrcitemsissues/docs/i_i_vol_5_no_3_2005.

Assemblée nationale du Québec. 2000a. "Débats de l'Assemblée nationale du Québec: Propos tenus par M. Yves Michaud à l'égard des communautés ethniques devant la Commission des états généraux sur la situation et l'avenir de la langue française au Québec." *Quebec History* (Marianopolis College, Montréal),

December 14. http://faculty.marianopolis.edu/c.belanger/quebechistory/docs/michaud/08.htm.

–. 2000b. "Pétition – Solidarité Yves Michaud: Défense de la liberté d'opinion et d'expression." *Quebec History* (Marianopolis College, Montréal), December 19. http://faculty.marianopolis.edu/c.belanger/quebechistory/docs/michaud/09.htm.

Auclair, A. 1995. "Le hijab ou l'intolérable tolérance: Au nom de quels et libertés le Québec devrait-il permettre aux immigrants de mettre la maison sans dessus dessous?" *Le Devoir,* May 4.

Auestad, Lene, ed. 2014. *Nationalism and the Body Politic: Psychoanalysis and the Rise of Ethnocentrism and Xenophobia*. London: Karnac.

Baillargeon, Normand. 1995. "Voile et sens." *Le Devoir,* February 21.

Balibar, Etienne. 1991. "The Nation Form: History and Ideology." In *Race, Nation, Class: Ambiguous Identities,* ed. Etienne Balibar and Immanuel Wallerstein, 86–106. London: Verso.

Bastien, P. 1995. "Une décision injuste." *La Presse,* March 1.

Bauman, Zygmunt. 1996. "From Pilgrim to Tourist – Or a Short History of Identity." In *Questions of Cultural Identity,* ed. Stuart Hall and Paul du Gay, 18–36. London: Sage.

Baumeister, Roy F. 1986. *Identity: Cultural Change and the Struggle for Self*. Oxford: Oxford University Press.

Beauchemin, Jacques. 2004. "What Does It Mean to Be a Quebecer? Between Self-Preservation and Openness to the Other." In *Québec: State and Society,* ed. Alain-G. Gagnon, 17–32. Toronto: University of Toronto Press.

Behdad, Ali. 1997. "Nationalism and Immigration to the United States." *Diaspora* 6, 2: 155–78. https://doi.org/10.1353/dsp.1997.0000.

Behiels, Michael D. 1985. *Prelude to Quebec's Quiet Revolution: Liberalism versus Neo-Nationalism, 1945–1960*. Montréal and Kingston: McGill-Queen's University Press.

Bélanger, Claude. 2000. "Ultramontane Nationalism: 1840–1960." *Quebec History* (Marianopolis College, Montréal), August 23. http://faculty.marianopolis.edu/c.belanger/quebechistory/events/natpart3.htm.

Bellah, Robert N. 1964. "Religious Evolution." *American Sociological Review* 29, 3: 358–74. https://doi.org/10.2307/2091480.

Benhabib, Seyla. 2002. "'Nous et les Autres' (We and Others): Is Universalism Ethnocentric?" In *The Claims of Culture: Equality and Diversity in a Global Era,* 24–48. Princeton, NJ: Princeton University Press.

Benjamin, Walter. 1973. *Illuminations*. London: Fontana.

Bensalem, Leila. 1994a. "Cessons de banaliser le hijab! Depuis la fin de la guerre froide et la mort du communisme, le champ est libre pour la nouvelle force montante que représente l'intégrisme." *La Presse,* December 3.

–. 1994b. "Le voile islamique ou le refus de s'intégrer à la société québécoise." *La Presse,* October 13.

Berger, Peter L. 1967. *The Sacred Canopy: Elements of a Sociological Theory of Religion*. New York: Anchor.

Berlant, Lauren. 2011. *Cruel Optimism*. Durham, NC: Duke University Press.

Beyer, Peter. 1985. "The Mission of Quebec Ultramontanism: A Luhmannian Perspective." *Sociological Analysis* 46, 1: 37–48. https://doi.org/10.2307/3710896.

Bhabha, Homi, ed. 1990a. *Nation and Narration*. London: Routledge.

–. 1990b. "The Third Space." In *Identity: Community, Culture, Difference*, ed. J. Rutherford, 207–21. London: Lawrence and Wishart.

Bilge, Sirma. 2013. "Reading the Racial Subtext of the Québécois Accommodation Controversy: An Analytics of Racialized Governmentality." *Politikon* 40, 1: 1–25. https://doi.org/10.1080/02589346.2013.765681.

Bisson, Marcien. 2007. "Mémoire." Brief submitted to the Consultation Commission on Accommodation Practices Related to Cultural Differences. Accessed May 2010. http://www.accommodements.qc.ca/documentation//memoires/Jonquiere/bisson-marcien.

Blain, Maurice. 1952. "Sur la liberté de l'esprit." *Esprit* 20: 201–13.

Boisvert, Réginald. 1950. "Domiciles de la peur." *Cité libre* 1: 10–19.

Bouchard, Gérard. 2012. *Interculturalism: A View from Québec*. Toronto: University of Toronto Press.

Bouchard, Gérard, and Alain Roy. 2007. *La culture québécoise est-elle en crise?* Montréal: Boréal.

Bouchard, Gérard, and Charles Taylor. 2007. *Accommodation and Differences: Seeking Common Ground: Quebecers Speak Out*. Québec City: Gouvernement du Québec.

–. 2008a. *Building the Future: A Time for Reconciliation: Abridged Report*. Québec City: Commission de consultation dur les pratiques d'accommodement reliées au différence culturelles, Gouvernement du Québec.

–. 2008b. *Fonder l'avenir: Le temps de la vonciliation*. Québec City: Commission de consultation sur les pratiques d'accommodement reliées aux differences culturelles, Gouvernement du Québec.

Boulanger, D. 1994. "Sous Le Foulard." *Le Devoir,* December 18.

Bourque, Gilles, and Jules Duchastel. 2000. "Multiculturalisme, pluralisme et communauté politique: Le Canada et le Québec." In *Mondialisation, citoyenneté et multiculturalisme,* ed. Mikhaël Elbaz and Denise Helly, 147–69. Sainte-Foy, QC: Presses de l'Université Laval.

Bourret, Gisèle. 1994. "Hidjab: Poursuivons le débat." *Le Devoir,* December 4.

Bouthillette, Jean. 1972. *Le Canadien français et son double*. Montréal: L'Hexagone.

Brah, Avtar. 1996. *Cartographies of Diaspora: Contesting Identities*. New York: Routledge.

Bramadat, Paul A. 2005. "Beyond the Trojan Horse: Religion, Immigration and Canadian Public Discourse." *Canadian Issues* (Spring): 78–81.

Brooke, Jams. 2001. "Resignation in Quebec Reflects Split in Nationalism." *New York Times,* January 13.

Brown, David. 1999. "Are There Good and Bad Nationalisms?" *Nations and Nationalism* 5, 2: 281–302. https://doi.org/10.1111/j.1354-5078.1999.00281.x.

Bruce, Steve. 2002. *God Is Dead: Secularization in the West*. Oxford: Blackwell.

Brunet, Michel. 1954. "Trois illusions de la pensée canadienne-française: L'agriculturalisme, l'anti-impérialisme, et le canadianisme." *Alerte,* 11: 135–46.

–. 1957. "Trois dominantes de la pensée canadienne-française: L'agriculturalisme, l'anti-étatisme et le messianisme." In *La présence anglaise et les Canadiens,* 113–66. Montréal: Beauchemin.

–. 1958. *La présence anglaise et les Canadiens*. Montréal: Beauchemin.

Butler, Judith. 1993. *Bodies that Matter: On the Discursive Limits of "Sex."* New York: Routledge.

–. 1997. *The Psychic Power of Life: Theories in Subjection*. Stanford, CA: Stanford University Press.

Caldwell, Gary. 1995. "Le local à l'heure de la mondialisation." L'Agora. November. http://agora.qc.ca/documents/leon_gerin–leon_gerin_par_gary_caldwell.

Calhoun, Craig. 1997. *Nationalism*. Minneapolis: University of Minnesota Press.

Cantin, Serge. 1997. *Ce pays comme un enfant: Essais sur le Québec (1988–1996)*. Montréal: L'Hexagone.

Casanova, José. 1994. *Public Religions in the Modern World*. Chicago: University of Chicago Press.

–. 2004. "Religion, European Secular Identities, and European Integration." *Eurozine,* July 29: 1–13.

Catholic Programme. 1871. *Quebec History* (Marianopolis College, Montréal), August 23, 2000. http://faculty.marianopolis.edu/c.belanger/quebechistory/docs/catholic/text-e.htm.

Cauchi, Mark. 2009. "The Secular to Come: Interrogating the Derridean 'Secular.'" *Journal for Cultural and Religious Theory* 10, 1: 1–25.

CBC. 2004. "Muslim Students in Montreal Denied Prayer Rooms." *CBC News,* October 15.

CCCI (Conseil des communautés culturelles et de l'immigration). 1993. *La gestion des conflits de normes par les organisations dans le contexte pluraliste de la société québécoise: Principes de fond et de procedures pour guider la recherche d'accommodements raissonables*. Québec City: Gouvernement du Québec.

CDP (Commission des droits de la personne). 1995. *Le pluralisme religieuse au Québec: Un défi d'éthique sociale*. Montréal: Commission des droits de la personne.

"Ce qu'Yves Michaud a vraiment dit." 2000. *La Presse*, December 19. http://faculty.marianopolis.edu/c.belanger/quebechistory/docs/michaud/02.htm.

Chiasson, Guy, and Junichiro Koji. 2011. "Quebec Immigrant Settlement Policy and Municipalities: Fine-Tuning a Provincial Template." In *Immigrant Settlement Policy in Canadian Municipalities,* ed. E. Tolley and R. Young, 148–91. Montréal and Kingston: McGill-Queen's University Press.

Choquette, Ernest. 1916. *La terre*. Montréal: Beauchemin.

Choudhury, Nafay. 2012. "Niqab vs. Quebec: Negotiating Minority Rights within Quebec Identity." *Western Journal of Legal Studies* 1, 1: 1–29. https://www.canlii.org/en/commentary/journals/24/690/.

Ciceri, Coryse. 1998. "Le foulard islamique à l'école publique: Analyse comparée du débat dans la presse française et québécoise francophone (1994–1995)." PhD diss., Université de Montréal.

Clément, Éric. 1994. "Une table ronde sur le foulard islamique à l'école laisse les participants sur leur faim." *La Presse,* December 8.

Cole-Arnal, Oscar. 1997. "Shaping Young Proletarians into Militant Christians: The Pioneer Phase of the JOC in France and Quebec." *Journal of Contemporary History* 32, 4: 509–26. https://doi.org/10.1177/002200949703200406.

Collectif de femme. 1994. "Va-t-on assisster au Québec à un phénomène de 'purification culturelle et idéologique'?" *La Presse,* December 8.

Cooper, Celine. 2013. "The Charter of Quebec Values: Anatomy of a Manufactured Identity Crisis." *Policy,* November/December, 24–26.

Corell, Synne. 2010. *Krigens ettertid: Okkupasjonhistorien i norske historiebøker*. Oslo: Scandinavian Academic Press.

Côté, J.D. 1995. "Hidjab et droit des collectivités." *Le Devoir,* March 7.

CRI (Conseil des relations interculturelles). 1997. *Un Québec pour tous ses citoyens*. Québec City: Gouvernement du Québec.

–. 2004a. *Laïcité et diversité religieuse: L'approche québécoise*. Montréal: Conseil des relations interculturelles.

–. 2004b. *Laicity and Religious Diversity*. Québec City: Gouvernement du Québec.

CSF (Conseil du statut de la femme). 1995. *Réflexion sur la question du port du voile à l'école*. Québec City: Gouvernement du Québec.

CTV. 2006. "Food Fight Infuriates Filipinos at Home and Abroad." *CTV News,* May 5.

Dagenais, M.N. 1995. "Le port du hijab: Des remous." *Le Journal de Montréal,* February 28.

Dakhlia, Jocelyne. 2001. "New Approaches in the History of Memory? A French Model." In *Crisis and Memory in Islamic Societies,* ed. Angelika Neuwirth and Andreas Pflitsch, 59–74. Würzburg: Ergon.

de Gaspé, Phillipe Aubert. 1864. *Les anciens Canadiens*. Montréal: Bibliotheque québécoise.

de Nevers, Edmund. 1896. *L'avenir du peuple canadien-français*. Montréal: Fides.

Deleuze, Gilles. 1962. *Nietzsche and Philosophy*. New York: Columbia University Press.

Derrida, Jacques. 1988. "Interpretations at War: Kant, the Jew, the German." In *Acts of Religion,* ed. Gil Anidjar, 137–88. London: Routledge.

–. 1992. *The Other Heading: Reflections on Today's Europe*. Bloomington: Indiana University Press.

–. 1995. "Faith and Knowledge." In *Religion,* ed. Jacques Derrida and Gianni Vattimo, 1–78. Stanford, CA: Stanford University Press.

–. 1996. *Monolingualism of the Other, or The Prosthesis of Origin*. Stanford, CA: Stanford University Press.
–. 2003. *Rogues: Two Essays on Reason*. Stanford, CA: Stanford University Press.
Dion, Léon. 1993. *Québec 1945–2000.* Vol. 2, *Les intellectuals et le temps de Duplessis*. Québec City: Presses de l'Université Laval.
Drouin, André. 2017. *Le code de vie d'Hérouxville – 2017: 10e anniversaire*. Trois Rivières: François A. Lachapelle.
Dufour, Pascale, and Ian A. Morrison. 2005. "The State of the Social Investment State in the Field of Employment Policy." *Canadian Journal of Career Development* 4, 1: 3–10.
Dumont, Fernand. 1995. *L'avenir de la mémoire*. Québec City: Chaire pour le développement de la recherche sur la culture d'expression française en Amérique, Université Laval.
Dupuis, Jean-Claude. 2003. "Remarques de Jean-Claude Dupuis sur l'exposé de Gilles Bibeau." In *L'antilibéralisme au Québec au XXe siècle: Les séminaires Fernand-Dumont,* ed. Gilles Gagné, 33–40. Montréal: Nota Bene.
Durham, Lord (John George Lambton). 1839. *Report on the Affairs of British North America*. London: J.W. Southgate.
Eid, Nadia F. 1978. *Le clergé et le pouvoir politique au Quebec: Une analyse de l'idéologie ultramontane au milieu du XIXe siècle*. Montréal: Cahiers du Québec/Hurtubise HMH.
Émery, Michel. 2007. "Mémoire." Brief submitted to the Consultation Commission on Accommodation Practices Related to Cultural Differences. Accessed May 2010. http://www.accommodements.qc.ca/documentation/memoires/Montreal-d/Emery-michel06-0085-pe-00.pdf.
Erikson, Erik H. 1968. *Identity, Youth, and Crisis*. New York: W.W. Norton and Company.
–. 1980. *Identity and the Life Cycle*. New York: W.W. Norton and Company.
"Êtes-vous en faveur du hijab à l'école?." 1995. *Le Journal de Montréal,* February 16.
Falardeau, Jean-Charles. 1964a. *L'essor des sciences sociales au Canada français*. Québec City: Ministère des affaires culturelles.
–. 1964b. "The Role and Importance of the Church in French Canada." In *French-Canadian Society,* ed. Marcel Rioux and Yves Martin, vol. 1, 342–57. Toronto: McClelland and Stewart.
–, ed. 1968. *Léon Gérin et l'habitant de Saint-Justin*. Montréal: Presses de l'Université de Montréal.
Faucher, Albert, and Maurice Lamontagne. 1964. "History of Industrial Development." In *French-Canadian Society,* ed. Marcel Rioux and Yves Martin, vol. 1, 257–71. Toronto: McClelland and Stewart.
Ferretti, Lucia. 1999. *Brève histoire de l'Église catholique au Québec*. Montréal: Boréal.
Fine, Sean. 2013. "Sikh Student Who Won Kirpan Case Now Considers Leaving Quebec." *Globe and Mail,* October 22.

Fontaine, Louise, and Yuki Shiose. 1991. "Ni citoyens, ni autres: La categorie politique 'Communautés culturelles.'" In *Citoyenneté et nationalité: Perspectives en France et au Québec,* ed. Dominique Colas, Claude Emeri, and Jacques Zylberberg, 435–43. Paris: Presses Universitaires de France.

Forty, Adrian. 1999. "Introduction." In *The Art of Forgetting,* ed. Adrian Forty and Susanne Kuchler, 1–18. London: Bloomsbury.

Foucault, Michel. 1969. *The Archaeology of Knowledge*. London: Routledge.

–. 1971. "Nietzsche, Genealogy, History." In *Essential Works of Foucault, 1954–1984,* vol. 2, *Aesthetics, Method, Epistemology,* ed. James D. Faubion, 76–99. New York: New Press.

–. 1978. "On Religion." In *Religion and Culture,* ed. Jeremy Carrette, 106–9. New York: Routledge.

Fournier, Marcel. 2001. "Quebec Sociology and Quebec Society: The Construction of a Collective Identity." *Canadian Journal of Sociology* 26, 3: 333–47. https://doi.org/10.2307/3341891.

–. 2002. "Quebec Sociology: A Discipline and Its Object." *American Sociologist* 33, 1: 42–54. https://www.jstor.org/stable/27700294.

Francis, R. Douglas, Richard Jones, and Donald B. Smith. 1992. *Destinies: Canadian History since Confederation*. Toronto: Holt, Rinehart, and Winston.

Fréchette, Louis-Honoré. 1880. *Papineau*. Montréal: Leméac.

Frégault, Guy. 1954. *La guerre de la Conquête 1754–1760*. Montréal: Fides.

Freud, Sigmund. 1921. "Group Psychology and the Analysis of the Ego." In *The Standard Edition of the Complete Psychological Works of Sigmund Freud Volume XVIII (1920–1922): Beyond the Pleasure Principle, Group Psychology and Other Works*, ed. James Strachey, 65–144. London: Hogarth Press.

Gagnon, Bernard. 2010. "Introduction." In *La diversité québécoise en débat: Bouchard, Taylor et les autres,* ed. Bernard Gagnon, 11–26. Montréal: Éditions Québec-Amérique.

Gagnon, Lysiane. 1994a. "Cessons de banaliser le hijab!" *La Presse,* December 3.

–. 1994b. "Le foulard islamique," part 1, *La Presse,* November 5.

Garnier, N. 1995. "Derrière le foulard, un rideau? À trop vouloir respecter les autres, on finit par ne plus se respecter soi-même." *Le Devoir,* February 4.

Gauvreau, Michael. 2000. "From Rechristianization to Contestation: Catholic Values and Quebec Society, 1931–1970." *Church History* 69, 4: 803–33. https://doi.org/10.2307/3169332.

–. 2005. *The Catholic Origins of Quebec's Quiet Revolution, 1931–1970*. Montréal and Kingston: McGill-Queen's University Press.

Geadah, Yolande. 1994. "Lever le voile sur le hijab." *Le Devoir,* September 29.

–. 1995. "Port du hijab à l'école: Il ne faut pas fonder le débat sur de fausses prémisses." *La Presse,* January 10.

Geertz, Clifford. 1963. "The Integrative Revolution: Primordial Sentiments and Civil Politics in the New States." In *Old Societies and New States: The Quest for Modernity in Asia and Africa,* ed. Clifford Geertz, 107–13. New York: Free Press.

Gellner, David N. 1964. *Thought and Change*. London: Weidenfeld and Nicholson.
Gérin, Léon. 1898. "L'habitant de Saint-Justin." Reprinted in *Léon Gérin et l'habitant de Saint-Justin*, ed. Jean-Charles Falardeau, 49–130. Montréal: Presses de l'Université de Montréal, 1968.
Gérin-Lajoie, Antoine. 1862. *Jean Rivard, le défricheur, suivi de Jean Rivard, économiste*. Montréal: Bibliotheque québécoise.
Geuss, Raymond. 1994. "Nietzsche and Genealogy." In *Nietzsche*, ed. John Richardson and Brian Leiter, 322–40. Oxford: Oxford University Press.
Godin, André. 2007. "Des grands enjeux éthiques pour mieux encadrer les accommodements raisonnables." Brief submitted to the Consultation Commission on Accommodation Practices Related to Cultural Differences. Accessed May 2010. http://www.accommodements.qc.ca/documentation/memoires/Sherbrooke/godin-andre-des-grands-enjeux-ethiques-pour-mieux-encadrer-les-accommodements-raisonnables.pdf.
Gouvernement du Québec. 1978. *La politique québécoise du développement culturel*. Québec City: Éditeur officiel.
–. 1981. *Autant façons d'être québécois: Plan d'action du gouvernement du Québec à l'intention des communautés culturelles*. Québec City: Ministère des communautés culturelles et d l'immigration.
–. 1990. *Au Québec pour bâtir ensemble: Énoncé de politique sur l'immigration et l'intégration*. Québec City: Ministère des communautés culturelles et de l'immigration.
–. 2015. *Criminalité au Québec: Principales tendances 2015*. Québec City: Ministère de la sécruité publique.
Groulx, Lionel. 1949. *Le nationalisme canadien-français*. https://www.fondationlionelgroulx.org/IMG/pdf/lionel-groulx-le-nationalisme-canadien-francais.pdf.
Gruda, Agnès. 1994. "Les pieds dans le voile." *La Presse*, December 30.
Guibernau, Montserrat. 1996. *Nationalisms: The Nation-State and Nationalism in the Twentieth Century*. Cambridge, UK: Polity.
Guindon, Hubert. 1988. *Quebec Society: Tradition, Modernity, and Nationhood*. Toronto: University of Toronto Press.
Hage, Ghassan. 2000. *White Nation: Fantasies of White Supremacy in a Multicultural Society*. London: Routledge.
–. 2003. *Against Paranoid Nationalism: Searching for Hope in a Shrinking Society*. Annandale: Pluto.
Hall, Stuart. 1996. "Who Needs 'Identity'?" In *Questions of Cultural Identity*, ed. Stuart Hall and Paul du Gay, 1–17. London: Sage.
Hamelin, Jean. 1960. *Économie et société en Nouvelle France*. Québec City: Presses de l'Université Laval.
Hamilton, Graeme. 2007. "The Hérouxville Code." *National Post*, December 30.
–. 2017. "Quebec Passes Bill Banning Niqab, Burka While Receiving Public Services." *National Post*, October 18.

Hamon, Édouard. 1882. *Exil et patrie: Drame en 5 actes*. Montréal: J. Chapleau et fils.

Heinrich, Jeff, and Valérie Dufour. 2008. *Circus quebecus: Sous le chapiteau de la commission Bouchard-Taylor*. Montréal: Boréal.

Helly, Denise. 2005. "La gestion de la diversité religieuse au Canada et le cas de l'Islam." *Revue marocaine d'études internationales* 13: 62–87. https://doi.org/10.1522/030584039.

Hobsbawm, Eric J. 1990. *Nations and Nationalism since 1780: Programme, Myth, Reality*. Cambridge, UK: Cambridge University Press.

Hobsbawm, Eric J., and Terence O. Ranger. 1983. *The Invention of Tradition*. Cambridge, UK: Cambridge University Press.

Honig, Bonnie. 2001. *Democracy and the Foreigner*. Princeton, NJ: Princeton University Press.

Hughes, Everett Cherrington. 1943. *French Canada in Transition*. Chicago: University of Chicago Press.

Huntington, Samuel P. 1993. "The Clash of Civilizations." *Foreign Affairs* 72, 3: 22–49. https://doi.org/10.2307/20045621.

Isin, Engin F. 2002a. *Being Political: Genealogies of Citizenship*. Minneapolis: University of Minnesota Press.

–. 2002b. "Citizenship after Orientalism." In *Handbook of Citizenship Studies*, ed. Engin F. Isin and Bryan S. Turner, 117–28. London: Sage.

–. 2004. "The Neurotic Citizen." *Citizenship Studies* 8, 3: 217–35. https://doi.org/10.1080/1362102042000256970.

Jean, Bruno. 2006. "The Study of Rural Communities in Quebec from the 'Folk Society' Monographic Approach to the Recent Revival of Community as Place-Based Rural Development." *Journal of Rural and Community Development* 1, 2: 56–68.

Jenson, Jane, and Denis Saint-Martin. 2003. "New Routes to Social Cohesion? Citizenship and the Social Investment State." *Canadian Journal of Sociology* 28, 1: 77–99. https://doi.org/10.2307/3341876.

Juteau, Danielle. 1996. "Theorising Ethnicity and Ethnic Communalisations at the Margins: From Quebec to the World System." *Nations and Nationalism* 2, 1: 45–66. https://doi.org/10.1111/j.1354-5078.1996.00045.x.

–. 2000. "Les ambigüités de la citoyenneté au Québec." Paper presented at McGill University, November 23. http://classiques.uqac.ca/contemporains/juteau_danielle/ambiguites_citoyennete_qc/ambiguites_citoyennete_qc.pdf.

–. 2002. "The Citizen Makes an Entrée: Redefining the National Community in Quebec." *Citizenship Studies* 6, 4: 441–58. https://doi.org/10.1080/1362102022000041268a.

Juteau, Danielle, and Marie McAndrew. 1992. "Projet national, immigration et intégration dans un Québec souverain." *Sociologie et sociétés* 24, 2: 161–80. https://doi.org/10.7202/001370ar.

Keohane, Kieran. 1992. "Symptoms of Canada: National Identity and the Theft of National Enjoyment." *CineACTION!* 28: 20–33.

Klein, Naomi. 2007. *The Shock Doctrine: The Rise of Disaster Capitalism*. New York: Henry Holt and Company.

Kristeva, Julia. 1982. *Powers of Horror: An Essay on Abjection*. New York: Columbia University Press.

–. 1990. *Nations without Nationalism*. New York: Columbia University Press.

–. 1991. *Strangers to Ourselves*. New York: Columbia University Press.

Kutty, Faisal. 1994. "Canadian Youths Return Horrified by Bosnian Misery." *Washington Report on Middle East Affairs*, November-December, 49, 83. https://www.wrmea.org/1994-november-december/anada-calling-canadian-youths-return-horrified-by-bosnian-misery.html.

Laborde, Cécile. 2005. "Secular Philosophy and Muslim Headscarves in Schools." *Journal of Political Philosophy* 13, 3: 305–29. https://doi.org/10.1111/j.1467-9760.2005.00225.x.

Lacan, Jacques. 1998. *The Seminar of Jacques Lacan*. Book 20, *Encore 1972–1973*. New York: W.W. Norton and Company.

Lacombe, Sylvie. 2003. "Exposé de Sylvie Lacombe sur le corporatisme." In *L'antilibéralisme au Québec au XXe siècle: Les séminaires Fernand-Dumont*, ed. Gilles Gagné, 41–51. Montréal: Nota Bene.

Laflèche, Louis François. 1866. *Quelques considérations sur les rapports de la société civile avec la religion et la famille*. Montréal: Senécal.

Lafond, Maurice. 1943. "À base de christianisme social." *Cahiers d'Action catholique*, special issue.

Lamarre, Jean. 1993. *Le devenir de la nation québécoise: Selon Maurice Séguin, Guy Frégault et Michel Brunet (1944–1969)*. Sillery, QC: Septentrion.

Lamontagne, Maurice. 1954. *Le fédéralisme canadien*. Québec: Presses de l'Université Laval.

Lamoureux, Diane. 2000. "Citoyenneté, nationalité, culture." In *Mondialisation, citoyenneté et multiculturalisme*, ed. Mikhaël Elbaz and Denise Helly, 111–29. Sainte-Foy, QC: Presses de l'Université Laval.

Laurendeau, André. 1947. "Quatrième état dans la nation." *L'Action nationale* 30 (October): 83–92.

–. 1953. "Y-a-t-il une crise du nationalisme? II." *L'Action nationale* 41, (January): 6–28.

Lavigne, Marie. 1995. "Hijab: Le conseil du statut de la femme explique sa position: 'Qui serait pénalisé par l'interdiction du port du voile à l'école?'" *La Presse*, May 26.

Le Moyne, Jean. 1955. "L'atmosphère religieuse au Canada français." *Cité libre* 12: 1–14.

Lenk, Helle-Mai. 2000. "The Case of Émilie Ouimet: News Discourse on Hijab and the Construction of Québécois National Identity." In *Anti-Racist Feminism: Critical Race and Gender Studies*, ed. Agnes M. Calliste and George J. Sefa Dei, 73–90. Halifax: Fernwood.

Leroux, Robert. 2001. "'La Nation' and the Quebec Sociological Tradition (1890–1980)." *Canadian Journal of Sociology* 26, 3: 349–73. https://doi.org/10.2307/3341892.

Lessard, Denis. 1995. "Un avis très censé." *La Presse*, February 16.

Létourneau, Jocelyn. 1998a. "'Impenser' le pays et toujours l'aimer." *Cahiers internationaux de sociologie* 105: 361–81.

–. 1998b. "Pour une révolution de la mémoire collective: Histoire et conscience historique chez les Québécois francophones." *Argument* 1, 1: 41–57.

–. 2000. *Passer à l'avenir: Histoire, mémoire, identité dans le Québec d'aujourd'hui*. Montréal: Boréal.

Lévesque, Lia. 1995. "Le port du hijab: À chaque école de décider." *La Presse*, May 26.

Levinas, Emmanuel. 1986. "The Trace of the Other." In *Deconstruction in Context: Literature and Philosophy*, ed. Mark Taylor, 345–59. Chicago: University of Chicago Press.

Linteau, Paul André, Ren Durocher, and Jean-Claude Robert. 1979. *Histoire du Québec contemporain*. Montréal: Boréal Express.

Lisée, Jean-François. 2007. "Pour un nouvel équilibre entre tous les 'Nous' Québécois." Brief submitted to the Consultation Commission on Accommodation Practices Related to Cultural Differences. Accessed May 2010. http://www.accommodements.qc.ca/documentation/memoires/A-N-Montreal/lisee-jean-francois.pdf.

Luckmann, Thomas. 1963. *The Invisible Religion: The Problems of Religion in Modern Society*. New York: Macmillan.

Mac Kay, Caroline. 1996. "L'identité nationale des Québécois." *Cahiers de recherche sociologique*, 27: 197–201. https://doi.org/10.7202/1002364ar.

Maclure, Jocelyn. 2003. *Quebec Identity: The Challenge of Pluralism*. Montréal and Kingston: McGill-Queen's University Press.

–. 2004. "Narratives and Counter-Narratives of Identity in Quebec." In *Québec: State and Society*, ed. Alain-G. Gagnon, 33–50. Toronto: University of Toronto Press.

Magnuson, Roger P. 1963. "Secular Trends in French Canadian Education." *Comparative Education Review* 7, 1: 43–46. https://doi.org/10.1086/444956.

Mahmood, Saba. 2005. *Politics of Piety: The Islamic Revival and the Feminist Subject*. Princeton, NJ: Princeton University Press.

–. 2008. "Secular Imperatives?" *The Immanent Frame: Secularism, Religion, and the Public Sphere*, May 7. https://tif.ssrc.org/2008/05/07/secular-imperatives/.

Mann Trofimenkoff, Susan. 1982. *The Dream of Nation: A Social and Intellectual History of Quebec*. Toronto: Gage.

Manzo, Kathryn. 1996. *Creating Boundaries: The Politics of Race and Nation*. Boulder, CO: Lynne Rienner.

Martin, David. 1978. *A General Theory of Secularization*. Oxford: Blackwell.

Martineau, Richard. 1995. "Leçons d'Alger." *Voir*, 25–31.

Marx, Karl. 1894. *Capital*. Moscow: Progress.

Marx, Karl, and Frederick Engels. 1848. "Manifesto of the Communist Party." In *Karl Marx and Frederick Engels: Selected Works*, Vol. 1: 108–37. Moscow: Progress.

Masuzawa, Tomoko. 2005. *The Invention of World Religions, or How European Universalism Was Preserved in the Language of Pluralism*. Chicago: University of Chicago Press.

McAndrew, Marie. 1995. "Multiculturalisme canadien et interculturalisme québécois: Mythes et réalités." In *Pluralisme et éducation: Politiques et pratiques au Canada, en Europe et dans les Pays du Sud, l'apport de l'éducation comparée*, ed. M. McAndrew, R. Toussant, and O. Galatanu, 33–52. Montréal: Publications de la Faculté des sciences de l'education, Université de Montréal.

–. 1996. "Diversité culturelle et religieuse: Divergences des rhétoriques, convergences des pratiques?" In *Pluralisme, citoyenneté et éducation*, ed. France Gagnon, Marie McAndrew, and Michel Pagé, 287–317. Montréal: Harmattan.

–. 2002a. "De l'interculturel au civique: 20 ans d'approche québécoise." In *Démocratie, multiculturalisme et citoyenneté*, ed. L.K. Sosoe, 537–40. Sainte-Foy, QC: Presses de l'Université Laval.

–. 2002b. "Le remplacement du marquer linguistique par le marquer religieux en milieu scolaire." In *Les relations ethniques en question: Ce qui a changé depuis le 11 septembre 2001*, ed. Jean Renaud, Linda Pietrantonio, and Guy Bourgeault, 131–48. Montréal: Presses de l'Université de Montréal.

–. 2006. "Le cas de l'école." Paper presented at the conference "L'affirmation religieuse menace-t-elle l'égalité des sexes? Diversité de foi, égalité de droits," Conseil du statut de la femme, Montréal, March.

–. 2007. "Reasonable Accommodation: Foundations, Guidelines and Issues." Paper presented at the conference "The Stranger Next Door: Making Diversity Work," Couchiching Institute on Public Affairs, Orillia, Ontario, August 9–12.

–. 2010. "Immigration and Diversity in Quebec's Schools: An Assessment." In *Quebec Questions: Quebec Studies for the Twenty-First Century*, ed. J. Rudy, S. Gervail, and C. Kirky, 287–304. Oxford: Oxford University Press.

McConnell, Michael W. 2000. "Believers as Equal Citizens." In *Obligations of Citizenship and Demands of Faith: Religious Accommodation in Pluralist Democracies*, ed. Nancy L. Rosenblum, 90–110. Princeton, NJ: Princeton University Press.

McCrone, David. 1998. *The Sociology of Nationalism*. New York: Routledge.

McInnis, Edgar. 1982. *Canada: A Political and Social History*. Toronto: Holt, Rinehart and Winston.

McLeod, Hugh. 2000. *Secularisation in Western Europe, 1848–1914*. New York: St. Martin's Press.

Meunier, E.-Martin, and Jean-Philippe Warren. 2002. *Sortir de la "Grande noirceur": L'horizon "personnaliste" de la Révolution tranquille*. Sillery, QC: Septentrion.

Milbank, John. 2004. "The Gift of Ruling: Secularization and Political Authority." *New Blackfriars* 85, 996: 212–38. https://doi.org/10.1111/j.0028-4289.2004.00009.x.

–. 2006. *Theology and Social Theory: Beyond Secular Reason*. Oxford: Blackwell.

Milot, Micheline. 2002. *Laïcité dans le Nouveau Monde: Le cas du Québec*. Turnhout, Belgium: Brepols.

–. 2006. "Une laïcité québécoise." Paper presented at the conference "L'affirmation religieuse menace-t-elle l'égalité des sexes? Diversité de foi, égalité de droits," Conseil du statut de la femme, Montréal, March.

Minces, Juliette. 1990. *La femme voilée: L'Islam au feminin*. Paris: Calman-Lévy.

Miner, Horace. 1939. *Saint-Denis: A French-Canadian Parish*. Chicago: University of Chicago Press.

Minville, Esdras. 1992. *La vie sociale*. Vol. 1, *Le nationalisme Canadien-Français*. Ed. François-Albert Angers. Montréal: HEC and Fides.

Montpetit, Édouard. 1938. *La conquête économique*. Vol. 1, *Les forces essentielles*. Montréal: Bernard Valiquette.

Morrison, Ian A. 2013a. "Christianity, Secularism and the Crisis of Europe." In *Europe after Derrida: Crisis and Potentiality*, ed. Agnes Czajka and Bora Isyar, 149–62. Edinburgh: Edinburgh University Press.

–. 2013b. "Rancière, Religion and the Political." *Citizenship Studies* 17, 6–7: 886–900. https://doi.org/10.1080/13621025.2013.834144.

–. 2014. "The Crisis and Governance of Religious Pluralism in the European Union." *Insight Turkey* 16, 3: 55–67.

–. 2016. "Religion." In *The Wiley Blackwell Encyclopedia of Race, Ethnicity, and Nationalism*, ed. John Stone, M. Dennis Rutledge, Polly Rizova, Anthony D. Smith, and Xiaoshuo Hou. Chicester, UK: John Wiley and Sons.

Moss, Jane. 1989. "Playing with History: Québec Historical Plays from the Quiet Revolution to the Referendum." *French Review* 63, 2: 337–46.

Nieguth, Tim, and Aurélie Lacassagne. 2009. "Contesting the Nation: Reasonable Accommodation in Rural Quebec." *Canadian Political Science Review* 3, 1: 1–16.

Nietzsche, Friedrich. 1874. "On the Uses and Disadvantages of History for Life." Reprinted in *Untimely Meditations*, ed. D. Breazeale, 58–123. Cambridge, UK: Cambridge University Press, 1997.

–. 1887. *On the Genealogy of Morality*. Cambridge, UK: Cambridge University Press.

Ouellet, Fernand. 1956. "Michel Brunet et le problème de la Conquête." *Bulletin des recherches historiques* 62, 2: 92–101. http://numerique.banq.qc.ca/patrimoine/details/52327/2657611.

–. 1958. "Le destin de Julie Bruneau-Papineau (1796–1862)." *Bulletin des recherches historiques* 64, 1: 7–31; 64, 2: 37–63. http://numerique.banq.qc.ca/patrimoine/details/52327/2657619.

Paiement, Alain C. 2007. "Mémoire." Brief submitted to the Consultation Commission on Accommodation Practices Related to Cultural Differences. Accessed May 2010. http://www.accommodements.qc.ca/documentation/memoires/Gatineau-d/paiement-alain07-0006-de-00.pdf.

Paré, Jean. 1994. "Quand l'habit fait le moine: La liberté de religion ne consiste pas à transformer églises, synagogues ou mosquées en centre d'achat de cultes: Les écoles pas d'avantage." *L'actualité*, November 1.

Parsons, Talcott. 1963. "Christianity and Modern Industrial Society." In *Sociological Theory, Values, and Sociocultural Change: Essays in Honour of Pitrim A. Sorokin*, ed. Edward A. Tiryakian, 33–70. New York: Free Press.

Pelletier, Alex, and Gérard Pelletier. 1944. "Caractères de la spiritualité étudiante." *Cahiers d'Action catholique*, special issue.

Pelletier, Gérard. 1952. "Crise d'autorité ou crise de liberté?" *Cité libre* 5: 1–10.

–. 1955. "Dialogue avec un suicidé." *Cité libre* 11: 1–11.

Perreault, Laura-Julie. 2006. "Les camionneurs sikhs pourront garder leur turban en tout temps." *La Presse*, March 9.

Plourde, Michel. 1993. *La politique linguistique du Québec, 1977–1987*. Montréal: Insitut québécois de recherche sur la culture.

Quinn, Herbert F. 1938. "The Bogey of Fascism in Quebec." *Dalhousie Review* 18, 3: 301–8.

Rancière, Jacques. 2001. "Ten Theses on Politics." *Theory and Event* 5, 3. https://doi.org/10.1353/tae.2001.0028.

–. 2004. "Who Is the Subject of the Rights of Man?" *South Atlantic Quarterly* 103, 2–3: 297–310. https://doi.org/10.1215/00382876-103-2-3-297.

Redfield, Robert. 1939. "Introduction." In Horace Miner, *Saint-Denis: A French-Canadian Parish*, xiii–xix. Chicago: University of Chicago Press.

Renan, Ernest. 1882. "What Is a Nation?" In *Becoming National*, ed. Geoff Eley and Ronald Grigor Suny, 42–55. Oxford: Oxford University Press.

Rioux, Marcel. 1955. "Idéologie et crise de conscience du Canada française." *Cité libre* 14: 1–29.

–. 1976. *La question du Québec*. Montréal: Parti pris.

Roitman, Janet. 2012. "Crisis." *Political Concepts* 1, 1. http://www.politicalconcepts.org/issue1/crisis/.

Rolland, Roger. 1951. "Projections libérantes." *Cité libre* 2: 33.

Rousseau, Jean-Jacques. 1762. *The Social Contract*. Reprint, New York: Penguin, 1968.

Roy, Fernande. 1993. *Histoire des idéologies au Québec aux XIXe et XXe siècles*. Montréal: Boréal.

Rudin, Ronald. 1997. *Making History in Twentieth-Century Quebec*. Toronto: University of Toronto Press.

Ryan, Claude. 1957. "L'Église catholique et l'évolution spirituelle du Canada français." *Chronique sociale de France* 65: 443–57.

Said, Edward. 1978. *Orientalism*. New York: Vintage.

Sarra-Bournet, Michel. 2001. *Les nationalismes au Québec du XIXe au XXIe siècle*. Québec City: Presses de l'Université Laval.

Séguin, Maurice. 1995. *Une histoire du Québec: Vision d'un prophète*. Ed. Denis Vaugeois. Guérin: Montréal.

Seljak, David. 1996. "Why the Quiet Revolution Was 'Quiet': The Catholic Church's Reaction to the Secularization of Nationalism in Quebec after 1960." *CCHA Historical Studies* 62: 109–24.

Smith, Anthony D. 1986. *The Ethnic Origins of Nations*. Oxford: Blackwell.

–. 1998. *Nationalism and Modernism: A Critical Survey of Recent Theories of Nations and Nationalism*. London: Routledge.

Spinner-Halev, Jeff. 2000. *Surviving Diversity: Religion and Democratic Citizenship*. Baltimore, MD: Johns Hopkins University Press.

Stasiulis, Daiva. 2013. "Worrier Nation: Quebec's Value Codes for Immigrants." *Politikon* 40, 1: 183–209. https://doi.org/10.1080/02589346.2013.768079.

Stavrakis, Yannis, and Nikos Chrysoloras. 2006. "(I Can't Get No) Enjoyment: Lacanian Theory and the Analysis of Nationalism." *Psychoanalysis, Culture and Society* 11, 2: 144–63.

Steinbach, Marilyn. 2010. "Eux autres versus nous autres: Adolescent Students' Views on Integration with Newcomers." *Intercultural Education* 21, 6: 535–47. https://doi.org/10.1080/14675986.2010.533035.

Swatos, William H., and Kevin J. Christiano. 1999. "Secularization Theory: The Course of a Concept." *Sociology of Religion* 60, 3: 209–31. https://doi.org/10.2307/3711934.

Tahon, Marie-Blanche. 1996. "Regards croisés sur les 'Musulmanes' au Québec." In *Les convergences culturelles dans les sociétés pluriethniques,* ed. Khadiyatoulah Fall, Ratiba Hadj-Moussa, and Daniel Simeoni, 169–88. Sainte-Foy, QC: Presses de l'Université du Québec.

Taylor, Charles. 1994. "The Politics of Recognition." In *Multiculturalism,* ed. Amy Gutmann, 25–73. Princeton, NJ: Princeton University Press.

Tazziolo, Martina, and Nicholas De Genova. 2016. "Europe/Crisis: Introducing New Keywords of 'the Crisis' in and of 'Europe.'" In *Europe/Crisis: New Keywords of "the Crisis" in and of "Europe,"* ed. Nicholas De Genova and Martina Tazziolo, 2–7. New York: Zone Books.

Therrien, Sophie. 2004. *Laicity and Religious Diversity: Québec's Approach: Report to the Minister of Citizen Relations and Immigration*. Montréal: Conseil des relations interculturelles.

Tilly, Charles. 1990. *Coercion, Capital and European States, AD 990–1990*. Reading, MA: Addison-Wesley.

Todd, Sharon. 1998. "Veiling the 'Other,' Unveiling Our 'Selves': Reading Media Images of the Hijab Psychoanalytically to Move beyond Tolerance." *Canadian Journal of Education* 23, 4: 438–51. https://doi.org/10.2307/1585757.

Toledo Freiwald, Bina. 2011. "'Qui est nous?' Some Answers from the Bouchard-Taylor Commission's Archive." In *Religion, Culture, and the State: Reflections on the Bouchard-Taylor Report,* ed. Howard Adelman and Pierre Anctil, 69–85. Toronto: University of Toronto Press.

Trudeau, Pierre Elliott. 1950. "Politique fonctionelle I." *Cité libre* 1: 20–24.

–. 1953. "Matériaux pour server à une enquête sur le cléricalisme." *Cité libre* 7: 9–31.

–. 1956. *La grève de l'amiante*. Montréal: Éditions Cité libre.

Trudel, Marcel. 1957. "La Nouvelle-France." *Cahiers de l'Académie canadienne-française* 2: 23–50.

Turner, Bryan S. 2002. "Religion and Politics: The Elementary Forms of Citizenship." In *Handbook of Citizenship Studies,* ed. Engin F. Isin and Bryan S. Turner, 259–75. London: Sage.

–. 2003. "Historical Sociology of Religion: Politics and Modernity." In *Handbook of Historical Sociology,* ed. Gerard Delanty and Engin F. Isin, 349–63. London: Sage.

Vaillancourt, Yves. 1994. "La tête dans le sable pour le voile islamique: Peut-on mettre sur un pied d'égalité le hijab, la kippa, le turban et même la croix chrétienne au cou?" *Le Devoir,* October 12.

Van Alphen, Ernst. 2011. "The Other Within." In *Alterity, Identity, Image: Selves and Others in Society and Scholarship,* ed. Raymond Corbey and Joep Leersen, 1–16. Amsterdam: Rodopi.

Vattier, Georges. 1928. *Contributions à l'étude de la psychologie des peuples: Essai sur la mentalité canadienne-française*. Paris: Librarie Ancienne Honoré Champion.

Verstraelen, Augustin. 1995. "Le foulard islamique." *Le Devoir,* April 19.

Weber, Max. 1920. *The Protestant Ethic and the Spirit of Capitalism*. Los Angeles: Roxbury.

–. 1927. "Citizenship." In *General Economic History,* ed. Frank H. Knight, 315–37. London: George Allen and Unwin.

Werbner, Prina. 2000. "Divided Loyalties, Empowered Citizenship? Muslims in Britain." *Citizenship Studies* 4, 3: 307–24.

Wilson, Bryan. 1966. *Religion in Secular Society*. London: Watts.

Woods, Allan. 2017. "'Trash Radio' Creates Culture of Intolerance in Quebec." *Toronto Star,* February 3.

Yack, Bernard. 1996. "The Myth of the Civic Nation." *Critical Review* 10, 2: 193–211. https://doi.org/10.1080/08913819608443417.

Young, Brian. 1994. *Quebec: A Socio-Economic History*. Toronto: Copp Clark.

Ziarek, Eva. 1995. "The Uncanny Style of Kristeva's Critique of Nationalism." *Postmodern Culture* 5, 2. https://doi.org/10.1353/pmc.1995.0017.

Žižek, Slavoj. 1993. "Enjoy the Nation as Yourself!" In *Tarrying with the Negative: Kant, Hegel, and the Critique of Ideology,* 200–38. Durham, NC: Duke University Press.

–. 2017. "The Seven Veils of Fantasy." In *Key Concepts of Lacanian Psychoanalysis,* ed. Dany Nobus, 190–218. London: Karnac.

Index